M000169518

SING, DANCE
AND PRAY

ADVANCE PRAISE FOR THE BOOK

'*Sing, Dance and Pray* is an informative and appealing narrative that recollects for us how Abhay Charan De grew from a boy in Calcutta into the renowned teacher and spiritual guide, Sri Bhaktivedanta Swami, even more famously known as Srila Prabhupada. The story of the International Society for Krishna Consciousness cannot properly be told without an understanding of the Society's revered founder and Hindol Sengupta has very successfully told this needed story in a simple manner that will be accessible to all who want to know more about this extraordinary and saintly figure. The book helps us to understand more clearly a very important moment in the arrival of Hinduism on the global scene'—Francis X. Clooney, S.J., Parkman Professor of Divinity, Harvard University

'If you're used to seeing Srila Abhay Charan De Bhaktivedanta Swami Prabhupada through the devotional lens that added all those extra names to the ones he bore at birth, you will be amazed. In this refreshingly independent book we hear how Prabhupada sounded when his followers weren't following him around with a microphone. Amid the glorious cacophony of the Lower East Side in the 1960s—the Grateful Dead, Santana, and The Who—we find him confiding this to his diary: "Sun Rise 5/34 am, Sunset 6/34 pm, Moonrise 7/01 . . . No income and No expenditure." Back in India his wife had been so angry about his disregard for home and family that she "pawned his sacred *Bhagavatam* to buy biscuits to have with her tea". Once he gets to New York a decade later we see him cooking for himself and whoever would join him. Hindol Sengupta gives us recipes for khichri, dal and chapatis. Thus the humble beginnings of what came to be called—with a suitably ornate Sanskrit ending—prasadam. Here we have Prabhupada from all sides and from the ground up. Now, when I see his life-size image glistening in gold in Vrindavan, I'll feel I know the man behind the metal'—Prof. John Stratton Hawley, Claire Tow Professor of Religion, Barnard College, Columbia University

'Abhay Charan [A.C.] Bhaktivedanta Swami Prabhupada's impact—both organizational [ISKCON] and written [Bhagavad Gita, Bhagavat Purana, *Chaitanya Charitamrita, Back to Godhead*, plus works in Bengali]—was stunning. In recognition, a special commemorative coin was released on 1 September 2021, his 125th birth anniversary. There was an amazingly productive period, especially from 1966 to 1977. His biography has been written in the past, typically by Westerners and those internal to the ISKCON organization [There is also the one by Joshua Greene, a devotee].

An external view, perhaps more objective, is always desirable. At the risk of sounding parochial, I think it requires a Bengali to appreciate the nuances. Having written on Swami Vivekananda, who followed a similar path in the West, Hindol Sengupta is eminently qualified. In his inimitable and engaging style, Hindol brings alive the life and message of *bhakti* that was Srila Prabhupada'—Bibek Debroy, economist and chairperson, Prime Minister's Economic Advisory Council

'The story of Srila Prabhupada, who left India at the age of seventy with Rs 40 in his pocket and ended up establishing the International Society for Krishna Consciousness [ISKCON], with dozens of branches around the world through which he has introduced millions of young men and women to Lord Krishna and Radha Rani, is indeed amazing. He is not well known even in India, except as the founder of ISKCON. Hindol Sengupta's book *Sing, Dance and Pray* is a truly inspirational story which presents Srila Prabhupada's life in the most engaging manner. The title is also appropriate because the Vaishnava tradition of singing, dancing and praying has come down from Mahaprabhu Shri Chaitanya to this very day. My wife and I had the privilege of meeting Srila Prabhupada, who kindly visited our house twice. Through this message I pay homage to him and express my appreciation for Hindol Sengupta's book. Jai Radhe'—Karan Singh, politician and philosopher

'Hindol Sengupta has accomplished the impossible task of bringing to life the legend of Bhaktivedanta Swami Prabhupada, who changed the landscape of the world by introducing Krishna consciousness through his profound wisdom and practice. Hindol's recounting excites the mind of the reader through his signature writing style. This riveting account of Prabhupada's life is a must-read book for everyone'—Lavanya Vemsani, Distinguished Professor, Shawnee State University, and member, executive board, Ohio Academy of History

'With this beautifully written, highly accessible and engaging book, Hindol Sengupta has done for A.C. Bhaktivedanta Swami Prabhupada what he did for Swami Vivekananda in *The Modern Monk* and for Sardar Vallabhbhai Patel in *The Man Who Saved India*. He has brought this important and compelling figure to life for the contemporary reader, showing the ongoing relevance of Srila Prabhupada's work for today's world. I promise that if you read this book, from the opening lines, you will find yourself hooked and unable to put it down. Sengupta has a gift not only for bringing his subjects to life, but also for creating a vivid sense of the times in which they lived. From the era of the Indian independence movement to the New York of the 1960s counterculture, one gets to breathe the air that Prabhupada breathed and experience the ways in which he both shaped and was shaped by his context. This book is an inspiration. Jai Sri Krishna!'—Jeffery D. Long, Carl W. Zeigler Professor of Religion, Philosophy and Asian Studies, Elizabethtown College, Pennsylvania

'The remarkable life of Srila Prabhupada deserved a serious and intellectually engaged biography. His attempt to create a movement by merging the Vedantic and bhakti traditions was intrinsically significant for the real world. And Prabhupada prompting Krishna worship globally is also inexplicably phenomenal, rivalling in scale the impact of the greatest of historic religious interlocutors. He has finally found a worthy biographer in Hindol Sengupta, who has combined an accessible, easy style with serious engagement with Prabhupada's deeper message'—Gautam Sen, former lecturer, London School of Economics

'With a rare gift for both depth and detail, Hindol Sengupta makes Prabhupada come alive as never before—the extraordinary tale of the extraordinary man who scattered the nectar of Krishna consciousness across the globe'—Makarand R. Paranjape, professor, English, Jawaharlal Nehru University

'Spreading the message of dharma beyond the Indian subcontinent has been a dream since Swami Vivekananda's Chicago address in 1893. This was successfully translated into reality by Prabhupada A.C. Bhaktivedanta. He turned Krishna consciousness into a global movement, touching unlikely parts of the world. While his works, especially his commentary on the Bhagavad Gita, are known, the life of this pioneering Hindu leader has received scant attention. Hindol Sengupta has filled the void with his biography of the founder of what is popularly known as the Hare Krishna movement. He [Sengupta] documents his [Prabhupada's] astonishing life, what influenced him and particularly the inspirational story of how he took the message of peace and brotherhood overseas. It is an astonishing story that deserves a prominent place in the annals of contemporary Hinduism' —Swapan Dasgupta, member of Parliament, Rajya Sabha

'Although American exposure to the Hindu tradition began several centuries ago, it was only during the latter half of the twentieth century that this exposure mushroomed and reached people all over the country. The majority of Indian spiritual teachers who came West during that time tended to focus on teaching aspects of Hindu yoga or Buddhist mind-centring practices. Sri Bhaktivedanta Swami [Srila Prabhupada] was unique for he came specifically to teach devotion to Lord Krishna. Through his lectures and his writings, he attracted a following almost wherever he went, even though he asked for more of a life-changing commitment from those he taught than most other teachers did. In the process, he left an indelible imprint on countless young Americans and then worldwide. For anyone wishing to know about his life, his teachings and the way he changed the world, these are all captured in Hindol Sengupta's *Sing, Dance and Pray*, an informative and worthwhile read'—Ramdas Lamb, Professor of Religion, University of Hawai'i, Mānoa

'*Sing, Dance and Pray* tells the fascinating story of Srila Prabhupada and of his creation, ISKCON. Hindol Sengupta's writing is fluid and rich with detail, tracing not only Prabhupada's life and career but immersing the reader in the sociopolitical and cultural contexts that shaped his path, from the burgeoning nationalist fervour of colonial India to the tumult of 1960s American life. A compelling tale, fluently told'—Shashi Tharoor, member of Parliament for Thiruvananthapuram Lok Sabha, chairman of the Parliamentary Standing Committee on Information Technology, and chairman, All-India Professionals' Congress

SING, DANCE AND PRAY

THE INSPIRATIONAL STORY OF
SRILA **PRABHUPADA**
FOUNDER-ACHARYA OF ISKCON

Hindol Sengupta

PENGUIN
ANANDA

An imprint of Penguin Random House

PENGUIN ANANDA

USA | Canada | UK | Ireland | Australia
New Zealand | India | South Africa | China

Penguin Ananda is part of the Penguin Random House group of companies
whose addresses can be found at global.penguinrandomhouse.com

Published by Penguin Random House India Pvt. Ltd
4th Floor, Capital Tower 1, MG Road,
Gurugram 122 002, Haryana, India

First published in Penguin Ananda by Penguin Random House India 2022

ISBN 9780670096732

Typeset in Adobe Caslon Pro by Manipal Technologies Limited, Manipal
Printed at Replika Press Pvt. Ltd, India

www.penguin.co.in

Contents

Contents

Introduction

The Art of Dying and Living

Summer 1967.

Soon after leaving San Francisco, the Learjet seemed like it might crash.

It wobbled, sputtered and rolled in the air. On the aircraft sat a man, whispering to himself. If he died that day, his death would create headlines around the world, and a tidal wave of grief from beleaguered fans. Few artistes before or after him have attained the fame that he had already seen with his band. He was a millionaire many times over.

As he sat in that plane, George Harrison, famed singer-songwriter, instrumentalist and one of the 'Fab Four' of The Beatles, faced with the possibility of his death, chanted again and again, Hare Krishna, Hare Krishna, Krishna Krishna, Hare Krishna, Hare Krishna, Krishna Krishna, Hare Hare/ Hare Rama, Hare Rama, Rama Rama, Hare Hare.[1] This was not unusual.

Only a few days ago, Harrison had spent six hours in a boat with his fellow Beatle, John Lennon, floating by the waters near Greece, all the while playing a ukulele and singing, again and yet

again, Hare Krishna, Hare Krishna, Krishna Krishna, Hare Hare/
Hare Rama, Hare Rama, Rama Rama, Hare Hare.[2]

Was one of the world's most famous singers of all time chanting
the Krishna mantra in joy, down the Aegean in a boat, or in mortal
fear, in a plane tottering in the skies above San Francisco?

By 1967, The Beatles were the world's most famous musical
group, on their way to becoming the biggest selling band of all-
time with a record of having sold six hundred million albums,
which has never been equalled.

But by the late 1960s, the Beatles were also embroiled in drug
and alcohol abuse, some of their personal lives were falling apart,
and their lifecycle as a band seemed to be coming to an end. In a
television interview in 1967 in England, the recording of which is
available on YouTube, John Lennon is seen saying that that the
band suddenly had money, after their songs became a sensation
around the world, 'and suddenly it wasn't all that good',[3] and in
same video, Harrison adds, 'by having the money we found that
money wasn't the answer because we had lots of material things
which people sort of spend their whole lives trying to get, we
managed to get them at quite an early age, and it was good really
because we learnt that that wasn't it, we still lacked something and
that something is what religion is trying to give to people'.[4]

The spiritual search had already begun for some of the
Beatles, with experiments in meditation, learning to play the sitar
and visiting Indian gurus. Harrison used the sitar, famously, in
the song 'Norwegian Wood' for The Beatles' 1965 album *Rubber
Soul*. But it was a record released in 1966 in America that Lennon
and Harrison heard which seems to have made the most profound
impact.

The record was called 'Krishna Consciousness'.

It featured monks chanting the name of Krishna—Hare
Krishna, Hare Krishna, Krishna Krishna, Hare Hare/ Hare Rama,
Hare Rama, Rama Rama, Hare Hare—led by an unusual leader, a
seventy-year-old first-time visitor to the United States of America.

In fact, the man, who was referred to as Bhaktivedanta Swami and who led the record, had many firsts to his name. 'Krishna Consciousness' was his first record; it was his first visit to America and his first-ever travel, in seven decades of his life, outside his home country, India.

Nothing about his background or achievements at that moment suggested that he could attract attention from The Beatles. But only months later, the chant of the elderly Bengali man from Calcutta* was being fervently repeated by George Harrison in his moment of dread.

In the years to come, such seemed to be the influence of the elderly monk, Harrison would create more philosophical music, in tune with his ever-increasing interest in Indian spirituality, and with songs like 'Inner Light' (1968), and a hit album called *Living in the Material World* (1973).

When Harrison died in 2001, only fifty-eight, at his bedside were disciples of Bhaktivedanta Swami, Mukunda Goswami and Shyamsundar Das, reading verses into the ear of the dying singer of the great Hindu treatise, the Bhagavad Gita, where Krishna, the avatar of Lord Vishnu, teaches the lesson of righteousness to the warrior–prince Arjun.[5]

Bhaktivedanta Swami had turned out to be one of the most powerful influences—if not the most powerful influence—in the life of one of the most prominent musicians of all time.

What had Harrison (and countless others) learnt from Bhaktivedanta Swami? One of the most important tasks of human life, explained the Swami, was to contemplate death or to learn the act of dying; to further elucidate, to prepare oneself for the inevitability of death. Material human life was but a deviation, a contamination and forgetfulness of the divine relationship of the soul with God. This is yoga literally translated to 'union', the process through which mere mortals, who are 'minus God'

---

* Known as Kolkata now.

in the Swami's words, can become 'plus God' again or associate
with God.[6]

For if there is one immutable truth of life, it is that it must
end in death. To contemplate this reality, to try and understand
the real purpose of life, to consider that human life is the greatest
opportunity towards God realization, this was a seminal message
of the Swami.

'As long as a man is in the full vigour of life, he forgets the
naked truth of death, which he has to meet. Thus, a foolish man
makes no relevant inquiry about the real problems of life. Everyone
thinks that he will never die, although he sees evidence of death
before his eyes at every second. Here is the distinction between
animalism and humanity. An animal like a goat has no sense of its
impending death. Although its brother goat is being slaughtered,
the goat, being allured by the green grass offered to it, will stand
peacefully waiting to be slaughtered next. On the other hand, if
a human being sees his fellow man being killed by an enemy, he
either fights to save his brother or leaves, if possible, to save his
own life. That is the difference between a man and a goat.

'An intelligent man knows that death is born along with his
own birth. He knows that he is dying every second and that the
final touch will be given as soon as his term of life is finished. He,
therefore, prepares himself for the next life or for liberation from
the disease of repeated birth and death.

'A foolish man, however, does not know that this human form
of life is obtained after a series of births and deaths imposed in the
past by the laws of nature. He does not know that a living entity is an
eternal being who has no birth and death. Birth, death, old age, and
disease are external impositions on a living entity and are due to his
contact with material nature and to his forgetfulness of his eternal,
godly nature and qualitative oneness with the Absolute Whole.

'Human life provides the opportunity to know this eternal
fact, or truth. Thus the very beginning of the *Vedanta-sutra* advises

that because we have this valuable form of human life, it is our duty—now—to inquire, What is Brahman, the Absolute Truth?

'A man who is not intelligent enough does not inquire about this transcendental life; instead, he inquires about many irrelevant matters which do not concern his eternal existence. From the very beginning of his life he inquires from his mother, father, teachers, professors, books and so many other sources, but he does not have the right type of information about his real life.'[7]

This message, this urge to seek the truth of life, captivated Harrison, as it would so many others.

There was nothing in the old Hindu monk's life till his ship reached New York in 1965, which suggested that he might have such influence. In fact, by all counts, Abhay Charan De, before he turned to monastic life and was given the name Bhaktivedanta Swami, had led a modest life.

He had been born to parents who would today be called middle-class parents, though there had been considerable money in the family history.[8]

He seemed destined to have a regular, normal life. De grew up in British-ruled India and did all usual things of the time—a vaunted Christian missionary education, an early marriage and a suitably mercantile job.

But De perhaps always had a feeling that something was missing. He was born in a family devoted to Vaishnavism. Vaishnavism is the stream of Hinduism that worships Vishnu, the preserver in the Hindu trinity. The avatar of Vishnu[9] preferred by many Vaishnavites is Krishna, the divine charioteer in the war of Kurukshetra in the Mahabharata and interlocutor in the Bhagavad Gita.

The worship of Krishna and his divine consort Radha was a hereditary act of faith for the Des. Krishna was the family deity, and while the young Abhay Charan had shown deep interest in spirituality even as a boy, it was inconceivable that he would turn to monkhood.[10]

And yet, a chance encounter with his spiritual master, Bhaktisiddhanta Saraswati Thakur, transformed De's life, and he renounced, in the age-old tradition of Indian asceticism, his family and his worldly belongings, to live as a sadhu, a mendicant in lifelong service of Krishna and to spread the word of Krishna.

If the story would just have been about Abhay Charan De becoming a monk and preaching in India, it would have been an interesting, though not a pathbreaking tale.

But De, who received the name Bhaktivedanta Swami, would have what can only be described as a late-life renaissance— at seventy, he would cross the high seas to preach the word of Krishna in America, in the West and around the world as his guru instructed him.

He arrived with neither cash nor contacts. And trawled the streets of New York chanting the name of Krishna, hoping to attract and convince a few Americans of the power of the name of God. He did more than gain a few followers.

He founded the International Society for Krishna Consciousness (ISKCON).

Soon in cities and towns across America, the sight of tonsured men in ochre robes and women in saris, singing and dancing, clanging cymbals, and playing the dhol, usually draped around their shoulders, created a wave which would, eventually, touch every part of the globe, and come to be known as the Hare Krishna movement, no doubt because its joyous devotees repeated, again and again, the mantra—Hare Krishna.

By around 1967–1968, as his fame started to spread in the West, Bhaktivedanta Swami née Abhay Charan De came to be known as Srila Prabhupada. The moniker has particular significance in Vaishnavism and other eastern philosophies. 'Prabhupada' means, in Sanskrit, the person who is devoted at the lotus feet of the lord, in this case, Vishnu. The reference of the lotus comes from the idea that the flower is born amidst dirt and mud and is yet itself untouched by the squalor that surrounds it. The feet of the lord are therefore that sacred point— which while being in touch with the dust of the world, remain unsullied by it—and thus a refuge for all those who seek a haven at it.[11] The way, or path, to receiving the lord's benediction is to submit completely at his lotus feet.

The name Prabhupada was given to Bhaktivedanta Swami to signify his utter sense of surrender to the will of Lord Krishna, ever at the feet of the lord. But this was not the first unique name he would receive. Even the term 'Bhaktivedanta', to those who study Hindu philosophy, would strike as a curious combination. Vedanta is usually understood (or misunderstood, as the Vaishnava Acharyas will argue) to describe a route of attaining the knowledge of the divine through contemplation on a formless, omnipotent, omnipresent Absolute Truth (The Vaishnava Acharyas too have written most elaborate and exacting commentaries on Vedanta that establish the transcendental form of Vishnu as the ultimate Absolute Truth). Or it is by knowing oneself, as the Brihadaranyaka Upanishad suggests, one knows the universe. The path of bhakti or devotion is almost always towards a divine with form—*sagun* as opposed to *nirgun*, or with transcendental qualities as opposed to without qualities.

Mostly, in Hindu philosophy, it is commonly understood that Bhakti and Vedanta stand at different ends of perceiving the truth about the divine.

By combining the two and making it 'Bhaktivedanta', the Vaishnavite scholars of Chaitanya tradition were conveying something important—here was a man who had, in a sense, brought these two impossible-to-converge elements uniquely together. Genuine bhakti or devotion is not sentimental but founded firmly on the understanding of Vedanta. Without decrying the merits of the Vedanta path, the Swami seemed to show how it culminates into bhakti. That the end of contemplation on Vedanta comes God realization which can only engender the deepest devotion or bhakti.

Though not discussed enough, this idea of convergence, controversial as it sounds, lay at the heart of Srila Prabhupada's theology. After Swami Vivekananda, who in 1893 created history with his speech at the Parliament of Religions in Chicago, the next most important date for what I would like to refer to as 'global Hinduism' surely would be 17 September 1965—the day Prabhupada arrived in New York.

In twelve short years, Prabhupada created a global movement that has far outlived him. In his own lifetime, he created a large following not only in the US and Europe but across all continents. Like Vivekananda, he continues to attract followers from around the world.

There are two ways of comparing the messages of these two men who played a pioneering role, across generations, in taking the message of Hinduism to the world.

One way to analyse this is that unlike Vivekananda Prabhupada's was in a sense a harder message to deliver to the West. Vivekananda preached a universal formless, quality-less divine consciousness that could be accessed by all human beings through deeper, more resonant contemplation on themselves.

A formless, quality-less divine that is found within every human being was easier to understand and less novel to the West than Prabhupada's message of Krishna as the only divine entity.

The other way to understand this is that maybe it was simpler to explain one true God in transcendental shape and form and quality to a predominantly Christian audience used to understanding the divine in this personalized manner.

No matter which way we look at it, though, it is impossible to deny that after Vivekananda (in the 1890s), the most influential Hindu figure in the West was Srila Prabhupada (in the 1960s). His spiritual achievements of establishing more than a hundred Krishna temples in barely a decade and that too between the age of approximately seventy and eighty years is striking.

Vivekananda was a young man in his thirties when he went to America. Prabhupada was a septuagenarian and his indefatigable energy is more evident.

Prabhupada's mission cannot be understood in its scope and size without considering two more things—his replication, in unique ways, the message of Chaitanya Mahaprabhu and his journey in publishing, which led to him to translate sixty volumes of religious literature in the last decade of his life, including one of the most definitive commentaries on the Bhagavad Gita called the *Bhagavad Gita as It Is*.

It is often forgotten today but the singing, dancing troupes of devotees that Srila Prabhupada led around the world, and who rejoice in streets and temples across the globe were, and even today, are re-enacting, reliving a process of worship through which Chaitanya Mahaprabhu and his followers took Bengal[12] by storm in the fifteenth century.

The idea that the same ecstatic devotional process could work in the twenty-first century was a leap of faith that ensured that Prabhupada would be remembered as one of the great innovators and risk-takers in the history of preachers for Hinduism.

Srila Prabhupada could not have known that what he was about to try would succeed in any shape or form. He confesses as much in his diaristic jottings from his arrival in America, 'I do not know why You have brought me here. Now You can do whatever You like with me. But I guess You have some business here, otherwise why would You bring me to this terrible place? How will I make them understand this message of Krishna consciousness? I am very unfortunate, unqualified and most fallen. Therefore, I am seeking Your benediction so that I can convince them, for I am powerless to do so on my own.'[13] The 'You' here is, of course, Krishna.

There is another and even more vital reason to consider Prabhupada a pioneer. That reason is his publishing legacy.

Already involved in writing and publishing, albeit at a small scale, before he reached America (where he arrived with two hundred copies of his books), Prabhupada would create a publishing empire which has sold and distributed around five hundred million books, including millions of copies of the Bhagavad Gita, and the

Srimad Bhagavatam (also known as the Bhagavat Purana which tells the tale of Krishna's reassertion of justice after a period when the forces of darkness overwhelm the divine beings).

It seems no one in history has done more for the promotion of these books, indeed perhaps for the sheer spread of Hindu texts, as Srila Prabhupada did. His legacy stands alongside that of Mahatma Gandhi in the promotion of the value of the word of the Bhagavad Gita, a book Gandhi considered his ultimate text of life lessons.

Books, worship through song and dance and some of the most delicious vegetarian food—these are potent symbols of the legacy of Srila Prabhupada. Even today, the best vegetarian food—for instance, at Oxford—is to be found at a centre for Hindu studies run by an ISKCON-affiliated scholar. Prabhupada was himself an excellent cook, and his devotion to present the best meal to Krishna, which could then be spread as prasadam[14] to countless devotees, won him many followers too. Today countless restaurants run by ISKCON around the world offer what they call a 'karma-free' meal—without any killing of animals—to the famished.

But none of this overshadows his primary achievement—that of building a worldwide movement in understanding the teachings of Krishna and to bring in a consciousness about Krishna. He certainly recognized that his greatest achievement was to bring in the figure of Krishna and make the very figure of Krishna a global spiritual icon.

As someone born in British-ruled India, Prabhupada recognized the value of turning the gaze, being able to reverse the preaching and reading about his life is to understand the complexity of the task he chose to fulfil, and the enormity of what he achieved in a very short time.

Srila Prabhupada speaks to us today because his message is untied to restrictions of time and space. Long before the modern concept of globalization became popular, Srila Prabhupada was a globalized, postcolonial saint, bringing the East—without ifs or buts—to the heart of the West. All, of course, in the glory of Krishna.

1

Calcutta Boy

It was a year that would prove to be the beginning of the end of the British Raj in India. The plague—which would, in time, prove to be so severe that it would take a capitalized reference, the Plague—began in Bombay[*] but by autumn 1896,[†] the first panic stirrings of the appearance of the plague on the outskirts of Calcutta were already shaking up the city.

The plague that had appeared was connected to a wider famine that spread across the country—from Bundelkhand to Madras, Rajputana to Hyderabad. It is often mentioned that Srila Prabhupada was born in 1896, in British-ruled India.

But that is telling an incomplete story. Between the 1700s and 1900s, India had a dozen major famines, often with an allied outbreak of plague and other pestilential diseases. It was a famine in Bengal which forms the backdrop of *Ananda Math*, the nationalist epic of Bankim Chandra Chattopadhyay, the father of Bengali

---

[*] Known as Mumbai now.

[†] '. . . the first alarm was raised in September 1896. There was a co-incidental sickness among rats in Burra bazaar and looking back with experience now gained in subsequent epidemics, the cases certainly were suspicious whatever in reality they were . . .,' from Srilata Chatterjee, 'Plague and Politics in Bengal', Proceedings of the Indian History Congress, 2005–2006, Vol. 66 (2005–2006), pp. 1194–1201.

literature, with the song 'Vande Mataram'.[*] In 1866, a famine
in Odisha[†] caused the death of a million people and 'became
an important turning point in India's political development,
stimulating nationalist discussions on Indian poverty'.[‡] It also
prompted the nationalist Dadabhai Naoroji to conduct seminal
research into how the British were draining India of its riches.[§]

It is important to note that the Bengal that Prabhupada was
born in was ripe with revolutionary fervour not only because of
the oppression of the British, including during the famines and
plagues, but it was ablaze with the power of revolutionary words.
Its most important writer was Chattopadhyay, who wrote some
of his most important work between 1885 and 1887, only a
decade before the birth of Abhay Charan. By the time the baby
Prabhupada was born, the words of Chattopadhyay and others,
along with the lived experience of the colonial yoke, had created a
turbulent atmosphere ripe for revolutionary change.

This context is important to understand the early life of Srila
Prabhupada and frame his later pronouncements about nationalism
and the globalization of spirituality, of the idea of universal peace.

Prabhupada was born in a city suffused with the power of the
colonial masters but where the hum of nationalism had started to
ricochet, though still in whispers. Prabhupada was born to devout
Vaishnavite parents, Gour Mohan De and Rajani, who named
him Abhay Charan, meaning 'He who seeks refuge at the feet
of the Lord'. The consciousness of Krishna, it may be said, was
embedded in his very name.

---

[*] 'Vande Mataram' went on to become the most famous revolutionary song
of the anti-colonial movement and was declared India's national song upon
independence.

[†] Known as Orissa earlier.

[‡] Dinyar Patel, 'How British let one million Indians die in famine', BBC.com, 11
June 2016, https://www.bbc.com/news/world-asia-india-36339524.

[§] Ibid.

The mercantile Des (Gour Mohan was a cloth trader) were an offshoot of the Mullick family, one of the wealthiest business families of its time. De was the original surname of the family, and Mullick, a deviation of the word malik, most likely, was given to an ancestor for dutiful service at some point in history by Muslim rulers of the region.

The Des lived and the young Abhay Charan grew up in a house—151 Harrison Road in north Calcutta. The Mullick family and its offshoots were what was known as suvarna vaniks or gold merchants, though of course the business interest of the clan had evolved far beyond just trading in gold. Their traditional home on Pathuriaghata Street could be more accurately termed a palace, and even the relatively newer residence, on Harrison Road, filled most of two sides of a major street. So wealthy were the Mullicks that one of them, on a whim, bought two zebras from the Calcutta Zoo and used them to tug his everyday carriage. The point was to show that zebras could be domesticated as effectively as horses.* It was the sort of idiosyncratic thing that only the truly wealthy could ever pull off.

But this was not the Mullicks' only claim to fame. They were also devout Vaishnavas, in a sense the keepers of the Gaudiya Vaishnava tradition in the city of Calcutta. Even today, the list of the temples and shrines that have been nurtured by the family for years is significant. His maternal grandparents' rather modest home—having two rooms with mud walls—in the Tollygunge area, including the willowy jackfruit tree, in whose shadow Abhay Charan De was born on 1 September 1896, is still preserved, and so is the Radha Govinda temple,† the temple next door to this childhood home, where Abhay Charan was taken as a boy every single day, as is the math or shrine started by Bhaktisiddhanta Thakur in Baghbazar in north Calcutta.

---

* See http://thegangeswalk.com/the-mullicks-of-pathuriaghata-episode-2/.
† Devoted to Krishna and his spiritual consort, Radha.

As our story moves forward, we will see how these twin influences, revolutionary fervour and an equal influence of bhakti, of utter devotion to Krishna, engendered by his family, would be the keys to understanding Srila Prabhupada's early life.

All evidence suggests that his childhood, if not spoilt with wealth, was well-to-do and cheerful in every way. Gour Mohan was in the cloth trade, in which he was moderately successful. Rajani was devoted to her family. As Vaishnavas, they lived a life full of piety, eating only vegetarian food, never touching tea or coffee, and the boy Prabhupada was taught at every step to be a good devotee to Krishna, including being taught to play the mridangam or the dhol. There seems to have been at least one instance when a Mullick relative suggested sending young Abhay Charan to England to study, but Gour Mohan would have none of it. His dream was to ensure that his son became a devoted proliferator of the word of Krishna, in music and text, dedicated to spreading the sacred message.[1] Abhay Charan would cross the seas but it would be many, many years later, and for a cause that would gladden his father's heart. In fact, taking from the old Mullick tradition[*] of being the organizers of the biggest rath yatras[†] in Calcutta into the world, and his own boyhood devotion of gathering children of his age group and having their own rath yatra, if not as towering and grand as the main one, then certainly as charming.

One incident seems to have made a mark in the boy Prabhupada's mind—the 1898 plague in Calcutta. One of the primary public

---

[*] The Mullick family keep up this tradition even today as noted in this newspaper article: *Times of India*, 'Kolkata's Marble Palace mosque run by trust dedicated to Jagannath', 7 July 2016.

[†] Originally organized from the Puri temple in Odisha celebrating Lord Jagannath, and his siblings Balabhadra (brother) and Subhadra (sister), it involves pulling gigantic chariots (raths) carrying the idols of the gods through the streets. The main yatra or journey is replicated by countless other smaller raths across the region. The festival is popular in many parts of India.

responses to the plague was the dissemination of hope, alongside the medicinal and sanitary response, through kirtans, processions of Vaishnavas, singing and dancing and playing the mridangam, walking in waves through the streets of Calcutta. Missionaries of that time like John Nicol Farquhar noted the work of organizations like the Shri Gauranga Samaj and men devoted to worship like Jagadbandhu Bhadra in gathering people from all walks of life and, more importantly, all castes,* into the kirtans cascading through the streets of Calcutta, a movement for psychological and devotional positivity, not unlike the efforts during the Covid-19 pandemic in our times. There was considerable devoted support for the kirtans among the intellectual elite of the city too. For instance, the freedom fighter and journalist Sisir Kumar Ghosh, the founder of *Amrita Bazar Patrika*, was an important figure in the Vaishnava world and a supporter of the kirtan programmes. He even wrote a book on Chaitanya Mahaprabhu.

Later, Srila Prabhupada would narrate those times as, 'In Calcutta there was a very virulent type of plague epidemic in 1898. So, Calcutta became devastated. All people practically left Calcutta. Daily hundreds and hundreds of people were dying. I was one year old or one and a half years old. So, one babaji,† he organized sankirtana,‡ Hare Krishna sankirtana all over Calcutta. And in the sankirtana, all people, Hindu, Muslim, Christian, Parsi, everyone joined. And they were going road to road, street to street, entering every house. So, the plague subsided. This is a fact. Everyone who knows history of Calcutta, know that the plague was subsided by sankirtana movement.'[2]

---

* Varuni Bhatia, the historian of religion, has noted in her 2017 book, *Unforgetting Chaitanya: Vaishnavism and Cultures of Devotion in Colonial Bengal,* that Bhadra even organized the doms or lower castes employed to cremate dead bodies to be part of the singing and dancing fests praising the name of the Lord. Such 'castelessness' in those years was unique.

† Ascetic; the reference here could be to Jagadbandhu Bhadra.

‡ Another word for kirtan.

It seems reasonable that Prabhupada, who was barely two years old when these kirtans against the plague took place, could have perhaps not vividly remembered them; he would have been told about them, and they were possibly momentous enough for many repetitions which made a strong impact on the child Prabhupada.

Especially since the devotional and performative power of the kirtans did not stop with the epidemic in 1898. The following year the city celebrated, in a grand fashion, the birth anniversary of Chaitanya Mahaprabhu. In fact, in March 1898, about a year before the celebrations, the *Amrita Bazaar Patrika* asked all Vaishnavas, whom they described as the 'majority of the population', to celebrate the birth date of Chaitanya Mahaprabhu with gusto. Ghosh himself weighed in, when he wrote in an issue of the paper, 'Brothers! It is our humble request that every Vaishnava[†] will sound the victory of the Light of Gauranga all over India. We must fill the heart of all its residents with the sweet melodies of kirtan; we must sing the songs of Lord Chaitanya; we must ourselves dance and make others dance as well in the ecstatic powers of devotional delight. The coming year the festival will be organized on a large scale in Calcutta by the Gauranga Samaj. We gratefully request the devotees in the provinces to similarly celebrate this occasion.'[‡]

The celebrations, therefore, would have been unmistakable and eminently memorable for all Vaishnavas in the city, and no doubt Abhay Charan heard the stories again and again.

Surrounded by the sound of Sanskrit, in the recitations of the scriptures, the epics, and of course, the mantra Hare Krishna, Hare Krishna, Krishna Krishna, Hare Hare/ Hare Rama, Hare

---

[*] Bhatia, *Unforgetting Chaitanya: Vaishnavism and Cultures of Devotion in Colonial Bengal*, 2017, p 153.

[†] Same as Vaishnav.

[‡] Bhatia, *Unforgetting Chaitanya: Vaishnavism and Cultures of Devotion in Colonial Bengal*, 2017, p 154.

Rama, Rama Rama, Hare Hare, the young Abhay Charan's world was suffused, in a sense, with Vaishnava piety; at least as far as Gour Mohan was concerned, the boy was being brought up to spread the word of Krishna.

There was food too—an endless supply of fruits, especially mango in season was a particular favourite, on which Prabhupada even had a philosophical insight. He said, 'In its unripe stage a mango is considered a mango, and when it becomes ripe and relishable it is still a mango. So even when a newcomer begins to chant Hare Krishna (sic) his activities are within the realm of love of God and are pleasing to Krishna. But activities of karma, jnana, and yoga are not pleasing to Krishna unless they are dovetailed with bhakti.'[3] And all kinds of vegetable delicacies made with pure ghee, especially kachori, a stuffed spicy pastry so loved by Abhay Charan that he got the nickname 'kachori-mukhi' or the boy whose face is stuffed with kachoris from his mother and grandmother. Abhay Charan was not only fond of eating his kachoris but also carrying them around and distributing them. This desire to feed would, in time, become a pioneering element of his great mission. We shall see in the course of this story that if books were one great material pillar of Srila Prabhupada's message, then surely food was an equally important element. Little wonder, then, that ISKCON still has a delectable recipe for making kachoris, something we will come across later in this book when we discuss the adventure that was Srila Prabhupada's culinary life.

Food makes an appearance even in his school life, even though Abhay Charan was not directly connected to the incident. He was sent to study, when he came of age, to Mutty Lal Seal's Free School. Now it is important, again, to put in context why he was sent to this school. Mutty Lal Seal is the distorted anglicized way of saying Moti Lal Seal. Seal was not only one of the richest suvarna vaniks and one of the richest people in Calcutta, but he was also one of the most devoted Vaishnavas. As inclined to

Vaishnava causes of pious charity as the Mullicks themselves, Seal not only supported rath yatras, but he also built a temple* of Lord Jagannath and Chaitanya Mahaprabhu that functions even today and started a free food programme for the needy that continues till date.†

The school that Abhay Charan was sent to was hailed in its time as a unique institution, built to bring together students from the gentry of Calcutta to give them a western, meaning anglicized education. A major German newspaper of the time, *Allgemeine Zeitung*, even cheered it 'as a revolution in the direction of open education and a mixing of civilizations'.‡

The school was initially run by Jesuit missionaries from St. Xavier's, but Mutty Lal Seal cut off the association with the Jesuits after an incident where the students were given food that was forbidden in their religion.§ What exactly this food was is a bit unclear but it was most probably meat. The *Bengal Catholic Herald* noted an angry letter to the Jesuits from one Kissen Mohun Mullick, secretary of the Free School, where he wrote, 'You must all be aware that the reception of European viands¶ are religiously considered indecent among Hindus, and that you were pledged not to enforce or encourage any practices among the boys calculated rudely to assail the prejudices of their parents and relations. And yet, with the full knowledge of all this the teachers themselves became parties to an indecent display on the part of the boys of eating and sporting with things the very touch of which

---

* The temple is called Thakurbari and it is located in the Belghoria area of Calcutta.
† http://www.motilalseal.com/msp/thakurbari/
‡ See https://play.google.com/books/reader?id=W9hDAAAAcAAJ&printsec=frontcover&output=reader&hl=en_GB&pg=GBS.PA2688-IA7, online records of the *Allgemeine Zeitung* from 1844.
§ See http://www.motilalseal.com/msp/seals-free-college/.
¶ Most likely used as a substitute for the word meat or meat-based dishes.

was forbidden to them by their social institutions." The letter accusingly noted that such incidents had happened repeatedly, and that Seal had no choice but to stop this by removing the Jesuit teachers from running the school.

So, from every side, the influences in the world of Abhay Charan were clear. The fervent piety, the early ripples of nationalism, the primacy of the printed word as a vehicle for the dissemination of ideas, and food, always the whiff of wholesome food.

Each of these would cascade through the life of Abhay Charan in his journey to becoming Srila Prabhupada. As we go along, the influence of these elements would be hard to miss in this story. Everyone, even saints, are products of their time, and so was Abhay Charan. But unlike ordinary folk, the godly retain a sense of uniform composure, of purpose and message, through their journey. That is perhaps the source of their strength—in a changing world to be an unchanging refuge of solace. Srila Prabhupada never relinquished any of the elements that so suffused his life, not least because they echoed with the sound of his beloved Krishna.

---

* See *Bengal Catholic Herald*, Volume 7, p. 177

2

A Different Kind of Revolutionary

August 1914.

When he was about eighteen years old, Abhay Charan De's Calcutta was aflame with the news of an arms robbery, perhaps the most daring in British-ruled India. The *Statesman*, the most venerable British newspaper of the time published from Calcutta called it, in its 30 August 2014 edition, the 'greatest daylight robbery'.[*]

Young revolutionaries fighting for India's freedom had managed to discover the landing date and transfer route of a major consignment of armaments to Messrs Rodda & Co., a prominent Calcutta arms dealer. They managed to intercept and steal, using an employee of the company who was also a revolutionary, fifty German-made Mauser C96 pistols and forty-six thousand rounds of ammunition.

The robbery was the handiwork of the Jugantar[†] faction of the fiercest revolutionary group, the Anushilan Samiti. Some of the most influential freedom fighters of the time belonged to these

---

[*] *The Statesman*, 'Kolkata's 'greatest daylight robbery' all but forgotten', 24 August 2013.
[†] 'Dawn of a new age' in Bengali.

groups—men like Aurobindo Ghosh and his brother Barindra, Rash Behari Bose, Sachindra Nath Sanyal, and even Subhas Chandra Bose. There was barely an attack on the British, an assassination, an arms robbery, that members of the Samiti and Jugantar, some of the cleverest young men in eastern India, did not have their fingerprints on. And echoes of the revolution rang through the corridors of one of the most prominent colleges in the country—Scottish Church—not least because some of the most influential figures for the revolutionaries were the monk Vivekananda, the scourge of the Empire, Subhas Chandra Bose and armed freedom fighters like Amarendranath Chatterjee.

The Scottish missionary Alexander Duff had started the Scottish Church College (first called General Assembly's Institution) in 1830 to create Indian men into perfect subjects of the Raj. But by the turn of the century, a different wind was blowing through its corridors.

And into these hallowed corridors stepped in Abhay Charan De. If he had caught whiffs of resistance to the Raj even during his schooling, no doubt he would have noticed that the mood among many at Scottish Church was even more rebellious.

Abhay Charan had been sent to Scottish Church to imbibe a sense of the spiritual, to be surrounded by an atmosphere of piety. But the Bible and catechism were not the only things that young Abhay learnt. He was enchanted by the romance of history, including historical fiction, admiring the work of Walter Scott and Bankim Chandra Chattopadhyay. Bankim, thought Prabhupada, was 'the Scott of Bengal'.[*]

Years later, there would remain in his accent traces of Scotland and an affinity for history, as noted by an interlocutor Dhananjaya, 'I could detect a slight Scottish accent in some of

---

[*] BBT Archives, Room conversation with Mr and Mrs James Williams, 23 July 1973, London.

Prabhupada's words. Later on, while I was massaging him, Srila Prabhupada asked me where I came from. I said "Scotland," and he started reminiscing about his education at Scottish Church College in Calcutta and how all his teachers were Scottish. He studied the Bible there and learned the catechism. He asked me if I knew any Scottish Lords. I said, "I don't know any Scottish Lords personally." He said, "Oh, one Lord Zetland* came to our college in Calcutta." He asked me if I studied British history, and I said, "Oh yes," and then he tested me. "When was the battle of Trafalgar?" I said, "1805," "When was the battle of Waterloo?" "1815." He said, "You know British history just like I know British history." He also asked, "How far is Scotland and Glasgow from London?" and I told him, "Approximately 400 miles." "How long did it take to go there by train?" "Approximately eight hours." He put me at ease in that way, because I really didn't know how to start a conversation with Srila Prabhupada when I was in the process of massaging him. That's the way he won over my heart too, because he related to me in a way I could appreciate and respond to.'†

In those years he took forward the lessons in devout theatrics that he had seen as a boy on the streets of Calcutta, performing and excelling in a play on Chaitanya Mahaprabhu and reading, and being moved by, among other things, Kalidasa's *Kumarasambhava*.[1] The young Abhay Charan saw, clearly, in the environment of the college, the cause, the consequences and resistance to British rule. He saw, for instance, racial segregation in everything including the common rooms used by teachers, between the English people and the Indians. It was a world where

---

* Lawrence John Lumley Dundas, the second Marquess of Zetland, a British Conservative politician who was an expert on India. He served as secretary of state for India in the late 1930s.
† Memories Anecdotes of a Modern Day Saint, Volume 1 by Siddhanta Dasa.

'the European population of Calcutta was markedly segregated from the other communities'.[2]

This differentiation, this distancing, this humiliation was, no doubt, underlined ever more strongly because of a fellow student, only one year senior to Abhay—Subhas Chandra Bose. Bose had come to Scottish Church after being thrown out from the other elite educational institution of that time, Presidency College. He was quiet and studious, and yet a leopard cannot change its spots. Though nationalist campaigning was forbidden at Scottish Church, Bose and his fellow nationalists found ways to preach the gospel of independence. For Abhay this was unmissably part of his education.

Later he would remember Bose fondly and argued that it was Bose's creation of the Indian National Army (INA) that compelled the British, with the fear of Indian soldiers rebelling throughout the country, to leave India.

In a conversation with guests in 1977, Srila Prabhupada recounted, 'They [the British] knew that "we are not going [from India]. So long as the non-violence is there, we are safe" . . . But Subhas Bose's protest was that "if you don't take to violence, then these people are never going". That was the difference of opinion between Subhas Bose and [the non-violent movement]. . . He managed to go out of India to Singapore . . . organized this INA.* And when the Britishers saw that "now the soldiers are [the] joining national movement, then we cannot rule over [India]", then they decided, "let us make some compromise[s], and as much [as] possible, do harm. Divide this India [into], Pakistan and India, and go away". This is [a] fact . . . So they decided that because without soldiers and police, how they can rule over [India]? And that, when they saw the soldiers are now joining Subhas Bose and

---

* The Indian National Army was an armed force formed by Indian collaborationists and Imperial Japan on 1 September 1942 in South-East Asia during World War II. Its aim was to secure Indian independence from British rule.

they are planning to come to India from Imphal, so they saw, "now it is impossible". They are politicians. They could understand . . . It is Subhas Bose's INA which compelled them to go away."

Essentially, what Srila Prabhupada was arguing is that Gandhian non-violent tactics or techniques were not the only reason that British rule ended in India. The role of revolutionaries like Subhas Bose, who raised an army to fight colonial rule, also scared the British rulers, who realized that the loyalty of Indian soldiers to the British government could no longer be taken for granted.

As noted from the fervour of his words, there was always a revolutionary spirit in Srila Prabhupada, an admiration for the kshatriya[†]—a word he used often—spirit. But for himself, he found a different medium or channel to focus the desire for independence. His freedom had a higher purpose, the freedom to submit in his entirety to Krishna. He had noted disdain for Hindu philosophical concepts, like karma, among his British teachers and lessons that suggested that until the arrival of the British, Indian culture and civilization, indeed Hindu culture and civilization, was derelict and debauched.

It is important to remember that Abhay and his fellow students were being taught under the shadow of definitive (at that time, that is) books like James Mill's *History of British India* (1818).[‡] Mill, who never visited India, never knew a single Indian language, yet went on to claim that 'a duly qualified man can obtain more knowledge of India in one year in his closet in England than

---

[*] BBT Archives, Room Conversation, 27 January 1977, Jagannatha Puri, Odisha.

[†] Warrior caste in the Hindu hierarchy of castes, though Prabhupada did not use it to suggest caste division but rather to underline a sort of 'indomitable spirit of the warrior'.

[‡] *The History of British India* is a three-volume work by James Mill, a Scottish historian, economist, political theorist and philosopher, charting the history of Company rule in India. It was first published in 1818.

he could obtain during the course of the longest life, by the use of his eyes and ears in India'.[3] Mill's work described Hinduism as steeped in ugly superstition with not a redeeming feature in sight—and it was to seep into the colonial consciousness as the key understanding of the colonized. Historian Thomas Trautmann has noted that 'James Mill's highly influential *History of British India* (1818)—most particularly the long essay "Of the Hindus" comprising ten chapters—is the single most important source of British Indophobia and hostility to Orientalism.'[4] It is under this shadow that the colonial gaze fell on students like Subhas and Abhay.

Young Abhay was conscious of these biases, and he understood that things could change only when freedom came, and for the world to respect the treasures of his beloved Bhagavad Gita, it would have to be respected and promoted by the people in power at home first.[5]

There was already, before him even at that time, one man who was already showing such reverence. His name was Mahatma Gandhi. Gandhi always carried the Gita, noted Abhay, and spoke of it as having had the most important influence in his life. Abhay, the devout Vaishnava boy, also approved of Gandhi's personal habits—his vegetarianism, his abstinence and his abhorrence of all intoxicants.[6] Gandhi seemed like a man worth emulating. After all, imagined Abhay, a man devoted to the gospel of Krishna could not be wrong, could he?

In the meantime, in keeping with the traditions of the time, his parents worked to find a suitable bride for him, and she was discovered in Radharani Datta, suitable not merely in name, carrying as she did the name of the consort of Krishna, but also socially acceptable as she came from the same suvarna vanik community. She was eleven when they were wed and Abhay, twenty-two.

There was also an examination to pass, a college to graduate from—and in this Abhay would show how sharply the revolutionary fire had burnt within him. Even though he took the examination and passed the course, when the time came for him to accept his degree, Abhay demurred.

No matter how important it might be for his career he would not accept a validation from the colonial masters. He had imbibed the non-violent path of protest and renunciation preached by Mahatma Gandhi.

Instead, on the coaxing of his father, he gained a position as an apprentice and manager at Dr Bose's Laboratories, a premier pharmacy of the time. In his own way, Dr Kartik Chandra Bose was a revolutionary too. Along with Prafulla Chandra Ray, he was one of the people who helped start Bengal Chemical and Pharmaceutical Works and became the company's first managing director.[7] These men broke the British monopoly on the chemicals and pharmaceutical business.

Abhay was now married. He had what, by all counts, qualified as a good job. And by his own later accounts, Abhay showed initial interest in the work.

He said, 'I wanted to become very big businessman, and there was good opportunity. I was very nicely associated with the chemical industry of India, Dr Bose's laboratory, Bengal Chemical, V.K. Farr, and all of them, they liked my business organization. Then I started a big laboratory in Lucknow. So that was golden days. But gradually, everything becomes dead, and at last my Allahabad business was lost. It was not lost on account of some, my debts; I had to hand it over to Dr Kartik [sic] Chandra Bose because I was his agent.'* But financial mishap may not have been the only reason. There is a sense that the ennui towards the material world was steadily rising. For instance, Prabhupada talks about, later in life, that at the same time he was giving up his business goals, he was getting more and more involved with ascetics like

---

* BBT Archives, Mayapur Temple Inauguration lecture, 17 March 1973, Mayapur.

'Sarvesva brahmachari and Atulananda brahmachari'* and would go regularly to their temple which happened to be near his home.[†]

But soon he grew weary of the work and disinterested in his marriage. It was clear to his father that the real calling of the son was elsewhere. Not that Gour Mohan minded. His son was showing all signs of a greater, more abiding devotion to his beloved Krishna, not least during a contemplative visit to the great temples of Puri, where Chaitanya had once danced in abandon, and where Abhay tasted the magnificent, fifty-six-course bhog offered to the deities, Jagannatha, Balabhadra and Subhadra, every single day.

A different call was emerging strongly, no doubt fuelled by the rebellion brewing in him. When Gandhi asked for a boycott of clothes made from cloth manufactured in British mills, Abhay had no hesitation in chucking his clothes into the bonfire of protest and embracing the freedom of khadi or Indian handspun as popularized by Gandhi himself rolling the charkha or thread spinning wheel.

This, though, was not merely the freedom of national revolution, but one step closer to Abhay Charan De shedding the world and moving towards his Krishna.

---

* Brahmachari or monks who have taken the vow of celibacy.
[†] BBT Archives, Mayapur Temple Inauguration lecture, 17 March 1973, Mayapur.

3

The Bookworm Monks

It is impossible to tell the story of Srila Prabhupada without talking about books. But the affinity for publishing millions of books, which his order continues even today, does not begin with him.

To understand this story better, we have to jump two generations and come upon a great personality called Bhaktivinoda Thakur.

Bhaktivinoda Thakur (1838–1914), born Kedarnath Datta, was one of the most prominent Gaudiya Vaishnava reformers and spiritual leaders of his time. Educated at Hindu College (also known as Presidency College, which we have encountered earlier in our story as a hub of revolutionary activity), Datta was a close associate with a veritable who's-who list of literary luminaries of his time—Ishwar Chandra Vidyasagar, Bankim Chandra Chattopadhyay and the prolific newspaper man Sisir Kumar Ghosh of *Amrita Bazar Patrika*. They were the leading lights of the Bengal Renaissance, a period of great cultural progress, which had, as its base, a technological intervention—printing.

To understand what Bhaktivinoda Thakur, and later his son Bhaktisiddhanta Saraswati Thakur, was trying to achieve is key to comprehending the impulses of Srila Prabhupada, for he built on the pivotal base that was created, first, by Bhaktivinoda Thakur.

One of the key features of the Bengal Renaissance was efforts made by its intellectual elite to formulate a new way of talking about the Hindu faith. It developed simultaneously with the arrival of the printing press in Bengal.

'Printing came to Bengal in 1777 when two presses were set up almost simultaneously, one in Calcutta by James Augustus Hicky (famous for later printing India's first newspaper, *Hicky's Bengal Gazette*) and another in the small town of Hooghly by Nathaniel Brassey Halhed and Charles Wilkins (famous for printing *A Grammar of the Bengal Language*). It is unclear which press was established first.'*

But what was distinctly clear is that printing transformed many things—literature in the Bengali language, for instance, written and printed, starting with Bankim, and politics, as the age of pamphleteering dawned and, more importantly, religion. Some of the first books printed in these presses were translations in vernacular languages of the Bible, eagerly produced by missionaries. The religious reformists among the Hindus, most of them highly educated, embraced the art of printing with what can only be described as Godspeed.

'But in 19th century Bengal, more than anything else, the language and its written literature became the object of immense scrutiny, surveillance and debate among the Bengali people and the rulers alike. For the British bureaucracy it was a language that had to be mastered for administrative convenience, and for gaining access to crucial local information. But for the native intelligentsia it became a bearer of Indianness, of cultural identity. In the active intellectual climate that had been stirred up following the encounter with the west, Bengali became the medium of self-expression of a conscious and articulate urban litterati [sic]. With

---

* See https://blogs.soas.ac.uk/archives/2019/06/28/the-first-printed-works-of-bengal/.

growing, numbers among the literate population, and a prodigious printing and publishing industry, increasingly large reader-writer groups jostled for recognition in the ongoing debates."

One of the native intelligentsia participating in this process was Kedarnath Datta, who worked for the British government for most of his life, rising to the level of a district magistrate, but whose lifelong exploration into the life and work of Chaitanya Mahaprabhu would, eventually, lead to a deeper embrace of devotional life and the name Bhaktivinoda Thakur. He had been given this title from the large Vaishnavite community in recognition of his immense scholarly contribution in the scholarly and devotional promotion of Vaishnavite thought. Like others of his intellectual ilk, Bhaktivinoda Thakur chose the path of writing and publishing to spread the word of the divine as he saw it.

He wrote one hundred books including '*Krishna-samhita* (1880), *Caitanya-sikshamrita* (1886) *Jaiva-dharma* (1893), *Tattva-sutra* (1893), *Tattva-viveka* (1893), and *Hari-nama-cintamani* (1900). Between 1881 and 1909, Kedarnath also published a monthly journal in Bengali entitled *Sajjana-toshani* ("The source of pleasure for devotees")'.†

Bhaktivinoda Thakur understood that in order to revive the movement of Chaitanya and the understanding of the Vaishnavite path would require what could perhaps be called a 'buy in' or acceptance, and devotion, from the elite of Bengal, and indeed outside Bengal. He was a pioneer in using what to him was the latest technology— printing and distribution of books—to reach a regional, national and global audience.

He not only wrote and published books on a major scale— certainly unprecedented in the Vaishnavite or perhaps any other

---

* Anindita Ghosh, 'Revisiting the 'Bengal Renaissance': Literary Bengali and Low-Life Print in Colonial Calcutta', *Economic and Political Weekly*, 19–25 October 2002, Vol. 37, No. 42, p 4329.
† Ravi M. Gupta (2014), Ravi M. Gupta (ed.), *Caitanya Vaiṣṇava Philosophy: Tradition, Reason and Devotion*, Burlington, VT: Ashgate.

Hindu tradition before him—he was also convinced that the message was so powerful that it would speak to people far away from the heartland of Hinduism.

But that is not all. He understood that for him to be taken seriously as a Vaishnavite pioneer, a pathbreaking monk if you will, he needed a source of credibility and the ability to effectively spread the word.

This he achieved through two ways—one, through diligent scouring of the Nabadwip area of Bengal, until he discovered Mayapur as the site of Chaitanya's birth and proceeding to initiate the building of a temple there,* and through sending out books, not only among the people and intellectuals of Bengal, and other parts of India, but also to Western scholars in England, Canada, Australia and America, to men like philosopher Ralph Waldo Emerson and German orientalist Reinhold Rost. His books appeared at Oxford University and McGill in Canada. At Oxford, Sanskrit scholar Sir Monier Monier-Williams, the Joseph Boden Professor of Sanskrit, reviewed a work of Bhaktivinoda Thakur in the journal of the Royal Asiatic Society.†

Bhaktivinoda Thakur is an important figure to understand because it is he who first defined the ambition of the message of Chaitanya to ring through the streets of the West. Writing in 1882, he noted, 'When in England, France, Russia, Prussia and America all fortunate persons by taking up kholas‡ and karatalas§ will take the name of Chaitanya Mahaprabhu again and again in their own countries, and raise the waves of sankirtana (congregational singing of Krishna's names), when will that day come! Oh! When will the

---

* This temple at Mayapur became in a sense the site of a new Gaudiya Vaishnavite resuscitation, and renaissance.
† Ferdinando Sardella (2013), *Modern Hindu Personalism: The History, Life, and Thought of Bhaktisiddhanta Sarasvati* (reprint ed.), New York, NY: Oxford University Press, pp. 94–96.
‡ Handheld drums.
§ Cymbals.

day come when the white-skinned British people will speak the glory of Shachinandana* on one side and on the other with his call spread their arms to embrace devotees from other countries in brotherhood, when will that day come!'†

It was Bhaktivinoda Thakur who, in 1896, wrote a book primarily addressed to devotees in the West, called *Gaurangalila-Smaranamangala*‡ or *Chaitanya Mahaprabhu: His life and Precepts*. And it is he who visualized a time when the world would recognize Chaitanya Mahaprabhu as a preacher of universal brotherhood, writing, 'Caitanya preaches equality of men . . . universal fraternity amongst men and special brotherhood amongst Vaishnavas, who are according to him, the best pioneers of spiritual improvement. He preaches that human thought should never be allowed to be shackled with sectarian views . . . The religion preached by Mahaprabhu is universal and not exclusive. The most learned and the most ignorant are both entitled to embrace it . . . The principle of kirtana invites, as the future church of the world, all classes of men without distinction of caste or clan to the highest cultivation of the spirit.'§ All of this is critical in the story as we shall see these ideas cascaded through Bhaktivinoda Thakur's son Bhaktisiddhanta Saraswati Thakur and on to Srila Prabhupada—the source of Srila Prabhupada's vision is unmistakable.

Bhaktivinoda Thakur was a contemporary of Vivekananda (1863–1902). But while Vivekananda's seminal voyage to America and his speech at the Parliament of Religions is very well known,

---

* Another name for Chaitanya.

† Thomas J. Hopkins; David A. Utz and Peter Gaeffke (eds.), 1984, *Identity and Division in Cults and Sects in South Asia: Proceedings of the South Asia Seminar*, Philadelphia, PA: Department of South Asia Regional Studies, University of Virginia.

‡ Self-published by author in 1896. See https://bit.ly/3r43WDI.

§ Sardella, Ferdinando (2013), *Modern Hindu Personalism: The History, Life, and Thought of Bhaktisiddhanta Sarasvati* (reprint ed.), New York, NY: Oxford University Press.

not enough is known about the contributions of Bhaktivinoda Thakur in changing public opinion about Hinduism at home, and especially abroad, through his publications.

Bhaktivinoda Thakur, as we noted, had a son, who also became a monk, an heir to his father in the Gaudiya Vaishnavite tradition. This illustrious son, born Bimala Prasad Datta, was known more by his monastic name Bhaktisiddhanta Saraswati Thakur.

Early in his life, Bhaktisiddhanta Saraswati changed the course of modern Gaudiya Vaishnavism through one seminal event. Before we go into that event, it is important to note a seminal fact about the lives of Bhaktivinoda Thakur, his son Bhaktisiddhanta, and Srila Prabhupada—none of them were Brahmins.

Bhaktivinoda Thakura and Bhaktisiddhanta Saraswati belonged to Kayastha community, a community in the Hindu caste system, which was known for its intellectual abilities (Vivekananda was a Kayastha), but in the religious pecking order, lower than the Brahmins or the priestly class which had a hegemony on theological knowledge. Srila Prabhupada belonged to the suvarna banik community.

In Vaishnavism, all that would change on 8 September 1911 at a mass gathering of traditional Vaishnavite scholars, all of them caste Brahmins, except Bhaktisiddhanta Saraswati, who was indeed the most qualified *brahmana* though not by caste. At this event, Bhaktisiddhanta challenged the supremacy of hereditary transmission of knowledge, and argued that it is true devotion and spiritual practice that mattered more than lineage. He presented a paper titled 'Brahmana o Vaishnava' (Brahmana and Vaishnava), which became a guiding document for the reinvigorated Gaudiya Vaishnavite tradition as started by his father.

Bhaktisiddhanta Saraswati was a prolific writer and publisher himself, not least because before his death his father had instructed him, 'The real service to Sri Mayapur can be done by acquiring printing presses, distributing devotional books, and sankirtana—

preaching. Please do not neglect to serve Sri Mayapur or to preach for the sake of your own reclusive bhajan . . . I had a special desire to preach the significance of such books as *Srimad Bhagavatam*, *Sat Sandarbha*, and *Vedanta Darshan*."

Under Bhaktisiddhanta Saraswati (1874–1937), the Gaudiya Math grew exponentially in stature. Not only did he personally write thirty books, many of them multi-volume tomes, but he also published a series of publications which appeared periodically in several languages like Bengali, English, Hindi, Odia and Assamese.

Bhaktisiddhanta Saraswati also made novel efforts to build centres for the Gaudiya Math in Berlin, London and Yangon (then known as Rangoon). In his own way, like his father, Bhaktisiddhanta Saraswati was both a mendicant and a social reformer. It was he who emphasized that traditional societal caste rules barring lower castes from entering temples should be abolished—everyone, he insisted, was welcome to bathe in the love of Krishna, and the greater the devotion (not the birth or lineage), the warmer should be the welcome and embrace of the devotee. Bhakti or devotion was the key; it unlocked the path to the realization of the divine.

This emphasis would prove invaluable—as it does even today—to attract followers from around the world to the world of Krishna consciousness; the doors are not shut to anyone. Anyone could enter as long as they chanted the holy mantra— Hare Krishna, Hare Krishna, Krishna Krishna, Hare Hare/ Hare Rama, Hare Rama, Rama Rama, Hare Hare. In fact, in this Bhaktisiddhanta Saraswati himself set an example by chanting the mantra one billion times—a feat that took ten years.

But like his father, Bhaktisiddhanta Saraswati did not deny the utility of modernism. Instead, he taught that anything—

---

* Phillip Murphy, Raoul Goff (eds.), *Prabhupada Sarasvati Thakur: The Life and Precepts of Srila Bhaktisidhanta Sarasvati* (first limited ed.), 1997, Eugene.

including any technology—that could be used to further the word of the boundless love of Krishna should, indeed must, be adopted to spread the message. The medium, as it were, should never be confused with the message.

It was due to the efforts of this father-and-son duo that the Gaudiya Math became as influential as the Ramakrishna Mission of Sri Ramakrishna and Vivekananda, as the twin pillars of revivalist Hindu movements that emerged from the Bengal Renaissance and transcended the old Brahminical boundary of the borders of India and began to take the message to the very heart of Europe.

This, in a sense, was the Empire talking back. Using the technology and the idiom that colonialism had brought to India, including English-language education, these Bengali spiritual scholars reversed the gaze. If missionaries were printing Bibles in Bengal in vernacular languages, they began taking the message of Hindu spirituality to the West in a format and voice that could be easily understood.

It is important to note here that their role in the Bengal Renaissance was seminal because they had used the churn brought about by British rule to throw away some of the worst shackles of orthodoxy (especially of caste hierarchy and prejudice) and established the primacy of knowledge, intellectual prowess and sheer devotion as the primary route to access divine grace.

It is also pertinent that the early followers of these movements came from a class in society in Bengal which came to be known as the *bhadraloks* or refined people. They were not always wealthy but almost always educated people and usually educated in British-run schools and colleges. They were reformists, people who were eager to try new things, new ideas that would shape the future of Bengal—but often they thought not only of Bengal, or India, but the entire world. Their education had engendered within them a certain openness of the mind and a temperament for progressive change.

Naturally, they sought such change, such reform, even in religion, a hugely influential part of their daily lives. The religion that they saw around them was steeped—more often than not— in prejudices and superstitions that was an ill fit with their new-found knowledge and intellectual pursuits.

Therefore, bookish-minded people, hungry for change, needed monks who spoke that language and wrote that grammar and idiom. And so, this was a powerful coming together of a new kind of elite (though several of them had old money, which they put to progressive use including in publications and education) and a new kind of ascetic with, more importantly, new methods of teaching and preaching, and with new tools.

It was in such a milieu that Abhay Charan De was coaxed one day to meet a monk who people said was very different from the many a bedraggled mendicant he had grown up encountering. That revered monk was Bhaktisiddhanta Saraswati.

4

'Who Will Hear Your Chaitanya's Message?'

The Indian National Congress, the main political movement leading India's freedom struggle from British colonialism, had agreed in its Calcutta session in September 1920 that the first major non-cooperation movement would be launched following Mahatma Gandhi's call against the Raj.

It was to be a demonstration of the power of peaceful resistance, satyagraha, but by 1922 it had been struck by a series of violent uprisings, including an incident at Chauri Chaura where several policemen had died. Gandhi called off the movement, but it marked a vital transition—the battle for Indian independence had become a mass movement. It would no longer be confined to the drawing rooms of the educated and their debating societies. The streets were alive with the chant of 'Vande Mataram'.

The man Abhay Charan was about to meet was also going through a fervent period. Bhaktisiddhanta Saraswati had taken upon himself the task of spreading the egalitarian but uncompromising word of Chaitanya Mahaprabhu. In 1918, he took sannyasa, adorning the robes of an ascetic. This, though little remarked upon even today, was the first instance of a monk in the Gaudiya Vaishnava tradition in more than four hundred years. With this decision, Bhaktisiddhanta Saraswati created a new

Gaudiya Vaishnava math, a new order devoted to the worship of Krishna in the manner prescribed by Chaitanya.

In 1920, Bhaktisiddhanta Saraswati renamed his first Calcutta ashram at the Ultadanga locality, from Calcutta Bhaktivinoda Asana to Shri Gaudiya Math—this is where he was destined to meet his most famous disciple. The transition to a more structured, methodical order not beholden to a one single living guru had begun to take shape. The venerable *Amrita Bazar Patrika* noted, 'Ardent seekers after truth are received and listened to and solutions to their questions are advanced from a most reasonable and liberal standpoint of view.'[*]

This propagation of a 'reasonable and liberal standpoint' is important to consider. The Bengal Renaissance which stretched well into the early twentieth century was a period of serious rethinking amidst the educated Hindus of Bengal.

'. . . the pervasive Hindu cultural identity that was reconstructed in the late nineteenth and early twentieth centuries in Bengal was the result of multiple interactions with colonial discourse . . . Western education, as also Orientalist fascination with India's glorious past, enabled the construction of this cultural identity by attempting to remodel the present into a closer resemblance to the putative past. Perceiving the essence of their identity as lying in a previous age, the articulate middle class transformed several Orientalist ideas in significant ways. Thus, the identity of this class in Bengal constructed for itself a universalist notion of Hinduism that erased differences between Hindus across class, time and geographical region. This cultural identity was specific to Bengalis, although at times its articulators conflated a pan-Indian Hindu identity with ingredients of "Bengaliness".[†]

---

[*] Sardella, Ferdinando (2013), *Modern Hindu Personalism: The History, Life, and Thought of Bhaktisiddhanta Sarasvati* (reprint ed.), New York, NY: Oxford University Press, p 92.

[†] Indira Chowdhury Sengupta, 'Colonialism & Cultural Identity: The Making of a Hindu Discourse, Bengal 1867–1905', School of Oriental and African Studies, London Department of History, 1993.

This reconstruction was seen prominently in reformist movements like the Brahmo Samaj and later the followers of the Sri Ramakrishna and the Swami Vivekananda-founded Ramakrishna Mission. The new Gaudiya Math of Bhaktivinoda Thakur and Bhaktisiddhanta Saraswati was in this mould. They approached a moribund and deeply sectarian system and exposed it to the sunshine of the true path of Chaitanya, to embrace wholeheartedly anyone who seeks to love Krishna.

So, when Abhay Charan was coaxed by a friend to meet a new monk, he did so immersed in a mood of revolution. But the monk he was meeting was in a particularly resolute frame of mind too. Bhaktisiddhanta Saraswati was only too aware of the opposition he faced from within his community, and the resistance from the orthodoxy to his radical new ideas. He would soon start a campaign to take the mission of the Gaudiya Math around the world. Missionary zeal was on the top of his mind.

When, without prompting, at first sight, Bhaktisiddhanta Saraswati asked him to use his education to spread the word of Chaitanya Mahaprabhu, Abhay Charan was startled. But he had his repartee ready—what use was the spreading of the message of Chaitanya when the land of Chaitanya was under foreign yoke?

This was not an unfair question. To the young Abhay Charan, devout as he was, it seemed only reasonable that any talk of spiritual upliftment should come after the fundamental task of freedom from colonial rule. What use was spiritual bliss if the body polity remained crushed?

But Bhaktisiddhanta Saraswati had a different point of view. The message of the divine, he argued, could not wait for the politics of mere mortals. Krishna's lessons could not be held back by the political circumstance of India; indeed, the word of the divine was not merely confined to people in India. It was for everyone. Every person around the world was entitled to listen to it and enrich their lives. The imagery of cities in the towns and cities of the

West reverberating with the sound of mridangas* and cymbals is deep-rooted within the movement that Abhay Charan De, later Srila Prabhupada, created. And it is easy to see why—this image, this graphic, sonorous picture was an inheritance passed on to him from his guru.

So, asked Bhaktisiddhanta Saraswati, what was keeping educated Vaishnavas like Abhay Charan from taking up the task of spreading the love of Krishna around the world?

If you see photos of Bhaktisiddhanta Saraswati, it is easy to see how his personality, even his sheer physical presence, would be startling but captivating for young Abhay. In almost every photo that exists of him today, he is staring at the camera with a piercing, questioning gaze through owl spectacles. His gaze is unwavering, as that of a professor, always slightly disappointed that his pupils do not quite measure up to his exacting standards. Usually, in the photos, he stands or sits ramrod straight. He appears to have been a lithe man and even though his head is shaved, one can see where the leonine references about him come from.

By the time he met Abhay Charan, Bhaktisiddhanta Saraswati was already fulfilling the task of his father—he had made the printing presses of the Gaudiya Math into a brhat mrdanga or giant drum through which he could broadcast the word of Krishna and Chaitanya across the country and around the world.

We have already noted in the earlier chapter that Bhaktisiddhanta Saraswati and his father played pioneering roles in sending books to theological scholars across the country and around the world. These books would now become the bridge between him and his newly acquired follower, Abhay Charan.

For the well-educated Abhay Charan, these books paved the path for his steady immersion into the world of the new Gaudiya

---

* A sort of traditional oblong drum hung from the neck and played by beating its two sides.

Math. But complete surrender to the cause was still some time away. There was, after all, a family to run.

By the 1920s, Abhay Charan was a father, embroiled, as all young parents are, in the vagaries of parenting and running a household. As a householder, Abhay Charan imagined that perhaps he could focus on running his business well and as he made more money, he would make that wealth available to spread the word as Bhaktisiddhanta Saraswati wanted, adding, as it were, to the reverb of the brhat mrdanga.

To expand his business, Abhay Charan moved the family to Allahabad where he joined hands with a local physician to start a pharmacy distribution and sales centre. Radharani and he were now parents of two children, a boy and a girl. Some members of his extended family, including his ageing father Gour Mohan, came to stay with the couple in their home in the old city of Allahabad.

Abhay Charan partnered with a local doctor to open a pharmacy called Prayag Pharmacy, after the old name for Allahabad. As he focused on expanding his business and earnings for the family, Abhay Charan travelled across northern India, his sphere of activity.

It was not that he had forgotten the words of Bhaktisiddhanta Saraswati but in his immediate family, especially his wife, he did not have anyone with whom he could share what was becoming an evermore urgent yearning in his heart for a devoted spiritual life.

His travels for work took him to the heart of Krishna worship, to Vrindavan, and he rejoiced. But his world in the early and mid-1920s was consumed by being the dutiful family man, fulfilling his *grihasta* duties.

However, the pull of the divine would not be kept away. In 1928, a small group of monks came to visit Abhay Charan at his shop. Later, Srila Prabhupada remembered this, '. . . from 1922 to 1933 practically I was not initiated, but I got the impression of preaching Chaitanya Mahaprabhu's cult.* That I was thinking. And that was the initiation by my Guru Maharaj. Then officially I was initiated in 1933 because in 1923 I left Calcutta. I started my business at Allahabad. So I was always thinking of my Guru Maharaj, that "I met a very nice sadhu." Although I was doing business, I never forgot him. Then, in 1928, these Gaudiya Math people came to Allahabad during Kumbhamela.† As the Kumbhamela is going to be held this year, a similar big Kumbhamela was held in 1928. In those days they came to open their branch in Allahabad, and somebody recommended that "You go to . . ." At that time I was running on my big pharmacy and I was very well known man in Allahabad as the proprietor of the pharmacy. So somebody recommended them that "You go to Abhaya‡ Babu. He is a very religious man. He'll help you." So when they entered my shop I was very much pleased that these men I met in 1922, and now they have come. In this way I became reconnected.'§

The monks from the Gaudiya Math had come to Allahabad to set up a new centre in the city, and who better to assist them but Abhay Charan? The guru whom he had found himself distanced from—through Bhaktisiddhanta Saraswati's incessant travels and his own domestic rigour—had, in a sense, come to his doorstep. There was no escaping him now. The call would have to be answered.

---

* It must be noted here that when Srila Prabhupada is saying this in 1976, the word 'cult' does not have the negative connotation that it has today. He merely means a religious grouping.
† A major Hindu festival that takes place once every twelve years in certain highly auspicious locations in India.
‡ Abhay, referring to himself.
§ BBT Archives, His Divine Grace Srila Bhaktisiddhanta Saraswati Goswami Prabhupada's Disapperance Day Lecture, Hyderabad, 10 December 1976.

Soon the Allahabad centre moved quite close to Abhay Charan's home and happily became an integral part of his daily life. So quickly did Abhay Charan allow this world to seep into his routine that is it easy to understand that this was what he had perhaps been missing for a long time—this singing, this playing of the mridanga, this chanting of Hare Krishna, Hare Krishna, Krishna Krishna, Hare Hare/ Hare Rama, Hare Rama, Rama Rama, Hare Hare. The void that had been created through him directing his energies towards his business and his family was getting filled drop by drop even though Bhaktisiddhanta Saraswati, who would become his guru, was not physically present there.

In 1930, the ailing Gour Mohan, the father of Abhay Charan, passed away. His last activity was to listen to the chanting of the monks of Gaudiya Math repeating the sacred mantra again and again.

With his father gone, saddened as he was, Abhay Charan may have realized that one more worldly tie that kept him away from his calling had fallen away.

5

'Forbearance Like a Tree, Humbleness Like a Straw'

As we proceed with this story, we will notice that while this is the tale of the life of Srila Prabhupada, it is, as we have already noted in previous chapters, the story of the reform and reinvention of Gaudiya Vaishnavism.

Note this verse from the Vaishnavite annals,

karma, tapa, yoga, jnana, vidhi-bhakti, japa, dhyana |
iha haite madhurya durlabha ||
kevala ye raga-marge, bhaje krishne anurage |
tare krishna-madhurya sulabha ||

Translated by Srila Prabhupada in his translation of the book *Chaitanya Charitamrita:*† The transcendental mellows generated from the dealings between the *gopis* and Krishna cannot be tasted by fruitive activity, yogic austerities, speculative knowledge,

* See https://flowingnectarstream.wordpress.com/2017/07/29/the-essence-of-gaudiya-vaishnavism/.
† A.C. Bhaktivedanta Swami Prabhupada, seventeen-volume set, published by Bhaktivedanta Book Trust, 1976.

regulative devotional service, mantra-yoga or meditation. This sweetness can be tasted only through the spontaneous love of liberated persons who chant the holy names with great ecstatic love.'

Note the emphasis and importance of austerity. Austerity had always been one of the cornerstones of the old Gaudiya Vaishnavite tradition. After Chaitanya Mahaprabhu renounced worldly life for the life of an ascetic devoted to Krishna, his wife Vishnupriya, for instance, described as a 'living icon", continued to adhere to 'to a high standard of austerity which impressed the devotees of the movement. In the Advaita-prakasha (Chapter 21), Chaitanya's disciple Jagadananda describes to him the daily activities of Vishnupriya: she would rise early each morning before daybreak with Sachi to bathe in the Ganges, but then remain indoors the entire day, never letting either the sun or the moon shine upon her. The devotees would never see her face except when she came to eat, and no one ever heard her speak. She would only eat Sachi's remnants and spent all her time absorbed in the repetition of the Holy Names while meditating on a picture of Chaitanya as he looked before taking the renounced order of life.'[†]

As Srila Prabhupada himself narrated, 'The Lord accepts the attitude of His devotee and sees how much he is prepared to serve Him. The devotee is at liberty to serve the Lord either in gross matter or in subtle matter. The important point is that the service be in relation with the Supreme Personality of Godhead. This is confirmed in the Bhagavad Gita (9.26):

patram pushpam phalam toyam yo me bhaktya prayacchati
tad aham bhakty-upahrtam ashnami prayatatmanah[‡]

---

[*] See http://www.harekrsna.de/woman-saints.htm#19.
[†] Ibid.
[‡] In Sanskrit, पत्रं पुष्पं फलं तोयं यो मे भक्त्या प्रयच्छति । तदहं भक्त्युपहृतमश्रामि प्रयतात्मनः ॥

'If one offers Me with love and devotion a leaf, a flower, a fruit or water, I will accept it. The real ingredient is bhakti (devotion). Pure devotion is uncontaminated by the modes of material nature. *Ahaituky apratihata*: unconditional devotional service cannot be checked by any material condition. This means that one does not have to be very rich to serve the Supreme Personality of Godhead. Even the poorest man can equally serve the Supreme Personality of Godhead if he has pure devotion. If there is no ulterior motive, devotional service cannot be checked by any material condition."

But the great insight of Bhaktisiddhanta Saraswati, when he set out to create a potentially global movement out of Gaudiya Vaishnavism was this: to bring in the reform that blended bhakti with the right level of austerity that can be practised by a global audience.

His 'aim was on preaching worldwide, (and) he knew that the renunciation of the Gosvamis was not possible for westerners; therefore he wanted to introduce the idea that devotees could live in a big palatial temple. He had accepted a large donation from a wealthy Vaishnava merchant and in 1930 had constructed a large marble temple in the Baghbazar section of Calcutta. In the same year, he had moved, along with his many followers, from his small rented quarters at Ultadanga to the impressive new headquarters'.[1]

Everything was Krishna's. All that one had, and all that one did was done as a service to Krishna. What was there to embrace or forsake? 'It was Rupa Goswami, the great disciple of Lord Chaitanya, who had written, "One is perfectly detached from all materialistic worldly entanglement not when one gives up everything but when one employs everything for the Supreme Personality of Godhead, Krsna"†.'[2]

---

* Sri Caitanya-caritamrta, Madhya-lila, Chapter 1.
† Krishna.

The application of this idea was efficiently and devotedly started, in a sense, by Bhaktisiddhanta Saraswati. The insight was sharp. What was holding back the word of Krishna from reaching every corner of the world? From being sung, as it were, on every street corner? Clearly, there were rigid ritualistic barriers to entry. Therefore, they must fall. Krishna was the embodiment of beauty, grace and love. This idea must reign supreme. 'Srila Bhaktisiddhanta* wanted to use the most modern printing presses. He wanted to invite worldly people to hear Krishna-katha in gorgeously built temples. And, for their preaching, devotees should not hesitate to ride in the best conveyances, wear sewn cloth, or live amidst material opulence.'[3]

In this spirit, Bhaktisiddhanta Saraswati pioneered the use of traditional dolls or dioramas in depicting the life of Krishna and Radha and putting up a major viewing of the same. These had been traditionally made but, in the spirit of Vaishnavism, Bhaktisiddhanta Saraswati used this in the service of his cause.

We shall note, as we go along, all these traits—building beautiful temples, reducing entry barriers, putting wealth and opulence in the service of Krishna, and the sheer, colourful beauty of the portrayal of the deity in the movement that Srila Prabhupada would go on to found—had their roots in the work of his guru.

As the 1930s began, the scope of work of Bhaktisiddhanta Saraswati expanded considerably. Not only did his movement now have three presses to fulfil the numerous publishing requirements, but it also started to publish a daily newspaper *Nadiya Prakasa* from Calcutta. There was also an English-language magazine called *The Harmonist*.

This was a period of Abhay Charan's life when he was slowly but firmly getting more and more acquainted with the movement

---

* Another moniker for Bhaktisiddhanta Saraswati, also referred to as Bhaktisiddhanta Saraswati Thakur.

of Bhaktisiddhanta Saraswati. He attended gatherings of the
group, and often was one of the last listeners to depart any place
where he saw Bhaktisiddhanta Saraswati give his lectures. And so,
when a time came when he heard that Bhaktisiddhanta Saraswati
was coming to his town, Allahabad, to inaugurate a new temple,
he knew that despite the reservations of his wife, the time had
come for him to be formally initiated into the order.

The pharmacist Abhay Charan was slowly turning from being
just a devotee, an increasingly ardent one at that, to becoming a
preacher. This transition would not be easy.

Not least because Bhaktisiddhanta Saraswati himself taught
the young, about-to-become preacher the perils of the path. This
is where the story gets very interesting and also throws up an
understanding of what these great men—Bhaktivinoda Thakur,
Bhaktisiddhanta Saraswati and, later, Srila Prabhupada—achieved.

Prabhupada recalled that Bhaktisiddhanta Saraswati had
told him that people had conspired to kill him (Saraswati).[4] But
why? According to Prabhupada it was because Bhaktisiddhanta
Saraswati was uncompromising about calling out the flaws of
the old Brahmin clans who ran Vaishnavism. According to him,
some of these groups even gathered money and tried to pay off
a policeman to look away when an attack was conducted. The
policeman revealed the plot to Bhaktisiddhanta Saraswati and he
was saved.[5]

The plain-talking Bhaktisiddhanta Saraswati was disliked by
many from the old order of Gaudiya Vaishnavism not only because
of his superior knowledge but also his penchant for sternly telling
off his opponents in debates.

To understand the stern nature of Bhaktisiddhanta Saraswati,
a story he told his disciples is worth repeating:

'A king used to maintain a group of monkeys to entertain his
sons. The monkeys were fed with sumptuous delicacies every day.
The leader of the monkeys was well-versed in the scriptures of

wise personalities, such as Sukracrya, Brhaspati and Canayaka, and he used to teach the other monkeys these scriptures.

'There was also a herd of sheep in the king's palace and the little princes used to ride them for fun. Some sheep were fond of stealing food from the palace kitchen, and the cooks in the kitchen quite often would be forced to beat the sheep to inhibit this mischievous behaviour.

'The monkey leader thought that the sheep's behaviour and the cook's reaction to that behaviour may in the long run result in disaster for the monkeys. He thought: "The sheep are extremely gluttonous and the cooks, on the other hand, are intent on beating them with whatever they find at hand. If the cooks at any time hit a sheep with a burning stick from the fire, the woolly body of the sheep would surely start burning."

"If a sheep, burning and in a frenzy, starts running around and by chance enters into the nearby horse stable, the hay inside first will catch on fire and in no time the entire stable along with its horses will be ablaze."

"One ancient expert Salihotra, who is well versed in animal husbandry, prescribes that burns on horse flesh can be healed by animal tallow obtained from monkeys. Accordingly, the king will then have the monkeys killed."

'Apprehending danger, the wise old monkey leader called all the monkeys and confidentially spoke, "In a place like this where the sheep and the cooks constantly confront each other, we, the monkeys, are sure to meet with destruction in the near future. So let us quickly take refuge in a nearby forest before we are destroyed."

'But the arrogant young monkeys did not have any respect for the wise old monkey's advice. They simply ridiculed the old monkey, "You must be under some sort of delusion due to your advancing age and so you talk like a lunatic. We are not interested in leaving the place for forest life, for in the forest we will only have distasteful fruits as our food. Here we eat varieties of Nectarian* foodstuffs. And we are served by the princes themselves!"

'Upon hearing the reply of the puffed-up young monkeys, the old monkey told them with tearful eyes, "O fools, you do not know the future results of your temporary pleasures. Your desires will ultimately cause your destruction! I will leave for the forest alone, for I don't want to witness your deaths."

'Saying thus, the monkey-leader started for the forest, leaving behind all the other monkeys.

'The fateful day soon followed. A greedy sheep entered into the kitchen, and a cook struck the beast with a burning stick of firewood. Seeing his wool ablaze, the sheep immediately began loudly bleating, and in a frenzy, ran straight into the nearby horse stable. As the sheep, its body now aflame, rolled desperately over the hay within the stable, the entire structure caught fire and many of the horses were burnt to death. Others ran amok, which resulted in great consternation throughout the palace.

'The king immediately summoned his veterinary surgeon to treat the remaining horses. The surgeon quoted Salihotra's prescription that monkey's tallow is essential for the quick healing of the burns suffered by horses. The king at once ordered that the prescribed treatment should be undertaken to save the horses, and accordingly he also issued instructions to kill the monkeys to collect their tallow.

'When the monkey leader received the above news, he became very depressed.

'Moral of this story: anyone who faithfully follows the instructions of his spiritual master and unflinchingly engages himself in devotional service to the Supreme Lord, will certainly attain the ultimate welfare. Those who contemplate that the ageing advisor (spiritual master) may be under delusion and may

---

* Like nectar; delicious.

not know more than a common person, and instead follow evil companions, will certainly meet a disastrous end."

Neither the fear of death from attacks from the opponents of Bhaktisiddhanta Saraswati nor the firmness of his teachings deterred Abhay Charan, who continued the often difficult process of balancing his role as a breadwinner and pharmacist with his inclination, and the urging of his fellow initiates, to do more, preach more for Bhaktisiddhanta Saraswati.

This mismatch was, in part, responsible for Abhay Charan's departure from his pharmacy at Allahabad which he had to give away to his supplier as debts of uncollected dues grew. Abhay Charan, now a father of three, moved to Bombay to set up a larger business, though leaving his wife and his family behind in Allahabad. The goal was to provide for his family.

But even in Bombay, he encountered fellow disciples of Bhaktisiddhanta Saraswati and the life of preaching tugged at him ever so strongly. He started writing poems in English which were published in *The Harmonist*. It was in this Bombay period that Abhay Charan would display the first skills that would one day take him to distant America and then around the world—he was an effective preacher in the English language.

One could see how the pieces of the jigsaw of Abhay Charan's life were slowly coming together, fitting in, one just right with the other.

But already within the followers of Bhaktisiddhanta Saraswati, there emerged, as is the wont when material prosperity comes, internecine squabbles and quarrels about petty questions of access to the resources that the order now possessed, including the houses and the temples. This was distressing to the master, Bhaktisiddhanta Saraswati, who told Abhay Charan that his

---

* See https://www.iskconbangalore.co.in/a-wise-old-monkey/.

dream—greater than any physical property—was books, to publish more and more books so that the world could be told the message.

In the Bengali language, Bhaktisiddhanta Saraswati told Abhay Charan, '*Amar iccha chila kichu bai karana* (I wanted to get some books done).'[6]

This would become a mantra, a task that Abhay Charan never forgot.

As an aside, it should be added here that perhaps one of the reasons Bhaktisiddhanta Saraswati was worried at the inner squabbling was that as a highly learned scholar of Gaudiya Vaishnavism, he would have known that something similar had happened when Chaitanya Mahaprabhu disappeared. Shortly after Chaitanya's disappearance, when some of his followers broke up into several factions, his genuine followers were 'led by devotees such as Nityananda, Advaita, Narahari Sarkara and the six Gosvamis* who had earlier been sent to Vrndavana† to continue the tasks of recovering lost sites of Krishna's activities'.[7]

Therefore, in the task that Bhaktisiddhanta Saraswati mentioned to Abhay Charan lay embedded that idea that beyond the material tiffs, the real essence of the message, the words that would convey the importance of the love of Krishna, and the reforms that had been led by both Bhaktisiddhanta Saraswati and Bhaktivinoda Thakur could be spread, undisturbed, through books.

But there was a caveat that would come with it. At the end of 1936, only weeks before the death of Bhaktisiddhanta Saraswati, Abhay wrote a letter to his guru asking what more he could do for the movement.

'You have many disciples, and I am one of them, but they are doing direct service to you. Some of them are *brahmacharis*,

---

* Great preachers of Chaitanya's movement.
† Vrindavana.

some of them are *sannyasis*, but I am a householder. I cannot. Sometimes I give monetary help, while I cannot give you direct service. Is there any particular service I can do?'[8]

Preach in English, replied Bhaktisiddhanta Saraswati. It was by preaching in this language that he would be of the greatest service to the cause, he told Abhay Charan. 'I have every hope that you can turn yourself into a very good English preacher if you serve the mission to inculcate the novel impression of Lord Chaitanya's teachings in the people in general as well as philosophers and religionists.'[9]

Within days, on the first day of 1937, Bhaktisiddhanta Saraswati was gone. His key parting message to his disciples was, 'You should live somehow or the other without any quarrel in this mortal world only for the service of the Godhead. Do not, please, give up the service of the Godhead, in spite of all dangers, all criticisms and all discomforts . . . You should always chant the transcendental name of Godhead with patience and forbearance like a tree and humbleness like a straw . . . There are many amongst you who are well qualified and able workers. We have no other desire whatsoever.'[10]

These would prove to be prophetic words.

His father was gone. His guru was gone. But Abhay Charan curiously did not feel alone. Despite his grief, something else had begun to fill his heart.

6

'Sugar Candy'

If you read the work of Srila Prabhupada, you will come across the word 'nescience'. During the course of writing this book, when I came upon this word, I wondered whether it was a common word or an amalgamation that I was not aware of.

It turns out that it is actually a word and means 'lack of knowledge or awareness; ignorance', according to *Merriam Webster Dictionary.*[*]

This word was in the motto of the magazine Abhay Charan De started soon after the passing of Bhaktisiddhanta Saraswati.

But why was the idea of ignorance keeping people away from the love and light of God so febrile in his mind? The reason is what happened to the Gaudiya Math of Bhaktisiddhanta Saraswati after he died.

Internecine conflict among various groups and subgroups broke out to the extent that lengthy court cases started where groups fought one another to control the real estate and material resources of the Math. It was the antithesis of what Bhaktisiddhanta Saraswati had asked of his pupils in his last message. Far from

---

[*] https://www.merriam-webster.com/dictionary/nescience.

living without any quarrel, as the guru had implored, the followers had turned the entire movement into one big property battle.

What had happened was something that plagues many a spiritual organization that grows swiftly. 'When the organization expanded there was money, many branches, prestige, then always problems occurred. In the early days, all the devotees were very seriously engaged in their sadhana—very serious about spiritual life. Later on, although the preaching was going on, they were building buildings and doing so many things, but the spirit was different. It even came to the point of arguing over which rooms in the Gaudiya Math building in Bhagbazar [sic] they should occupy.'[1] The conflict in the Math even led to the sale of the previous printing press started in Calcutta by Bhaktisiddhanta Saraswati.

Dejected by what he saw around him at the Math, Abhay Charan kept remembering his last instructions from his guru— preach in English. Bhaktisiddhanta Saraswati had encouraged him to speak and write in English about the cause, spreading the love of Krishna, and this is what Abhay Charan turned to, penning his early thoughts on the importance of the love of Krishna. Some of his first writings were introductions to the Bhagavad Gita, to the great teachings and love of Krishna, but this soon progressed to the big dream—a complete translation and commentary on the Bhagavad Gita. Abhay Charan had only himself to organize the writing and publishing of any such work. In fact, even the financing was his responsibility as the squabbling Maths—yes, there were now several of them as warring factions broke away— could barely help.

But one thing did happen. Even as word of his early enthusiasm in doing this pioneering work of translating and explaining Krishna bhakti in the English language spread, and the quality of his devotion and deep scholarship from a practitioner's point of view came to notice, he came to acquire a new honorific of

Bhaktivedanta*—the man who had brought the scholastic rigour of Vedantic studies to the all-encompassing devotional ocean of Bhakti.

All this was happening against the backdrop of historic conflict within and without the Math. War raged within the Math even as British India went to battle against Germany as the Second World War enveloped India too. Scarcity of food and other materials like paper raged across Calcutta. Abhay Charan struggled, first, to find enough rations for his family and for his business, he saw the impact of hunger as beggars choked the streets of Calcutta, and saw his city bombed, night after night, by the Japanese.

Writer Eugenie Fraser noted in *A Home by the Hoogly*: 'The following morning we went off with the twins to Calcutta to see what damage was caused by the bombing. On our way we were met by the astonishing sight of a great exodus from Calcutta. Men, women and children, cars and lorries of all descriptions, donkeys, goats tethered to carts, parrots in cages on top of lorries, one solid mass of humanity were moving along the trunk road, all terrified out of their wits trying to reach a place of safety anywhere away from Calcutta.'[2]

The bombing was a 'devastating blow to the morale of the inhabitants' of Calcutta, noted historian Joydeep Sircar, and around one and a half million people fled from the city. The dock areas where the bombing was particularly intense, many of the workers in the docks and the British government in Calcutta estimated that around 2,50,000 people fled the city by road, and another 1,00,000 by rail.[3] It must be noted that all this happened from December 1942, and the food shortages that started in Bengal grew much worse, and led to the infamous famine in Bengal where between one and four million people died as the British prioritized food for their army rather than the starving Indians.

---

* This is why in ISKCON materials even today he is often referred to as AC for Abhay Charanaravinda.

This experience of war, hunger and acute deprivation all around him, when taken into context, explains Srila Prabhupada's description of conflict, war and what could save mankind from these.

Prabhupada wrote: 'Davanala means forest fire. Forest fire. You have got experience. You have seen, might have. In the forest, nobody goes to set fire, but it takes place. Everyone knows it. Similarly, within this material world, nobody wants to be unhappy. Everyone is trying to be very happy, but he is forced to accept unhappiness. This is the position. Therefore it is called Davanala. Davanala means nobody willingly sets fire, but there is fire in the forest. Similarly, in this material world, everyone is trying from time immemorial—even at the present moment. There is some occasional war, world war, and they manufacture some means. In our days, when we were young men, there was a League of Nations. Perhaps some of you may know. When the nineteen hundred, nineteen . . ., when the First World War was finished, these nations, they formed a League of Nations. League of Nations means just to arrange for peaceful living between the nations. So there was forest fire again. Nobody wanted war, but there was Second World War. Again. And again they are trying to, the League . . . What is that? United Nations. But the war is going on. The Vietnam war is going on, the Pakistan war is going on, and many others are going on. So you may try your best to live very peacefully, but nature will not allow you. There must be war. It is not possible. In the history, especially in European history, there were so many wars—Carthaginian War, Greece War, Roman War, Seven Years' War between France and England, and Hundred Years' War . . ., so . . ., so far we have read in the history. And the war feeling is going on, not only between nation and nation, between man to man, neighbour to neighbour—even between husband and wife, father and son, this war is going on. This is called Davanala, forest fire. Forest fire means in the forest nobody goes to set fire, but automatically, by the clash, friction of the dried bamboo, there is electricity and it catches fire. Similarly, although we do not want unhappiness, still, by our dealings we create enemies and friends, and there is fight, there is war. This will continue. This is called samsara-davanala.* Try to understand. So *guru* means spiritual master means who can deliver one from this forest fire. Just like when there is a forest fire, the animals are very much disturbed, and they die mostly. The snakes, they die immediately. So this forest fire, samsara-davanala, is going on perpetually, and the person or the authorized person who can deliver you from this forest fire of material existence, he's called *guru*, or the spiritual master.'[4]

Only the guru, only the Godhead could come to the rescue, this is the recurrent theme in the publication that he would start during this time. It was called, unsurprisingly, *Back To Godhead*. For that is where Abhay Charan De hoped to transport himself and his readers, far from the world of strife, back to a world of faith, where the most important thing was devotion.

Abhay Charan wrote: 'The defect of the present-day civilization is just like that. This is actually the civilization of Nescience or illusion and therefore civilization has been turned into militarization. Everyone is fully concerned with the comforts of the body and everything related with the body and no one is concerned with the Spirit that moves the body, although even a boy can realize that the motor-car mechanism has little value if there is no driver of the car. This dangerous ignorance of humanity is a gross Nescience and has created a dangerous civilization in the form of militarization. This militarization which, in softer language, is Nationalization is an external barrier to understanding human relations. There is no meaning in a fight where the parties do fight only for the matter of different coloured dresses. There must be therefore an understanding of human relation without any consideration of the bodily designation or coloured dresses.'[5]

* Many such 'forest fires'.

It is interesting to note the influences that Abhay Charan drew which did not shut out but spoke to his times. For instance, he quoted the Archbishop of Canterbury, 'In every quarter of earth men long to be delivered from the curse of War and to find in a world which has regained its peace, respite from the harshness and bitterness of the world they have known till now. But so often they want the Kingdom of Heaven without its King. The kingdom of God without God. And they cannot have it.

'OUR RESOLVE MUST BE BACK TO GOD [sic]. We make plans for the future for peace amongst the nation and for civil security at home. That is quite right enough and it would be wrong to neglect it. But all our plans will come to shipwreck on the rock of human selfishness unless we turn to God. BACK TO GOD [sic], that is the chief need of England and of every nation.'[6]

Abhay Charan is not the only one who took such cues, as citizens of a colonially ruled country, from England, one of their main social influences. The same is seen across that period in the writings of all major figures, including Mahatma Gandhi, Jawaharlal Nehru and even earlier with men like Rammohun Roy and Vivekananda during the Bengal Renaissance.

Quite like them, Abhay Charan borrowed the idiom, the style but not the message. The message—like Gandhi's—was his, and his alone.

The presence of the image of his guru in the very logo of the publication authenticated his history and his path. He was Bhaktisiddhanta Saraswati's pupil and his path was illuminated by the teachings of his guru.

This was not going to be some light, frothy teaching. As Abhay Charan noted (warned?), 'Sugar-candy is never sweet to those who are suffering from the disease of the bile. But still, sugar-candy is the medicine for bilious patients. The taste of sugar-candy will gradually be revived if the bilious patient goes on taking sugar-candy regularly for the cure of the disease. We recommend the same process to the readers of *Back to Godhead*.'[7]

BACK-TO-GODHEAD

AN INSTRUMENT FOR TRAINING THE MIND AND EDUCATING
HUMAN NATURE TO RISE UP TO THE PLANE OF THE SOUL SPIRIT

First Appearance on the Vyas Puja Day 1944

PARTS I, II, III & IV

Edited & Founded under direct order of

His Divine Grace Sri Srimad Bhakti Siddhanta Saraswati Goswami Prabhupada

BY

ABHAY CHARAN DE

THACKER, SPINK & CO. (1933) LTD.
3, ESPLANADE, CALCUTTA

Back to Godhead cover page, 1944

If struggling and managing to get paper (highly rationed during the war) for his forty-four-page publication gives us a glimpse of the resolute and entrepreneurial nature of Abhay Charan, his ambition, too, is unmistakable.

When he faced a paper shortage for the second and third edition of the magazine, he wrote to government authorities citing a British example: 'Can we not therefore sacrifice a few reams of paper in the midst of many wastages, for the same purpose in order to derive greater benefit for the humankind? I request that the Government should take up this particular case in the light of spiritualism which is not within the material calculation. Even in Great Britain the Government has immensely supported a similar movement called The Moral Re-Armament Movement without consideration of the scarcity of paper which is more acute there than here.'[8]

After all, this was no ordinary publication. From the very beginning, Abhay Charan's vision and promise was of a global movement, a coming together of all races, creeds and kinds to ensure that conflicts ended keeping Krishna in the centre.

'From this foretelling we can hope that the cult of *Samkirtan* will take very shortly a universal form of religious movement, and this universal religion—wherein there is no harm in chanting the Name of the Lord nor is there any question of quarrel—will continue for years, as we can know from the pages of authoritative scriptures.'[9]

And that's not all.

With the publication of the magazine, the back cover already announced pre-orders for his magnum opuses—a detailed exposition of the Bhagavad Gita, with elaborate commentary and full of colour images, in three parts and spread across 1200 pages, in 'royal size' and 'first class Morocco binding'.[10] That's not all. Another work, in two volumes, and with equally expensive production value, on the life of Chaitanya Mahaprabhu was also put up for pre-order.

He had not completed these works. But Abhay Charan was showing the skills that would help him one day take the Gaudiya Mission around the world—the skills to mount projects on a major scale and ensure that the promise itself leads to the successful delivery.

There is one more thing that Abhay Charan did with the publication of his magazine which is striking in the history of ideas of that time—and which has barely been remarked upon—he took on Gandhi and his idea of absolute non-violence.

7

'Rotten Politics'

Abhay Charan De, later Srila Prabhupada, was a child of conflict. By this we mean that he was born at a time when conflict was almost the natural state. He grew up in colonial India at a time when the nationalist movement was taking root and spreading rapidly. He saw the effects of nationalist mobilization. He saw strikes and protests, both violent and non-violent. He saw war. It was a very turbulent time.

But one of the things that has been rarely commented upon is Abhay Charan's responses: Abhay Charan as a philosopher who saw violence around him and the theological impulses that it triggered.

One of them is his thoughts on the violence/non-violence dichotomy. This, of course, was a predominant theme of his time because of the interventions of one man—Mahatma Gandhi.

Gandhi had made non-violence the defining dogma of the Indian National Congress. The propagation of the adoption of non-violence in the national movement gave it a unique lustre. Gandhi was critiqued for this position by several revolutionaries, including Abhay Charan's college senior Subhas Chandra Bose, who challenged Gandhian tactics to fight British imperialism and even Gandhi's leadership of the Congress. But Abhay Charan's engagement was not at the level of politics. It was more subtle, more spiritual.

Watching the horror of Japanese bombing, Abhay Charan reflected, 'The exodus of the residents of Calcutta to other places out of fear of being raided by the Japanese bombs, is due to the same tendency of non-destructible (sic) existence. But those who are thus going away do not remember that even after going away from Calcutta saved from the raids of the Japanese bombs, they are unable to protect their bodies as non-destructible in any part of the material universe, when the same bodies will be raided by the bombs of material nature in the form of three-fold miseries.

'The Japanese also—who are threatening the Calcutta people with ruthless air-raids for increasing their own happiness by possession of lands-o (sic) not know that their happiness is also temporary and destructible as they have repeatedly experienced in their own fatherland. The living beings, on the other hand, who are designed to be killed, are by nature eternal, impenetrable, invisible, etc. So all those living entities who are threatened to be killed as well as those who are threatening to conquer are all alike in the grip of the "Maya" (sic) potency and are therefore in the darkness.'[1]

What is Abhay Charan saying? He is saying, as a man surrounded by the flames of war, that both the victor and the vanquished, no matter who they are, are finally losers in this. For both of these people prioritize ephemeral life over the quest to discover and offer their devotion to the divine.

The world is in the grip of maya; the illusion holds for both the victor and the vanquished. Abhay Charan is urging the insight that the very fundamentals of war are flawed, as are the human beings conducting the battle. In victory there is defeat and so it is in defeat.

'Without light, any amount of speculation of the human mind (which is also a creation of the material nature) can never restore the living entities to permanent happiness. In that darkness any method of bringing peace in the world . . . can bring only temporary relief or distress, as we can see from all creations of the External Potency. In the darkness non-violence is as much useless as violence, while in the light there is no need of violence or non-violence.'[2]

Abhay Charan is probably one of the very few people—if not the only one—who is arguing this as he watches a World War unfold, and Gandhian non-violence takes precedence in India's freedom movement.

A younger Abhay Charan had been intrigued, even captivated, by the figure of Gandhi. Here was a modern-day saint who revered, and quoted, the Bhagavad Gita, at every given instance. Here, at last, seemed someone who could, literally, practise the ethics he was preaching. But with time, and his own spiritual journey, Abhay Charan came to see things a bit differently.

He recognized why when Subhas Chandra Bose told Bhaktisiddhanta Saraswati, 'So many people you have captured. They are doing nothing for nationalism,' the monk replied, 'Well, for your national propaganda you require very strong men, but these people are very weak. You can see, they are very skinny. So don't put your glance upon them. Let them eat something and chant Hare Krishna.'[3]

Abhay Charan realized that political freedom by itself was not enough. The question to ask was: What were the people who were receiving such political freedom likely to do with this liberty? Where would their ethics and morals be grounded? What would lie at the heart of their lives?

'Without light, any amount of speculation of the human mind (which is also a creation of the material nature) can never restore the living entities to permanent happiness. In that darkness any method of bringing peace in the world . . . can bring only temporary relief or distress, as we can see from all creations of the External Potency. In the darkness non-violence is as much useless as violence, while in the light there is no need of violence or non-violence,' he wrote.[4]

Abhay Charan was not against India's freedom movement. But he sought the influence of a greater life, which to him could only come from utter and complete devotion to the divine, and the understanding that without that submission, violence and non-violence would merely remain a political dichotomy with political endgame. The mere act of non-violence would not be enough to elevate those who practised it, unless they were more deeply rooted in the metaphysical reasoning behind non-violence (or violence for that matter), truly comprehending the idea that it is not our mere action but the divine flow of life that matters.

The succinct summation of this is to be found in something Abhay Charan wrote about Winston Churchill's comments about creating a better world. 'We are pleased to find that leaders of world politics such as Mr. Churchill* have nowadays begun to think of a humane world and trying to get rid of the terrible national frenzy of hate. The frenzy of hatred is another side of the frenzy of love. The frenzy of love of Hitler's own countrymen has produced the concomitant frenzy of hatred for others and the present war is the result of such dual side of a frenzy called love and hatred. So when we wish to get rid of the frenzy of hate, we must be prepared to get rid of the frenzy of so-called love. This position of equilibrium free from love and hatred is attained only when men are sufficiently educated,' he wrote.

It is important to remember that these comments were made at a time when the fascist shadow threatened to destroy the world. To comprehend and propagate the futility of any action without the direction and strength of inner spirituality at a time of global warfare was curious, but to go a step further and preach this to Gandhi was even more striking.

---

* Winston Churchill, the British Prime Minister.

'I tell you as a sincere friend that you must immediately retire from active politics if you do not desire to die an inglorious death. You have 125 years to live as you have desired to live but if you die an inglorious death it is no worth. The honour and prestige that you have obtained during the course of your present lifetime, were not possible to be obtained by anyone else within the living memory. But you must know that all these honours and prestiges (sic) were false in as much as they were created by the Illusory Energy of Godhead called the Maya. By this falsity I do not mean to say that your so many friends were false to you nor you were false to them. By this falsity I mean illusion or in other words the false friendship and honours obtained thereby were but creation of Maya and therefore they are always temporary or false as you may call it. But none of you neither your friends nor yourself know this truth,' [5] Abhay Charan wrote in his very first letter to Gandhi on 7 December 1947.

This was not Gandhi's moment of glory. Two nations had been created through a religious fracture, something that Gandhi would never accept. His greatest apostles, Jawaharlal Nehru and Vallabhbhai Patel, had disobeyed Gandhi's refusal to accept partition and had embraced it to create an independent, though broken, India. Even within the Congress, Gandhi's political strength was fading, though moral strength remained resolute but was often applied at the threat of suicide via starvation. In the new government of independent India, Prime Minister Nehru and his deputy Patel quarrelled incessantly. The edifice that Gandhi had built over decades was crumbling, the riots he had tried to stop between Hindus and Muslims were incessant. Massacres during Partition had killed about a million people, one of the greatest death tolls in civilian strife in history. The father of India's ostensibly non-violent freedom movement was surrounded, and haunted, by the spectre of violence all around him.

Abhay Charan wrote to him: 'So you are also in a plight to find out a proper solution for the present political tangle created by your opponents. You should therefore take a note of warning

from your insignificant friend like me, that unless you retire
timely from politics and engage yourself cent percent in the
preaching work of Bhagavad Gita, which is the real function of the
Mahatmas, you shall have to meet with such inglorious deaths as
Mussolini, Hitler, . . . or Lloyd George met with . . . you can easily
understand as to how some of your political enemies in the garb
of friends (both Indian and English) have deliberately cheated you
and have broken your heart by doing the same mischief for which
you have struggled so hard for so many years. You wanted chiefly
Hindu-Moslem unity in India and they have tactfully managed to
undo your work, by creation of the Pakistan and India separately.
You wanted freedom for India but they have given permanent
dependence of India. You wanted to do something for the
upliftment of the position of the Bhangis* but they are still rotting
as Bhangis even though you are living in the Bhangi colony. They
are all therefore illusions and when these things will be presented
to you as they are, you must consider them as God-sent. God has
favoured you by dissipating the illusion you were hovering in and
by the same illusion you were nursing those ideas as Truth.' [6]

The tone that Abhay Charan took in his letter was sharp, even
forceful, though polite. The point about caste was particularly
cutting. It echoed the criticism that Bhimrao Ramji 'Babasaheb'
Ambedkar† placed at Gandhi's doorstep—that his grand
gestures and platitudes did precious little to really eliminate caste
discrimination.

He even questioned the fact that Gandhi never chose to accept
a spiritual master or a guru. 'I know that you never underwent such
transcendental teaching except some severe penances which you
invented for your purpose as you have invented so many things
in the course of experimenting with the relative truths. You
might have easily avoided them if you had approached the Guru

---

* Lower castes, 'untouchable' caste of that time.
† An exceptional scholar and author of India's constitution, himself from a lower
  caste.

as above mentioned . . . But your sincere efforts to attain some Godly qualities by austerities, etc. surely have raised you to some higher platform which you can better utilise for the purpose of the Absolute Truth. If you, however, remain satisfied with such temporary position only and do not try to know the Absolute Truth, then surely you are to fall down from the artificially exalted position under the laws of Nature. But if you want really to approach the Absolute Truth and want to do some real good to the people in general all over the world, which shall include your ideas of unity, peace and non-violence, then you must give up the rotten politics immediately and rise up for the preaching work of the philosophy and religion of "Bhagavad Gita"* (sic) without offering unnecessary and dogmatic interpretation on them . . . I would only request you to retire from politics at least for a month only and let us have discussion on the Bhagavad Gita. I am sure, thereby, that you shall get a new light from the result of such discussions not only for your benefit but for the benefit of the world at large-as I know that you are sincere, honest and a moralist.'[7]

How did an unknown Vaishnavite get the courage to write such things to Gandhi? What prompted this confidence? There are few answers available, but the fact that this was perhaps the beginning of a life of gumption that Abhay Charan, now in his fifties, was about to lead. Even though his business had, in the best of times, been second priority to him and, therefore, more often than not, stuttered, the fervent flames of his Vaishnavite belief triggered a certain spirited confidence in him and, more importantly, his cause.

Gandhi never responded. And soon afterwards he was assassinated by a radical Hindu. The communal harmony that he had sought to bring about even by threatening to take his own life had, in fact, finally taken his life.

He was walking towards a prayer meeting when he was killed. As Abhay Charan had warned, proximity to politics had led to his destruction.

---

* The Bhagavad Gita.

8

The Reluctant Pharmacist

As Abhay Charan's fame as a writer grew with the various divisions of the Gaudiya Math, what was happening to his life as a pharmacist?

It meandered on. A factory in Lucknow initially did well, but then petered out. An outfit in Allahabad had a similar fate. Something was not going right.

Consistently, the only thing that seemed to draw him in was the Gaudiya Math and preaching about the Bhagavad Gita, and the love of Krishna.

His family, especially his wife, took a dim view of what they saw as his neglect of familial responsibilities in favour of his gradual metamorphosis as a full-time preacher.

But Abhay Charan was quickly shedding the last vestiges of familial ties, unconcerned by both emotional pull and the emotional blackmail of the humdrum of everyday life of a family man. By the time* Abhay Charan published the second edition of *Back to Godhead*, he had an agent, the Calcutta-based Thacker, Spink and Company.† This firm could do one thing that had always been Abhay Charan's dream—sell books in Europe and America.

---

* March 1952.
† With branches in Burma (now Myanmar) and in what is now Bangladesh. It was, for a while, owned by the Maharaja of Darbhanga.

But it was going to be another nearly two decades before Abhay Charan would actually be able to set foot on foreign land. In the meantime, by the time he was in his mid-fifties, Bhaktivedanta Abhay Charan, now renowned as A.C. Bhaktivedanta across ISKCON, was a full-time preacher. You could say that by the time he had hit his mid-life, he had fulfilled the one cherished goal in his life—to become a full-time orator of the love, and words, of Krishna. The solace he offered, the solace he found, was Krishna.

One of the first places where the preacher Abhay Charan Bhaktivedanta gained followers was Jhansi. This might seem like a curious choice of place—why not traditional Vaishnava centres like Mathura or Vrindavan? But Jhansi had an illustrious history connecting it to Krishna worship. The Chandela Rajputs, founders of the kingdom of Jhansi, claimed to trace their lineage to Chandravanshis, or the lineage of the moon, and of Krishna.

Not just that, perhaps the most important character in Jhansi's history, the daredevil queen, Lakshmibai, who fought the British colonial rulers to ensure the freedom of her kingdom in 1858, is said to have proclaimed on the eve of battle, 'We fight for independence. In the words of Lord Krishna, we will if we are victorious, enjoy the fruits of victory, if defeated and killed on the field of battle, we shall surely earn eternal glory and salvation.'[1]

So it was that in Jhansi that Abhay Charan Bhaktivedanta, the preacher, first started to give shape to the movement for Krishna in the way that he had dreamt of.

But what happened in the process is illustrative of the early struggles of A.C. Bhaktivedanta, the preacher. His pious earnestness gathered some early devotees easily, and wherever he went to preach and sing kirtans with them, he was welcomed. In many homes, both in towns and villages, he was asked to return, and welcomed as a man of God would.

He was even given access to a building which he found useful to house his 'League of Devotees'.

But successful as he was as a local preacher, Bhaktivedanta was no closer to his dream, the dream that his guru had left him, of taking the word of Krishna to the world, in English. His repeated appeals over the years to various government entities asking for support for this cause had had little response.

His private businesses had tottered nearly to closure and at home he continued to be misunderstood, divided in instinct between wanting to do the right thing for his family, and abandoning familial life altogether for a life in service of the divine.

Two tipping points occurred.

In Jhansi, the building where he had set up base, so to speak, of the League of Devotees, and which he understood as having been given as a gift to him, turned out not to be so. The owner demanded that he buy out the property. But Bhaktivedanta could not afford to do that. Years of paying for his preaching work, and then for the publications, from his intermittently successful businesses had reduced him to penury.

At home, conflict came to a head when his wife, Radharani, pawned his sacred Bhagavatam to buy biscuits to have with her tea, to which she was attached. This storm would no longer remain in the teacup.

Abhay Charan Bhaktivedanta left. He left Jhansi. First he went to Jhargram, and then to Mathura and Vrindavan, where he found refuge with another disciple of Bhaktisiddhanta Saraswati, and continued to show his skills in writing and editing—not always as a lofty Vaishnavite scholar but, in the best possible way, he was a storyteller, giving access to the love of Krishna to anyone who sought it. This move away from home resulted in the final stepping into the shoes that he had perhaps been preparing his whole life—the monastic vows of a sannyasi—no more would he have to maintain a foot in two boats. His family life had capsized. But he had found an anchor in Krishna.

Soon, Bhaktivedanta moved to Delhi, at around sixty years old, to take over the running of *Sajjana-toshani*—this was a quasi-academic journal, but his dream was to make it like the *Illustrated Weekly*, the slickest Indian magazine of its time, or even America's finest publications, *Time* or *Life*. The reality on the ground, though, was not in his favour. In Delhi, he found a deeply divided house in the Gaudiya Math, and his ambitions to expand and better the publishing programme finally led to his—and there is no other way to write this and demonstrate what happened—expulsion.

He was, perhaps in the eyes of his contemporaries or even his seniors in the deeply divided Gaudiya Math, too clever, too polished, too ambitious, even too devout. There may have even been a latent sense, from his history of having run businesses and often contributed financially to the community, that he did not really need the support, in material terms, of the splinter groups of the order.

But this was far from the truth. Having left his familial life behind, Abhay Charan Bhaktivedanta had been driven nearly to penury. His ambitions of reaching the world remained intact but for now he could barely find a refuge for himself.

As an aside, it is important to remember that Bhaktivedanta was also living through times of great poverty in large parts of India after independence. 'Between 1950–1980, the economy barely grew at about 1 per cent per capita per annum. Not surprisingly, poverty did not decline by much. In 1951–1952, the first year of the National Sample Survey (NSS), the headcount ratio of poverty in India was deemed to be close to 45 per cent of the population. Some thirty-two years later, in 1983, the poverty ratio had stayed "constant" at 43 per cent.'[2]

But it was in Delhi, through relentless efforts, that Bhaktivedanta—not least assisted by a public meeting he held at the city's wealthiest spiritual institution, Birla Mandir—slowly began to rekindle his aspiration.

Birla Mandir meeting was an early source of reinvigorating some small support through which Bhaktivedanta was able to restart his work, especially his publishing. It is important to understand why. Birla Mandir was built in about five years from 1933 onwards by Jugal Kishore Birla, a prominent member of one of India's great business families with deep and enduring ties with the national movement. Jugal Kishore's younger brother, Ghanshyamdas (G.D.) was a friend of Sardar Vallabhbhai Patel and Mahatma Gandhi. It was at Birla House, the mansion of the family in central Delhi, where Gandhi had been holding a prayer meeting when he was assassinated.

The Birlas were among the wealthiest people in the land, and the temple was their first great act of spiritual institution building, and therefore was the religious refuge for prominent Hindus across India's capital. It is from here that Bhaktivedanta was able to start building a small group of benefactors.

After four years of silence, *Back to Godhead* began to speak again. Bhaktivedanta was able to gather just about enough funds to start publishing the magazine again. Sometimes he may not have had enough money for food or clothing, but whatever he could gather went into publishing.

It is to be noted that, like Gandhi, Bhaktivedanta was not enamoured by the mechanized progress of industrial society. It seemed to him that the colonial processes and structures had continued even though the Britishers were gone. The edifice remained, even though the architects had left.

This meant—to him, and to Gandhi—that the very soul of Indian civilization, which they felt lay its spiritual heritage, had been replaced for an endless and futile pursuit for the material. But even if everyone else forgot this, Bhaktivedanta was determined to remind them.

There was no one else working on *Back To Godhead* but him. He would produce the content, procure the paper, take it to the printer (sometimes fail to even pay for the paper) and then hawk it quietly on the streets, selling it to anyone who might want to buy it. He would tell them why it was so important. He used his very meagre funds to even post it not just around India but across the world in the hope that one day, someday, someone might read and truly hear.

During this time of barely being able to make do, Bhaktivedanta divided his time between Delhi and Vrindavan. In Vrindavan, he resided first at Vamsi Gopal temple, where his tiny rooftop room gave him a clear view of the Yamuna, whose waters had cradled Krishna himself, and then, later, he stayed at Radha Damodar temple. Abhay Charan Bhaktivedanta remained at Radha Damodar temple for six years and it was his final Indian point of refuge before he embarked upon his journey to America.

The history of this temple is worth noting. Radha Damodar temple is one of seven most important temples in Vrindavan, the holy land of Krishna, twin town to the equally sacred Mathura. It is said that Chaitanya Mahaprabhu's own disciple, Rupa Goswami, carved by hand the deities of Radha Damodar temple. Rupa Goswami gave the *murtis* to Jiva Goswami, another fervent disciple, who proceeded to start the temple in 1542 CE. The worship at the temple has continued unbroken since then—barring a short period when, fearful of an attack from the zealot Mughal emperor Aurangzeb, the deities were transferred for safekeeping to Jaipur. They were returned to the temple in 1739 CE.

It was in this temple, in a ground-floor room, which is still preserved today and opens with a view to the main altar, that Abhay Charan Bhaktivedanta began writing his detailed commentary to the Bhagavatam—all eighteen thousand verses. It was here that he cooked in a small kitchen, preparing the pure vegetarian dishes that would become the signature prasad of his movement.

He calculated that such a work of translation and commentary would fill sixty volumes! Remember that this is a man who, for all practical purposes, was penniless and struggled at that time, more often than not, to even publish a magazine regularly.

Then, who would produce a sixty-volume series, who would buy it and who would read it? But these concerns were immaterial and prosaic for Bhaktivedanta. How could one compromise with the word of God?

To bring this endeavour to life, Bhaktivedanta moved from Radha Damodar temple in Vrindavan to the gullies near Jama Masjid in Delhi, to a location called Chippiwada. It was a place not only replete with the bazaar that usually surrounds historic monuments, but was also a mini hub of assorted small publishers. It was with one of them that Abhay Charan Bhaktivedanta, having gathered some small initial donations, started the process of publishing, in fits and starts, his marathon journey of publishing sixty volumes of commentary and translation of the Bhagavatam.

The cover of the first edition of the first volume had been designed by a local designer following detailed instructions from Bhaktivedanta.

The cover page of the first Volume of *Srimad Bhagavatam*, pre-edition 1965

As the first volume got published, Abhay Charan Bhaktivedanta created a work plan for himself, which is in a sense followed by monks of his order even today—conceptualize books, publish books and then physically sell books. Often he would run out of money or patience and yet, from carrying reams of precious printing paper to cajoling publishers to give him credit, Bhaktivedanta rose to every challenge.

For it was he who sent his own books for reviews, sent them to people who might be motivated to donate for future volumes, sent them to opinion makers, including Dr Zakir Hussain, the vice president of India, who replied, 'I have read your book Srimad Bhagavatam with great interest and much profit.'[3]

There was an entrepreneurial energy in all this, though Abhay Charan was already in his sixties. But was this frenzied writing, publishing and especially selling suitable for a monk? Bhaktivedanta pre-empted this question in the beginning of the second volume of his translation and commentary on the Bhagavatam. He explained that people 'conclude sometimes mistakenly that we are also doing the same business in the dress of a mendicant! But actually there is a gulf of difference between the two kinds of activities. This is not a business for maintaining an establishment of material enjoyment. On the contrary it is an humble attempt to broadcast the glories of the Lord at a time when the people need it very badly . . . So even though we are not in the Himalayas (as ascetics might be), even though we talk of business, even though we deal in rupees and paisa, still, simply because we are 100 per cent servants of the Lord and are engaged in the service of broadcasting the message of His glories, certainly we shall transcend and get through the invincible impasse of Maya and reach the effulgent kingdom of God'.[4]

This is the spirit which propelled Abhay Charan Bhaktivedanta to ask Lal Bahadur Shastri, the Indian prime minister, to buy copies of his translations. And the prime minister, charmed by the sincerity of the elderly monk, ensured that fifty copies each were bought of the two volumes Bhaktivedanta had managed to publish till that time. And it is this indefatigable spirit that took him to a shipping company scion Sumati Morarjee of the Scindia Steam Navigation Company in Bombay.

The initial idea had been, as always, to raise funds to publish more volumes. But soon the latent ambition arose—could he perhaps finally fulfil the dream of his guru and take the holy word to foreign shores, especially America?

He had already been badly rebuffed in an earlier attempt to present the sacred message in Japan. Invited to the Congress for Cultivating Human Spirit in Tokyo in 1961, all attempts by Abhay Charan Bhaktivedanta to raise funds to attend the programme failed—though he had prepared all the materials for such an endeavour, and even though he personally reached out to Indian President Sarvepalli Radhakrishnan for assistance. No support had come from any quarter.

But now, by 1965, he not only had three volumes of his translations and commentaries on the Bhagavatam ready, but had even managed to find a sponsor, Gopal Aggarwal, in Pennsylvania who had issued him a letter of invitation upon his father's* request, and even procured a passport. All that remained was for him to find support for his travel. And the Scindia Steam Navigation Company Ltd had, well, ships.

But at every step, there were hurdles. Abhay Charan Bhaktivedanta was told he was too poor or too old, what if he died in a foreign land or even in transit, he did not have the right sponsor (only a private individual and not an institution), he did not have the right papers. Also, was it right for a Hindu sannyasi to cross the seas? Was it even acceptable?

---

* His father was a businessman in Mathura and was known to Abhay Charan Bhaktivedanta.

None of this would stop Bhaktivedanta. He was almost seventy years old and had in his monastic life suffered many a setback and humiliation. He had overcome them all by the mercy of Lord Krishna and now, at long last, the path seemed unambiguous. Go, he must.

The call, if it ever had to come, had arrived. The seat on the ship, *Jaladuta*, was provided by the Scindia Steam Navigation Company Ltd. A benefactor bought him some warm clothes. He had five hundred pamphlets describing his mission and two hundred sets of the first three volumes of his translations and commentaries of the Bhagavatam—far from his sixty-volume target.

But that balmy August in 1965, Bhaktivedanta Swami was propelled by his mission and the recognition that he had failed to create the movement he thought he would of Krishna bhakti across India. He had tried his best but somehow success in creating a wider movement had eluded him. The only thing to do was to heed the instruction of his guru and change his geography.

Bhaktivedanta Swami had only a very nebulous idea of the 'foreign' when he embarked upon this mission. He had only really seen parts of India in his whole life and had little understanding of what could, or would, await him in the United States. He knew of course that his guru had tried to seed this idea—but he would have also known that none of those efforts had really become sustainable or taken real root. Nothing in his life till that point suggests that it could have given him the confidence or the energy to be thrust into such an arduous task. He had, it must be remembered, barely ever succeeded in winning many followers, disciples or even donors in his home country. His record as a preacher, as devout and fervent as he was, was at that time distinctly patchy. All of this is important to underline for it gives us an unambiguous picture of the motivations that drove this elderly, frail monk. His power and confidence, if any, were almost entirely driven from his very personal faith in his beloved Krishna and the words of his guru. As a Bengali he would have known the famous Bengali saying *'bishashe milaye bostu, torke bohu dur'* or, loosely translated, that which seems impossible in a debate becomes real through sheer faith. This adage fit his journey aptly.

As ever he was certain of the historicity of his effort—and even went to newspaper offices to inform them of his upcoming momentous journey. Most ignored him, and only one published a small article.

No matter.

A few clothes in a suitcase, an umbrella, some dried cereals (would he even find food that he could eat in America?), and up climbed Abhay Charan Bhaktivedanta, a tonsured monk in saffron sannyas robes, undeterred up the gangway of the black cargo ship.

The impossible mission of his life—to broadcast the glories of Krishna all over the world—had begun.

9

Downtown Monk

Before going into the details of the rather dramatic crossing of the oceans by A.C. Bhaktivedanta aboard the *Jaladuta* in 1965, it is important to put his journey in context. Seventy-two years after Swami Vivekananda made the same difficult voyage, it was still a rarity.

'Emigration to the United Kingdom and Northern America started during colonial rule in India. However, the number of emigrants was insignificant, both in relation to emigration from India, and to total immigration to those countries. Between 1820 and 1900, no more than 700 persons moved from India to the United States. In the following 30 years, this number rose to a still insignificant 8,700; most were Punjabi Sikhs who worked in agriculture in California. Anti-Asian legislation in 1917 and 1924 banned immigration from south or southeast Asia, including India, and ensured that Asians would not qualify for naturalization or land ownership.'[1]

This journey was wondrous to A.C. Bhaktivedanta long before he touched American shores. In the last chapter we noted that for all his life, Bhaktivedanta had only really seen India. So much so that even the arrival of the *Jaladuta* in Cochin gave him new perspective, almost as if he were seeing Kerala with foreign eyes.

'Out of the group of islands two big islands joined by an iron
over-bridge are known as Cochin and Ernakulam. The iron over
bridge was constructed by the Britishers very nicely along with
railway lines. The railways line is extended up to the Port. There
are many flourishing foreign firms and banks. It is (?) [sic] Sunday,
the bazar was closed. I saw a peculiar kind of plantain available in
this part of the country. The island known as Cochin is not an up
to date city. The roads are like narrow lanes. The part of the city
where the foreigners are residing are well situated. The buildings
factories, etc. all big and (?) well maintained. The mohamedan[*]
quarters are separate from the Hindu quarters as usual in other
Indian cities. The part known as Ernakulam is up to date. There
is a nice park on the bank of the gulf and it is named Subhas Bose
Park. It is good that Subhas Babu[†] is popular in this part of the
country. I saw the Kerala High Court and the public buildings,
the High Court being situated in Ernakulam it appears that the
city is capital of Kerala. This . . . part of India resembles Bengal
scenario and the city Ernakulum also Cochin appears to me like
old Kalighat or Tollygunge area of Calcutta. The culture is Indian
as usual.'[2]

The last sentence is telling. So new was Prabhupada to the rest
of the world, as compared to his familiar north Indian haunts, that
'Indian culture' in Kerala was worth noting to him.

Such a man was travelling via ship to America and getting
seasick frequently and, if that wasn't all, in the course of the journey,
he suffered two heart attacks. Even before he had started from
Bombay, one of his benefactors had warned him that he might
die in the process of trying to achieve this impossible dream—and
even before he landed in America, he had already gone through
near-death experiences.

---

[*] Muslim.
[†] Subhas Chandra Bose, the freedom fighter.

But even that experience could not have prepared him for the country he landed in.

To understand what happened to A.C. Bhaktivedanta in America and what he did there, we first have to understand the state of America when the monk from India landed there.

The conflict in Vietnam had already dragged on for about a decade since the mid-1950s by the time Bhaktivedanta arrived at Boston Harbour. In the early 1960s, American President John F. Kennedy pushed more resources into battle in Vietnam, and the failure of a breakthrough victory only meant greater angst and protest at home. With the failure of the Bay of Pigs invasion in 1961 and the Cuban Missile Crisis, chances of a third world war or at least conflict using nuclear weapons between the United States and the Soviet Union had become a real possibility. 'The risks to world peace seemed so significant at this time, that an extensive peace movement developed throughout the 1960s, particularly through the intervention of young people and students. Young people wanted autonomy and self-determination. They did not want to live in a world involved in major armed conflict.'[3]

Within America, the response to this war-addicted climate was the rise of subcultures which would experiment with everything from Eastern mysticism to psychedelic drugs, poetry, music and, more importantly, massive protest rallies for peace and against war.

If we distil the messages of the movement that came to be known through many varying names over the years from 'Beat' to 'hippie', a few are immediately apparent. There is the desire for a different way of life, a different way of thinking, of freedom from the oppression of society and government and even the economic system. There is the determined refusal to authorize state-sanctioned violence (though ironically some of the protesters clashed with the police and became quite violent), there is the attempt to create building blocks of a 'non-commercial world' in everything from the focus on handmade things, like tie-and-dye clothing (another element borrowed from India), vegetarianism and natural birth,* the focus on meditation and non-Abrahamic forms of spirituality and, more importantly, music.

When you look at all these elements carefully, you understand something that is rarely ever said about A.C. Bhaktivedanta, that like Vivekananda he was, in many ways, the right person, in the right place at the right time. Vivekananda gained from the flowering of interest in Eastern philosophies led by scholars like Max Mueller and others in the late nineteenth century and therefore his message found a certain influential, academically elite audience that helped it spread across the English-speaking world. His key early benefactors were the educated wealthy, including a Harvard professor who introduced him to the Parliament of Religions. In A.C. Bhaktivedanta's case, his earliest followers were unemployed hippies attracted to the sonorous sannyasi to find a refuge from the tumult all around them and in their heads.

Bhaktivedanta's early life in the United States is usually described in terms of the difficulties he had in finding appropriate shelter, often having to share space with people who did not quite understand his calling or his message. But the way to really think about the story is that he appeared to give the right message to the right people at the right time.

His first days were spent with Gopal Aggarwal and his wife Sally, an American, at Butler County, Pennsylvania, where the famous four-wheel drive, the Jeep, had been invented in 1940 as a vehicle for tough-haul jobs of the US Army. It was a time when A.C. Bhaktivedanta was under the impression that he would remain in America maybe, at most, for about a month. Even though he was clear about his mission in the West—propagating the good word of Krishna—several of his early hosts imagined that

---

* As opposed to caesarean birth.

he had merely come to raise funds for his publishing and would soon return.

But it was here, at Butler, Pennsylvania, that A.C. Bhaktivedanta found his first audience. It was here that one of the most written-about spiritual figures in modern times first appeared in the American local press: the Indian 'swami' who had come to America to preach 'bhakti yoga', noted the *Butler Eagle*.[4] Even in that very first article, there were clear signs of why A.C. Bhaktivedanta would start to attract followers in America.

First, in a country obsessed at that time with war or peace, Bhaktivedanta stood out by saying that the question was immaterial to his message.

'The Swamiji is equally philosophical about physical discomforts or wars: "It's man's nature to fight," he shrugs. "We have to adjust to these things; currents come and go in life just as in an ocean".'[5] His message was also non-threatening, 'His religion remains Hindu. He does not ask his listeners to change their religious affiliation, but merely to become "better Jews or Christians," etc.'[6] To his predominantly Christian audience who wanted to know if he accepted that Jesus Christ was the son of God, he said, yes of course—and then added, deftly, that he himself was the son of God.[7] This suited everyone's beliefs, and purposes, just fine. In making his audience comfortable, A.C. Bhaktivedanta did not step away from the fundamentals of his own system of belief.

Also, the philosophy he pitched so closely resembled the evolutionary theory that his audience knew so well that it would have made sense to them. He taught to those first audiences at the home of the Aggarwals, 'A simplified version of his theory is that life progresses from aquatic to plant, to reptile to bird, to beast to "beastly" human being and finally, to civilized man. "After this life there is a still better life on other planets," predicted the visitor. He believes that the highest possible state will be to go to God, or eternal life.'[8]

Bhaktivedanta was in Butler for only around twenty-one days but during this time one of his recollections, as he later told of it in a conversation in 1976, is illuminating. '. . . some time, that one piece of wire lying in one place, one piece of bamboo was lying in another place, and one dry shell of a squash was lying. So one intelligent man collected. So this dry shell became the tambura's what is called . . .

'Hari-sauri (his interlocutor): I don't know. Like sound chamber. What do you call it?

'Prabhupada:* Sound chamber may be called. So with that dry squash he made the sound chamber. The bamboo he fixed up and the wire upon it, and then it became a "tin, tin, tin, tin . . ." (laughs) Our organization is like that. I was loitering in the street. Somebody was over there, somebody was there. Not combined together. International Society String Band. Yes. Separately we are all useless. Eh?'[9]

As we go along this story, we shall see that is such an apt image for what A.C. Bhaktivedanta did in those early days—quite literally, he formed bonds with people loitering on the streets, banded them together with the love of Krishna and created a new kind of music, his very own kirtan of Krishna consciousness.

It was when he moved to New York, to stay first with one Dr Ramamurti Mishra, a follower of Advaita Vedanta or the impersonal divine consciousness, which of course Bhaktivedanta objected to and argued with his host against, that his singing was first commented upon as one of the most luminous aspects of the monk.

Whether one agreed with him or not, few could resist the power of his voice singing in complete devotion. There was ecstasy in his singing that suffused the air. Even Mishra's Advaita Vedanta

---

* As in Srila Prabhupada, as he would come to be known.

students could not help getting up and dancing and chanting when they heard his 'ambrosial' voice.[10]

Even though a few people had started to come for some of his prayer sessions, A.C. Bhaktivedanta was, for the most part during this period, utterly alone and almost penniless. He survived on the sale of the few copies of his books that had managed to reach buyers; his many letters, not least to his old Gaudiya Math fellow monks and his benefactor who had ensured that he reached America on a ship, Sumati Morarjee, and to many others, received little or no response.

The tone and verve of these letters have the innocence that a child, or a monk, could only muster. Bhaktivedanta always sounded convinced that his reasoning for wanting to buy a building in New York—only weeks after he had landed—for an international centre devoted to Krishna consciousness would be embraced wholeheartedly. 'There is scope and there is necessity also and it is the duty of every Indian specially the devotees of Lord Krishna to take up the matter [11],' he wrote in one letter to Morarjee, and '. . . it is the duty of every devotee of Lord Krishna to help me by all means.'[12] But every political figure, including the prime minister of India and some of the wealthiest people of India, turn him down.

No help came from anywhere. Every person he wrote to either answered with silence, or politely declined. Meanwhile A.C. Bhaktivedanta moved from Mishra's apartment to a small room in a yoga studio and then to another room nearby. Even though this meant that he managed to attain some privacy, his penury perhaps became even more acute.

The infamous New York blackouts came, the blizzards of the East Coast froze the city, and on its dirty streets, almost utterly alone, roamed a dhoti-clad man in a borrowed coat, still hopeful, still ambitious for his Krishna.

New York in the 1960s was crime-infested and choking with trash. 'Mindlessly walking along the street in New York in the

'(19)60s, you might feel a gust of wind and then a handful of grit in your face. Or you would find, strolling along, that the smell of dog poop was following you. Stopping to look around, more often than not you'd find the poop on your shoe. You had unknowingly stepped in it a few yards back and tracked it all the way. Sometimes you would step in some gum, and you'd realize it when your shoe would stick a little at every step.'[13] Srila Prabhupada also made similar observations.

It was a 'time in New York's history when people could touch the air and nobody would want to put their feet in most of the waterways. Before the great clean-up began, New York had abandoned blocks that dotted the landscape, creating vast areas absent of urban cohesion and life itself during the 1970s. The fastest-growing cause of death in New York during the 1960s was pulmonary emphysema. There were ashes and tiny particles of scraps and garbage from incinerated garbage. Many power plants in the city were fuelled with coal and heavy grades of oil, which led to noxious emissions.'[14]

So dirty was New York that its sanitation department created its own quarterly magazine in the 1960s called *Sweep!*[15] It is worth remembering that the pathways on which Prabhupada roamed, well, even the air there was unbreathable. As one writer from that time has written, 'In the 1960s, my playmates and I stopped everything when it began "snowing" ash from incinerated garbage. We chased tiny scraps of partly burned paper that floated in the air as if they were blackened snowflakes. According to a study published in 2001, the quantities of lead in the sediments of the Central Park Lake correlated strongly with the vast quantities of particles emitted from garbage burned in Manhattan during the 20th century. The study found 32 garbage incinerators that were operated by the city, and 17,000 others in apartment houses . . . Many power plants in the city were fueled with coal and heavy grades of oil, which led to noxious emissions.'[16]

Before the Environmental Protection Agency was created in 1970, New York was one of the filthiest big cities in the world. It wasn't just environmental decay; there had been an overarching social and economic downfall of the city. The electricity crisis that Bhaktivedanta stoically faced was part of a major energy crisis. On 9 November 1965, the same year that Bhaktivedanta landed in America and only months after his arrival, he lived through one of the biggest blackouts across northern and eastern America which was so notorious that it even inspired a film, *Where Were You When the Lights Went Out?*.

It was a time when New York had lost both its resident National League baseball teams; both the Dodgers and the Giants moved to California.

In the year that Bhaktivedanta arrived in America, the country removed the notorious national-origin quotas, thus creating grounds for a large Asian-American community in the city. As the population grew and moved towards the suburbs, many of the old industries like textiles began to shutter, leaving behind wasteland neighbourhoods, polluted, drug-infested and crime-afflicted.

But that was not the only thing that was happening in New York at that time. It was also a period of great creative flourishing— especially in poetry and music. It was a time when artistes like Paul Simon, Neil Diamond and Lou Reed were trying their luck in the city. Many of them began to develop their reputations through gigs at Greenwich Village and East Village, at coffee houses and bars. Greenwich Village and other sites of action brought together writing, music, poetry and other creative forms joining the spirit of anti-war protest to youthful artistry and politics. It was the time of Bob Dylan, Andy Warhol and Allen Ginsberg, a time of great ideas and churning.

This backdrop is necessary to understand the next part of our story. It helps us understand why not only the message but also the form that A.C. Bhaktivedanta used was so ripe for reception.

10

A Swami among Hippies

We cannot leave the New York story there. We must now talk about a neighbourhood called the Lower East Side, for this, as we shall soon see, will be a definitive geography of A.C. Bhaktivedanta in winning hearts and minds in America.

'At the close of the 1950s, housing conditions and the class, ethnic and racial makeup of residents on the Lower East Side stood in stark contrast to the homogeneous residential suburban hamlets that had transformed the outlying regions of northern New Jersey, New York City and Connecticut. Across the northeast United States, growth in suburban development showed little indication of saturation. The inner cities, meanwhile, continued to lose their middle-class populations and poverty levels among remaining residents (both old and new) worsened. On the Lower East Side, first and second-generation eastern Europeans made do with the limitations of tenement living while holding on to their ethnic restaurants, bakeries, butcher shops, churches and bookstores . . . Many of the social problems encountered in the 1950s, including limited employment opportunities, declines in community infrastructure (such as schools, playgrounds and parks) and juvenile delinquency, continued to plague the Lower East Side in the early 1960s. By 1965, the popular media referred to the Lower East Side streets and avenues above Houston Street as the East Village. East Village applied to the area's hippie community and not to the older white ethnic and Puerto Rican residents. By 1966 a rite of passage for many neophyte hippies was a pilgrimage either to Haight-Ashbury on the west coast or to the East Village. The streets and avenues north of Houston Street attracted the burgeoning countercultures that offered a variety of social, political and cultural challenges to mainstream society. The characterization of the Lower East Side as different, authentic, anti-suburban and uncorrupted held appeal to a number of youth movements, together loosely identified as the hippie movement. In the East Village, St. Mark's Place was the center of hippie culture. Along the sidewalks, hippies performed, recited poems, chanted or engaged in "be-ins" and "be-outs." A "be-in" or "be-out" combined elements of performance, protest, entertainment and audience participation. "Happenings" actively included the audience in a performance piece. The Film Makers' Cinematheque on Lafayette Street was often the site of happenings presented by the artists Claes Oldenburg and Robert Rauschenberg, among others. Active performance pieces were also included with a showing of experimental film. The Grateful Dead, Santana and The Who were among the many musical acts who performed at The Filmore East on Second Avenue. Andy Warhol transformed the Polish meeting club, the Dom, on St. Mark's Place into an experimental club.'[1]

Note the themes in this little historical description above—poverty, squalor but also music, art, breakthrough, even historic, creativity. This juxtaposition must be clearly understood to comprehend what happened next in the life of Bhaktivedanta. His first follower was a jobless young man on dole who was interested in God—Robert Nelson.

Nelson followed him around as A.C. Bhaktivedanta, the monk, marched up and down the streets of New York looking for a building worth tens of thousands of dollars, where he barely had pennies, to set up his dream temple.

One can see how Nelson and Bhaktivedanta, now being referred to as 'Swami' by many who met him, would land up at The Paradox restaurant-lounge-general-hang-about-place for people looking for an alternative way to live.

The Paradox had two great advantages—it had cheap food and tea was free. It was, or at least advertised itself as, 'the world's first macrobiotic restaurant';[2] for macrobiotic, read vegetarian.

Who came there?

Well, among others, Yoko Ono, the woman who would later be the partner of John Lennon, the legendary singer-songwriter of The Beatles. Ono and folksinger Loudon Wainwright III worked here, 'and Abbie Hoffman described it as "a neat cheap health joint that will give you a free meal if you help peel shrimp or do the dishes" . . . one of Yoko Ono's conceptual pieces at The Paradox, "People would climb inside these huge black burlap bags, singly, or with a partner, and then do whatever they wanted, providing a floor show for patrons while they ate their brown rice and sprout salad".[3]

It was two Paradox regulars, Harvey Cohen and Bill Epstein, who had earlier heard Bhaktivedanta speak at Dr Mishra's who urged him to move base to the Lower East Side.

But it would perhaps have not happened if it hadn't been for a robbery. Bhaktivedanta had a small tape recorder and typewriter and one day they were stolen from his room. Thus, he was convinced through this incident, which surprised and shocked him, about the wisdom of Bill and Harvey to move to the Bowery, the great hub of the artistic but spiritually adrift. Cohen had come to possess a loft there through inherited money, and offered to rent it to David Allen, a perfectly pleasant young man who, nonetheless, had a bit of a wavering point of view on psychedelic drug-induced nirvana as long as Allen agreed to share it with a septuagenarian monk from India.

Thus, it came to pass that the scholar of Vrindavan, the devotee of Krishna, came to be housemates with a twenty-one-year-old trying to find himself.

How does one explain what the Bowery is? Perhaps it could be understood by this quote by Theodore Roosevelt from 1913, 'The Bowery is one of the great highways of humanity, a highway of seething life, of varied interest, of fun, of work, of sordid and terrible tragedy; and it is haunted by demons as evil as any that stalk through the pages of the *Inferno*.'[4]

There was also a common ditty about it, *A Trip to Chinatown*:

The Bow'ry, the Bow'ry!
They say such things,
And they do strange things
On the Bow'ry! The Bow'ry!
I'll never go there anymore![5]

That seemed rather apt for the Bowery full of the homeless, drunk or restless people that A.C. Bhaktivedanta started to live with at the Bowery, stepping consistently either over trash, or slumped human bodies in stupor.

One element of his life in New York in the early days is worth noting, especially since it does not seem to find too much mention—how acutely conscious of money A.C. Bhaktivedanta is throughout that period.

As an example, here are three days' worth of diary jottings:

Sunday 3 April

Sun Rise 5/38 am. Sunset 6/30 pm. Moon Set 5/08 am.

Chaturdasi

From Ananda Ashram came back to New York. Passed night at my apartment. Dr Mishra gave me a tape-recorder which is not working.

no expenditure, No income.

Monday 4 April

Sun Rise 5/36 am. Sunset 6/31 pm. Moon Set 5/46 am.

Poornima

Today I went to see Mr Bogart. His publisher Mr Laughton interested in publishing Srimad Bhagavatam. Mr Bogart offered me a typewriter and Tape Recorder. I took them. Typewriter nice. Tape Recorder defective.

Today I have replied the letter of State Department regarding visit to the President.

Then I came to Paul's place.

There was meeting and Kirtan, Hari Katha.

No income. Expenditure .30*

Tuesday 5 April

Sun Rise 5/34 am. Sunset 6/34 pm. Moonrise 7/01

Prabhupada: The whole day I was at Paul's place. He is a nice boy. I prepared Paratha he was pleased to have it. He is anxious to follow the principles of Vaishnavism. I shall help him to my best. In the evening we held kirtan together. He is hopeful.

No income and No expenditure.[6]

When in June, the collection goes up significantly one time, to $19, it is described as 'best than all previous classes'.[7]

---

* 30 pence.

Even Robert Nelson recalled being told that the recipe for roti or chapati[8] would cost him a donation. Well, unemployed Robert could not raise one hundred dollars, but Bhaktivedanta showed him the recipe anyway, and urged him to wash his hands before eating, and to eat with his right hand only.[9]

And so it went on and on. There was no escaping it. A.C. Bhaktivedanta is unconscious, mostly, of material comfort but he was acutely aware of the fact that, without money, his mission might remain unaccomplished. The struggle to raise funds was real. The aim was not to make his own life easier. Bhaktivedanta seems to have lived stoically in every arrangement that had been thrown at him, but the ambition to build for Krishna never dimmed.

At the Bowery, to its creative and some just lost souls, Bhaktivedanta brought the joy of, even if momentarily, a touch of divinity. The music was always rousing, the kirtans, the smell of burning incense sticks pervaded the air. He taught, he preached, he cooked—it was almost as if the bhakti of Krishna was impossible to imagine without the solace of a full stomach and the sound of music. This was a lesson understood only too well by his audience.

There is an important thing to highlight here. From the beginning, since A.C. Bhaktivedanta created what perhaps would today be called 'safe spaces' in some of the most unsafe parts of New York. Safe spaces for the artistes, the vagabonds, the seekers and the lost. In his incense-perfumed prayer meetings, in talking about the love of Krishna, in sharing the music of devotion, the kirtan, Bhaktivedanta created—and for this he is rarely given credit—a multiracial safe space, where anyone, no matter colour of their skin, would be welcomed as long as they were receptive to the message of A.C. Bhaktivedanta on the importance of the love of Krishna.

In hindsight, it was an astonishing act—a septuagenarian Indian monk leading multiracial gatherings in one of the most poor and violent areas of New York during a decade torn by racial strife. 'Between 1964 and 1971, civil disturbances (as many as 700, by one count) resulted in large numbers of injuries, deaths, and arrests, as well as considerable property damage, concentrated in predominantly Black* areas. Although the United States has experienced race-related civil disturbances throughout its history, the 1960s events were unprecedented in their frequency and scope. Law enforcement authorities took extraordinary measures to end the riots, sometimes including the mobilization of National Guard units. The most-deadly riots were in Detroit (1967), Los Angeles (1965), and Newark (1967). Measuring riot severity by also including arrests, injuries, and arson adds Washington (1968) to that list. Particularly following the death of Martin Luther King in April 1968, the riots signaled the end of the carefully orchestrated, non-violent demonstrations of the early Civil Rights Movement.'[10]

The underlying reason for this violence was deep-seated inequity, among other prejudices, which had been festering since World War II. 'In the early 1960s, African Americans in cities nationwide were growing frustrated with the high level of poverty in their communities. Since the years immediately following World War II (1939–45), middle-class white Americans had been leaving the cities for nearby suburbs. Businesses that had once provided jobs and tax funding in the cities were leaving as well. At the same time, more than three million job-seeking African Americans moved from the South to the cities of the North and the West. Increasingly, the downtowns of large cities became home to lower-income minorities, many of them southern Blacks. Unemployment among African Americans was well above

---

* 'Black' is a term used by some communities, and sometimes by all persons of colour, to describe themselves. It is a term which now had a long history in having been reclaimed and reappropriated by persons of colour and is in widespread mainstream usage. Its usage in this chapter is not pejorative; is not intended as a racial slur; and is not intended to cause offence or to hurt the sentiments of any individual, community, section of people, group, race, caste or religion.

the national average, and one-half of all Black Americans lived
below the poverty line (as opposed to one-fifth of whites). Not
surprisingly, tensions ran high in Black communities . . . Major
riots occurred in Birmingham, Alabama , in 1963; New York City
in 1964; Watts in Los Angeles, California , in 1965; and Chicago,
Illinois, in 1966. In 1967 alone, Tampa, Florida; Cincinnati,
Ohio; Atlanta, Georgia; Newark, Plainfield, and New Brunswick,
New Jersey; and Detroit, Michigan, all had riots. Riots erupted in
more than 110 U.S. cities on April 4, 1968, the night civil rights
leader Martin Luther King Jr. (1929–1968) was assassinated.'[11]

This bloodletting unravelled even though 'Lyndon Johnson
[1963-69], brought with him to the Presidency a vision of a
country no longer divided into rich and poor, Black and white, the
powerless and the wielders of power. Out of the despair following
JFK's assassination, Johnson inaugurated programs that aimed at
closing the gap between rich and poor, and concomitantly between
Black and white Americans by launching an all out "War on
Poverty." His American Opportunity Act included such programs
as "Upward Bound," and "Headstart" that remain fixtures in
American education even today. Part of Johnson's plan focused on
the empowerment of local action initiatives, or CAP's (Community
Action Programs), to combat poverty in individual communities.
Placing local Black leaders (supported by federal stipends) in charge
of implementing such programs sometimes drew the resentment
of local white politicians and members of the law enforcement
community. This resentment often resulted in official toleration
of acts of uniformed brutality on Black people, behavior that too
often went unpunished. As animosities continued to fester, an
already frustrated and angry Black population in America's cities
violently took that sense of unfairness to the streets in the form of
demonstrations, looting, and the destruction of property'.[12]

But in the small, sonorous spiritual services of Bhaktivedanta,
these gaps were closed, even if momentarily, and a higher power

invoked. This spirit of service and sensory worship blurred the lines that were so acutely drawn on the streets. In fact, some of Bhaktivedanta's early followers were Black, including, importantly in this phase of his journey, a thirty-year-old Black Cornell student from the Bronx, Carl Yeargens.

It was in Carl Yeargens' home, which Yeargens shared with his partner, that A.C. Bhaktivedanta sought refuge when his earlier roommate David Allen, in a drug-induced frenzy, went hysterical. And it was in the presence of people like Yeargens, and other students and artistes, that Bhaktivedanta was first written about in the influential 'counterculture' publication *The Village Voice*. Here he got to speak about the dream of his 'American church'.

By the end of May, A.C. Bhaktivedanta and his followers had agreed 'about incorporation of The International Society for Krishna Consciousness.'[13] In June, *The Village Voice* announced this ambition in its article about Bhaktivedanta. Thus, it came to pass that unwittingly and in part through his natural affection for anyone who came to him, A.C. Bhaktivedanta became, in his own way, a part of the counterculture of America at that time, teaching his pupils that the war of Kurukshetra was not quite akin to the war in Vietnam. These were complex metaphysical ideas—Arjun was not just a warrior or a soldier, but his task was emboldened and sanctified for he was doing it, he was fighting the battle for Krishna. This would not have been easy to explain to his followers in the Lower East Side, but Bhaktivedanta soldiered on nonetheless.

An important thing was happening—he had to place his devotion to Krishna in a new cultural context and find words and examples that would speak directly to pupils in this alien land. Food, therefore, served as an important glue. For Bhaktivedanta, empathy for man naturally flowed from enthusiasm for God. For one such gathering, he noted, 'I cooked 12 different items and all present, more than sixteen ladies and gentlemen, ate with great pleasure.'[14] This kind of passion for feeding people would continue throughout his mission. This would remain one of his great legacies, the refusal to send anyone away hungry. Food for Bhaktivedanta was a bridge, not only between God and man but between people too. He used food to bridge differences—often seemingly irreconcilable ones—in those tense years in America. The fingerprint of his influence was still small but what it lacked in numbers, it made up in sheer novelty—who really could have ever imagined?

Even though for months he had received no support from any quarter in India and had to desert the site where his work as a preacher was just getting grounded, hope was in sight.

Days after *The Village Voice* article was published, A.C. Bhaktivedanta was told by his assorted gaggle of students and followers that a new site for his work had been found, along with a new home for him.

This home was to be a twin set—a store or what the Americans called a shopfront which used to sell nostalgia gifts, and a small apartment across the road on Second Avenue in East Manhattan. This was to be the first official site of his preaching which did not have to double up as also his home.

By this time, he was already drawing more than just casual visitors; after all, he now had people willing to fund his venture, small as it was, and register the society in America. And by the end of June, he noted in his diary that one of his followers 'proposed to become a Vaishnava and married with his girlfriend'.[15] He had come not to convert anyone. Indeed, his early followers were of all kinds—Christians, Jews, non-sectarians, agnostics, even atheists. Yet, within months of his presence, the imperative to his path and his role as a guru had grown significant, at least among some of them.

This was going to be much more than his home. It would be the home—the first home—of ISKCON.

11

Sami Krishna

In starting ISKCON, A.C. Bhaktivedanta had defined seven founding principles:

To systematically propagate spiritual knowledge to society at large and to educate all people in the techniques of spiritual life in order to check the imbalance of values in life, and to achieve real unity and peace in the world.

To propagate a consciousness of Krishna as He is revealed in Bhagavad Gita and Srimad Bhagavatam.

To bring the members of the society together with each other and nearer to Krishna, and thus to develop the idea within the members and humanity at large that each soul is part and parcel of the Supreme Personality of Godhead.

To teach and encourage the sankirtana movement, congregational chanting of the holy name of God, and to reveal the teachings of Lord Chaitanya Mahaprabhu.

To erect for the members, and the society at large, a holy place of transcendental pastimes, dedicated to the Personality of Godhead.

To bring the members closer together for the purpose of teaching a simple and more natural way of life.

With a view towards achieving the aforementioned purposes, to publish and distribute periodicals, magazines, books and other writings.[1]

He never really could achieve any of these goals—which he had had even in India—with any real scale in his home country. But, as we shall see as our story progresses, he was able to fulfil at least half of his set of goals within less than twenty-four months after arriving in America.

It may have amused A.C. Bhaktivedanta that the place of worship that he was gaining on Second Avenue, Lower East Side replaced a store called 'Matchless Gifts', for that is what he believed he had brought to America.

The early recipients of the matchless gifts of Bhaktivedanta were young men like Carl Yeargens, Bill Epstein, Harvey Cohen, Howard Wheeler, his roommates Keith and Wally and others like them. What was common between these men were that they were all young, in their twenties or early thirties, and they were all seeking more than what their immediate surroundings and culture were able to offer. They were seeking a centredness, perhaps it is best called love.

Why did this need emerge?

Because, as we have noted before, America was in those years experiencing a resurgence in counterculture. It is important to define what counterculture is. The scholar Paul Oliver noted, 'The term counterculture tends to be used where a sub-culture evolves which is significantly different from conventional society in terms of values and patterns of behaviour. Such a counterculture exhibits antipathy towards the established institutions of society. It could be argued that countercultures have existed since society has existed, since only through periodic challenges to the prevalent power structures, can society change . . . Indeed one might further argue that it is part of the concept of a counterculture that it seeks to subvert the existing society . . . There was . . . at the beginning of the 1960s an increasing demand for freedom, equality, and autonomy in many areas of life. Where inequalities were deeply embedded within the existing social structure, as for example with race and gender in equalities, the coming decade would see a concentrated challenge to these existing cultural norms.'[2]

But this kind of springing up of interest, as we have been noting, and as the American scholar of Hinduism Jeffery Long has pointed out, had a predecessor: in the late nineteenth and early twentieth century, several Americans took keen interest in Hinduism, 'even to the point of participating in the movement for Indian independence, taking up monastic vows, or both . . . The main difference between the countercultural movement of the earlier period—the late nineteenth and early twentieth centuries—and that of the 1960s seems largely to be one of scale. Westerners drawn to, for example, the Vedanta Society (of Vivekananda) . . . in the early decades (of the organization) numbered in the thousands or tens of thousands, at the most. Westerners drawn to the counterculture of the 1960s, though, numbered in the millions'.[3]

And one of the key people who brought about this surge was A.C. Bhaktivedanta and his ISKCON.

At Second Avenue, the site of the first real worship centre, many of the young visitors were transfixed by the 'cool tranquillity'[4] that Bhaktivedanta exuded. In a bewildering and disturbing world of violence and, perhaps even more importantly, impermanence, the swami, as he came to be known, offered a message of permanence, something that would not alter even if all other things did.

The homeless, the LSD-laden and the drunk interrupted some of his meetings but the sonorous voice of A.C. Bhaktivedanta rose above the din. Boys with nowhere else to go, like Don or Rapahel, found refuge in his home. They helped clean and cook, and they helped make arrangements for his preaching when they could not help with the expenses. He was asked about Camus, Nietzsche, Kafka, about the *Tibetan Book of the Dead*, even Bob Dylan, and through it all Bhaktivedanta explained that he only wished to speak of the Bhagavad Gita, of the lessons of Krishna and their application in everyday life, in its strife and hardships.

'What about the Buddha?' he was asked.

'Do you follow him?' he asked his interlocutor.

'No,' came the response.

'No, you just talk,' replied Bhaktivedanta, with a touch of exasperation. 'Why don't you follow? Follow Krishna, follow Christ, follow Buddha. But just don't talk.'[5]

Like Krishna, in the Gita, A.C. Bhaktivedanta preached a gospel of action to his followers, something to actually do, pray, sing, dance, but not merely talk.

Stephen Goldsmith, a young Jewish lawyer, was roped in to register the society, make it tax-free and the men around, those hippies, several of them became trustees, now part of ISKCON.

Through this process, A.C. Bhaktivedanta continued to hold his preaching sessions at his makeshift temple at 26, Second Avenue. Sometimes he was asked about Camus, sometimes about sex, sometimes people on drugs floated by, but Bhaktivedanta looked past them all to focus on his task—spreading the word of Krishna. Build and publish for Krishna. During his spare time, he continued his fervent translation work—sixty volumes, the target remained intact.

The storefront-turned-temple was decorated with bric-a-brac from India, including a statuette of Hanuman, carpets on the floor and paintings on the wall.[6] He cooked, he cleaned, he preached, building the first small community of ISKCON in that run-down Manhattan neighbourhood. In a New York full of discontented youth, A.C. Bhaktivedanta had managed to find some devoted helpers, the first of his followers.

Here we must, in our story, talk a little about what A.C. Bhaktivedanta was offering to his followers apart from spiritual and musical guidance—food, prasadam. For a man who had worried that he would find little to eat in America that was not meat or meat-based, Bhaktivedanta was pleased to find himself in the middle of a food revolution too.

As we have noted before, with the Paradox restaurant, demand for vegetarian food was growing with the alternative, non-violent lifestyle movement. Bhaktivedanta was pleasantly surprised to find all his essential ingredients, from basmati rice to spices for his vegetarian dishes, and khichdi, a tasty Indian-style savoury porridge laden with spices.

To understand what he was cooking and why so many seemed to love it, it is worth sharing the recipes of the three of the most common dishes A.C. Bhaktivedanta cooked—khichdi, dal and chapati. This is the description of the dish that is used by ISKCON even today.

Khichari[*]

Khichari is a nutritious stew featuring *dal* and rice. There are two main varieties thin (geeli[†] khichari) and thick (sookha[‡] khichari). Whichever way you prepare khichari, it will soon become a delicious favourite. The following recipe is for the thicker variety. Khichari is an ideal breakfast food, wonderful when accompanied by yogurt and fresh hot Puffed Fried Breads (Pooris) or toast. Always serve khichari with a wedge of lemon or lime. Not only does this add a delightful nuance of flavour, but it lends nutritional advantage also: there are good sources of iron in the dal and vegetables in khichari, and

---

[*] Khichdi.
[†] 'Wet' in Hindi.
[‡] 'Dry' in Hindi.

the lemon juice, rich in vitamin C, helps your body absorb it. This recipe is mildly spiced. Adjust your own spicing as required.

- PREPARATION TIME: 5 minutes
- COOKING TIME: 30–40 minutes
- YIELD: Enough for 6–8 persons
  - 1/3 cup (85 ml) split mung beans
  - 1 cup (250 ml) basmati or other long-grain white rice
  - 3 tablespoons (60 ml) ghee or oil
  - 1/3 cup (85 ml) raw cashew pieces or halves
  - 2 teaspoons (10 ml) cumin seeds
  - 1 tablespoon (20 ml) fresh hot green chili, minced
  - 2 tablespoons (40 ml) minced fresh ginger
  - 1 teaspoon (5 ml) turmeric
  - 1 teaspoon (5 ml) yellow asafoetida powder
  - 1 small cauliflower (about 400 g, or 14 ounces) cut into small flowerets
  - 5–6 cups (1 ¼–1.5 litres) water
  - 1.5 teaspoons (7 ml) salt
  - 1 tablespoon (20 ml) butter
  - 2/3 cup (165 ml) cooked green peas
  - 1 cup (250 ml) tomatoes, peeled and chopped
  - 1/2 cup (125 ml) chopped fresh coriander leaves

1. Wash and drain the dal and rice.
2. Heat the ghee in a heavy 4-litre/quart non-stick saucepan over moderate heat. Fry the cashews in the hot ghee until they turn golden brown and remove them with a slotted spoon. Put them aside. Fry the cumin seeds in the ghee. When they turn golden brown add the chilies and ginger. Sauté them for a few seconds; then add the turmeric and asafoetida. Add the cauliflower pieces and stir fry them for

1 minute. Finally, add the dal and rice, stirring with the spices and vegetables for 1 minute.

3. Add the water and bring to a full boil over high heat. Reduce the heat to low, partially cover, and slowly cook, stirring occasionally, for 30–40 minutes or until the dal and rice are soft. If the khichari dries out too much, add up to one cup (250 ml) warm water. Before removing the khichari from the heat, fold in the salt, butter, cooked green peas, chopped tomatoes, toasted cashews, and the chopped fresh coriander leaves, allowing them to warm for one minute. Serve hot.[7]

Split-Mung (Beans) Dal

Used extensively in soups, stews, and sauces in Indian vegetarian cuisine, split mung beans are rich in vegetable protein, iron, and B vitamins. When you combine dal with a food that has a complementary protein (grains, seeds, nuts, or milk products), the usable protein in the dal increases dramatically. Serve this simple puree like soup as an entree to a western-type meal or serve it as part of a traditional Indian meal such as Sautéed Rice with Poppy Seeds, North Indian Curried Cauliflower and Potatoes, Griddle-Baked Bread, Mixed Vegetable and Yogurt Salad, Creamy Condensed-Milk Rice Pudding, and Lemon, Mint, and Whey Nectar.

- PREPARATION TIME: 10 minutes
- COOKING TIME: About 1 hour
- YIELD: Enough for 4 persons
  - 3/4 cup (185 ml) split mung dal (without skins)
  - 6 cups (1.5 litres) water
  - 1/2 teaspoon (2 ml) turmeric
  - 1 teaspoon (5 ml) ground coriander

- 2 teaspoons (10 ml) minced fresh ginger
- 1 teaspoon (5 ml) fresh hot green chili, minced
- 2 tablespoons (40 ml) ghee or oil
- 1.5 teaspoons (7 ml) cumin seeds
- 1/4 teaspoon (1 ml) yellow asafoetida powder
- 1 teaspoon (5 ml) salt
- 2 tablespoons (40 ml) chopped fresh parsley or coriander

1. Wash and drain the split mung beans.
2. Place the mung beans, water, turmeric, ground coriander, minced ginger and chili in a heavy 3-litre/quart saucepan and, stirring occasionally, bring to a full boil over high heat. Reduce the heat to moderately low, cover with a lid, and boil for one hour or until the beans become soft.
3. Heat the ghee or oil over moderate heat in a small pan. Sauté the cumin seeds in the hot oil until they turn brown; then add the asafoetida powder and sauté momentarily. Pour the seasonings into the *dal*. Add the salt and remove the soup from the heat, allowing the spices to soak for a few minutes. Add the minced fresh herbs and stir well. Serve hot.[8]

Chapati

Chapatis are one of India's most popular breads. They are enjoyed especially in the northern and central regions of India. They are partially cooked on a hot griddle and finished over an open-heat source. Chapatis are made from a special wholemeal flour called atta, available from Indian grocers. If unavailable, substitute sifted wholemeal flour. You can spread melted butter or ghee on the chapatis after they are cooked. Chapatis are usually served at lunch or dinner and are great whether served with a 5-course dinner or just with a simple dal and salad.

- PREPARATION TIME: 5–10 minutes
- DOUGH RESTING TIME: ½–3 hours
- COOKING TIME: 25–35 minutes
- YIELD: 12 chapatis
  - 2 cups (500 ml) sifted chapati flour
  - 1/2 teaspoon (2 ml) salt (optional)
  - water
  - extra flour for dusting
  - melted butter or ghee (optional, for spreading over chapatis after they've been cooked)

1. Combine the flour and salt in a mixing bowl. Add up to 2/3 cup (165 ml) of water, slowly pouring in just enough to form a soft kneadable dough. Turn the dough onto a clean working surface and knead for about 8 minutes or until silky-smooth. Cover with an overturned bowl and leave for ½–3 hours.
2. Knead the dough again for one minute. Divide the dough into a dozen portions. Roll them into smooth balls and cover with a damp cloth.
3. Preheat a griddle or non-stick heavy frying pan over moderately low heat for 3–4 minutes. Flatten a ball of dough, dredge it in flour and carefully roll out the ball into a thin, perfectly even, smooth disk of dough about 15 cm (6 inches) in diameter.
4. Carefully pick up the chapati and slap it between your hands to remove the excess flour. Slip it onto the hot plate, avoiding any wrinkles. Cook for about 1 minute on the first side. The top of the chapati should start to show small bubbles. Turn the chapati over with tongs. Cook it

until small brown spots appear on the underside (about a
minute).

5. If you are using gas, turn a second burner on high, pick
    up the chapati with your tongs, and hold it about 5 cm (2
    inches) over the flame. It will swell into a puffy balloon.
    Continue to cook the chapati until it is speckled with black
    flecks. Place the cooked chapati in a bowl or basket, cover
    with a clean tea towel or cloth and continue cooking the
    rest of the chapatis. When they're all cooked and stacked,
    you might like to butter them. Serve chapatis hot for best
    results or cover and keep warm in a preheated warm oven
    for up to 1/2 hour.[9]

As his followers grew, so did his contacts in New York, and soon an
invitation through an acquaintance came for A.C. Bhaktivedanta
and his group to participate in a vigil for peace (as part of the
war protests) at the United Nations. This was held on 6 August
1966, the anniversary of the Hiroshima bombing.[10] As a spiritual
leader, Bhaktivedanta was, at that time, in the right place at the
right time. Even though he and his followers would not be able to
sing the kirtan, which is what they would have liked to do, even
a peace vigil, silent as it was, provided an occasion for a public
outing as a community. Instead of singing, A.C. Bhaktivedanta
asked his followers to softly chant the Hare Krishna mantra and
later remarked that if only everyone would chant the mantra 'they
won't have to artificially try for peace'.[11]

    Their efforts were noticed in the *New York Post*, though
Bhaktivedanta was named as 'Sami Krishna'.[12]

    Bhaktivedanta spent his time praying, writing and preaching,
and slowly a congregation built around him. They had started
by being intrigued and interested in him, but now one by one
they expressed the desire to be initiated. But not many of
them understood what having a guru meant. To initiate his

first disciples, A.C. Bhaktivedanta prepared an entire sequence
of rituals and explained the importance of the guru (next only
to God) to them.

He had requested them to chant the Hare Krishna* mantra
softly throughout the ceremony, and the chanting had now become
a continuous drone, accompanying his mysterious movements as
head priest of the Vedic rite.

He began by lighting a dozen sticks of incense. Then he
performed purification with water. Taking a spoon in his left
hand, he put three drops of water from a goblet into his right
and sipped the water. He repeated the procedure three times. The
fourth time he did not sip but flicked the water on to the floor
behind him. He then passed the spoon and goblet around for the
initiates, who tried to copy what they had seen. When some of
them placed the water in the wrong hand or sipped in the wrong
way, Swamiji patiently corrected them.

'Now,' he said, 'repeat after me.' And he had them repeat, one
word at a time, a Vedic mantra of purification:

om apavitrah pavitro va
sarvavastham gato 'pi va
yah smaret pundarikaksham
sa bahyabhyantara shucih
sri vishnu sri vishnu sri vishnu

The initiates tried falteringly to follow his pronunciation of
the words, which they had never heard before. Then he gave
the translation: 'Unpurified or purified, or even having passed
through all situations, one who remembers the lotus-eyed
Supreme Personality of Godhead is cleansed within and without.'
He repeated the sipping of water three times, the drone of the

---

* Another name for Krishna.

Hare Krishna mantra filling the room as the goblet passed from initiate to initiate and back again to him, and three times he led the chanting of the mantra: *om apavitrah* . . . Then he raised a hand, and as the buzzing of the chanting trailed off into silence, he began his lecture.

After the lecture, he asked the devotees one by one to hand him their beads, and he began chanting on them—Hare Krishna, Hare Krishna, Krishna Krishna, Hare Hare/Hare Rama, Hare Rama, Rama Rama, Hare Hare. The sound of everyone chanting filled the room. After finishing one strand, he would summon the owner of the beads and hold the beads up while demonstrating how to chant. Then he would announce the initiate's spiritual name, and the disciple would take back the beads, bow to the floor and recite:

nama om vishnu padaya krishna preshtaya bhutale
srmate bhaktivedanta svamin iti namine

'I offer my respectful obeisances unto His Divine Grace A.C. Bhaktivedanta Swami, who is very dear to Lord Krishna, having taken shelter at His lotus feet.' There were eleven initiates and so eleven sets of beads, and the chanting lasted for over an hour. Prabhupada gave each boy a strand of neck beads . . . Wally received his beads and his new name (Umapati), he returned to his place beside Howard and said, 'That was wonderful. Getting your beads is wonderful.' In turn, each initiate received his beads and his spiritual name. Howard became Hayagriva, Wally became Umapati, Bill became Ravindra Svarupa, Carl became Karlapati, James became Jagannatha, Mike became Mukunda, Jan became Janaki, Roy became Raya Rama and Stanley became Strayadhisa.'[13]

What was A.C. Bhaktivedanta doing? He was transplanting an ancient Indian tradition to an alien land. He was redefining spiritual processes that would work in a foreign culture. He was putting down rituals and norms for his new organization in that novel country. He was explaining, through word and deed, to these young men that to become disciples was to truly immerse oneself into the cause and knowledge of the guru. No longer would they be able to maintain any semblance of a dual life where the focus was diluted—to be initiated would mean complete devotion to Krishna and the guru.

It was around this time that A.C. Bhaktivedanta would meet a man who would be the first real catapult of the elderly preacher's mission in the West. Allen Ginsberg could have been, indeed for many he was, the emblem of the counterculture movement. A Columbia University graduate, Ginsberg, a poet and writer, was one of the three people, with William S. Burroughs and Jack Kerouac, who were the pioneering lights of the Beat Generation. The Beat Generation, from the 1950s, brought together people interested in breaking the bonds of absolutist capitalism, materialism as the sole defining criteria of life, choice of different kinds of living, and engagement with Eastern faiths.

In 1956, Ginsberg produced a poem called *Howl* which became a counterculture anthem, seized often by customs and police, and chanted by the disillusioned young. Some of the most memorable lines of the poem sound like, yes, a howl of agony against the soullessness of a materialistic world:

What sphinx of cement and aluminum bashed open their skulls and ate up their brains and imagination?

Moloch! Solitude! Filth! Ugliness! Ashcans and unobtainable dollars! Children screaming under the stairways! Boys sobbing in armies! Old men weeping in the parks!

Moloch! Moloch! Nightmare of Moloch! Moloch the loveless! Mental Moloch! Moloch the heavy judger of men!

Moloch the incomprehensible prison! Moloch the
crossbone soulless jailhouse and Congress of sorrows! Moloch
whose buildings are judgment! Moloch the vast stone of war!
Moloch the stunned governments!

Moloch whose mind is pure machinery! Moloch whose
blood is running money! Moloch whose fingers are ten armies!
Moloch whose breast is a cannibal dynamo! Moloch whose ear
is a smoking tomb![14]

Bhaktivedanta had been thinking on similar lines. In a letter to a
pupil, who asked him how America had such material progress,
the monk answered:

'Actually, there is no material advancement in the USA.
Material advancement means there is ample opportunity for
eating, sleeping, mating and defending. Superficially, it appears
that in the USA there is sufficient provision of eating, sleeping,
mating and defending, but actually nobody is safe even in his good
apartment. I have got practical experience in New York. Several
times my typewriter and tape recorders were stolen and the police
could not take any action. There are many persons in the Bowery
street, they have no shelter to live.

'So if a certain fraction of the people are supposed to be
very materially happy at the cost of others, that is not material
advancement. Had it been so, then why there are so many
persons confused and frustrated? So actually there is no
material advancement here. Here, I am seeing practically that
Gaurasundara, such a nice intelligent and qualified boy, he has
to work hard 12 hours simply for his subsistence. I think there
are many instances like that, so this is not material advancement.
You can call it capitalist advancement, and the reaction for such
advancement is communism. Such movement is simply suppressed
in your country, but actually the reaction is this. So the Western

type of civilization, industrialism and capitalism, is no material advancement. It is material exploitation.

'When one gets the bare necessities of life, namely peaceful home, sumptuous eating, necessary sex life, and feeling of security, then it is called material advancement. In the absence of such four preliminary necessities of life, it is not at all material advancement— just try to understand. According to Vedic civilization, a man is supposed to be rich when he has got sufficient grains and cows. Here we have neither sufficient grains or cows, but you have got sufficient quantity of papers only—falsely thinking that it is money. When there is some catastrophe, this bunch of papers will neither supply milk or grain. They will be seen only and the man will starve.'[15]

The emotions in Ginsberg's *Howl* and A.C. Bhaktivedanta's opinion about the material culture in America are useful to study side by side for they allows us to understand what these two unlikely men would have seen in one another. Even though Ivy League-educated, Ginsberg was a misfit in traditional American society: a homosexual, a poet, fervently anti-violence, anti-war, against mindless materialism and seeking a deeper, more profound way to live.

Bhaktivedanta was of the firm opinion that his path was the only one that could resolve, at once, the kind of doubts, apprehensions and hunger that someone like Ginsberg had. Faced with the listlessness of 1960s America, Bhaktivedanta was not disillusioned. On the contrary, it reinforced his belief that more than ever the word of Krishna had to be given to the world—it needed it.

12

The 'High' of Krishna

Apt for the tumultuous time in which they met, Allen Ginsberg was introduced to A.C. Bhaktivedanta through a psychiatrist.

In his diary, Bhaktivedanta noted of his earliest connection with Dr Edward Harnick, thus:

> Dr Edward Harnick Psychiatrist supplied one set of books
> Bhagawatam through Keith
> Dr Edward Harnick
> c/o Einstein Psychiatric Institute
> 11 West 73rd Street
> N.Y.C.

Clearly, the psychiatrist was a purchaser of a set of Bhaktivedanta's books. Ginsberg too noted his interactions with Dr Harnick:

> Peter Orlovsky* and I met Harnick at a group that I knew called the GAP, Group for the Advancement of Psychiatry. We had been to their conference. They had invited us to talk about hippies and they wanted to know what was this generation

---

* Ginsberg's partner.

thing. It was like a breakthrough between the poets and the new culture and the psychiatry groups. So we'd given a big poetry reading and made friends with a lot of them, and sang Hare Krishna* with them, the whole thing.

Over the years Harnick and I developed a pleasant friendship and worked out an arrangement that if I knew anybody particularly gifted among the younger generation that was getting screwed up in the Lower East Side for drugs or busts or madness or whatever, that rather than have them go through the whole horror mill of Bellevue and not know what to do, to put them in touch with him and the Einstein Clinic, so he could intervene to make sure that they had a safe refuge. When Kirtananda's† case came up, at that time he wasn't the only one in trouble. There were a lot of hippies going through the same problem, wandering the street, flipping out. It was a question of finding a psychiatrist who had a little political clout in the New York psychiatric community among the hospitals, whom we could talk to and explain what the situation was, that this guy was a devotee practising traditional Vaishnava‡ practice, and that's why he looked so funny in the American context, but it was all right, he wasn't crazy, he was just doing his thing. Harnick was good. He picked up fast and could intervene.

When A.C. Bhaktivedanta met Allen Ginsberg, he was starting to settle in a routine. He had some followers, but few were really trained into understanding the unique relationship between the guru and the disciple—the guru–shishya parampara—or the age-old tradition of the guru and the pupil. At the kirtans and prayer meetings, few contributed monetarily—as is customary in

---

* Hare Krishna.
† One of A.C. Bhaktivedanta's followers had been facing some trouble with authorities as many in the wider hippie movement had been.
‡ Vaishnava.

Hindu tradition—and often all the chores had to be done by A.C. Bhaktivedanta himself, including cooking for not small groups of people—and cleaning up afterwards.

Still, it was a beginning. A.C. Bhaktivedanta even managed to get a couple, Mike and Jan, rechristened after their initiation as Mukunda and Janaki, get married according to Hindu rituals, complete with a ceremony before the sacred fire.[1] He taught them and others about the importance of the matrimonial vows in Hinduism, the importance of the fire, how to cook prasad and yes, why they must repeatedly wash their hands before doing any work for Krishna.

He even started taking his disciples and openly singing in parks the mantra of Hare Krishna, Hare Krishna, Krishna Krishna, Hare Hare/ Hare Rama, Hare Rama, Rama Rama, Hare Hare. This, too, had never been done before. It was one thing to conduct ceremonies quietly in one corner of Manhattan, and quite another thing to hit the parks and the streets, as it were.

But there he was, opening his voice and singing aloud, breaking the trepidation of his followers, and urging them to do the same, of the mantra in public spaces in Manhattan. This was a new sound, a new music, rising above the roar of revolution and counter-revolution. The lilt, the lift of the words, the reverberation of all those Rs in the mantra would have been strange—and sometimes they drew the attention of the police—but something was being proved, something celestial.

That in the streets of foreign lands, the kirtan of Chaitanya Mahaprabhu could be sung and they could ring with the chants of Krishna.

But the question was of scale. Whatever A.C. Bhaktivedanta was doing was local, confined to a small area of traction and even though his work had received some press attention, its footprint was still very small.

That would change with the arrival of Allen Ginsberg.

Apart from their common connection with Dr Harnick, Ginsberg also received pamphlets that were being distributed by the pupils of A.C. Bhaktivedanta. This was autumn 1966.

What had happened in Ginsberg's life by that time?

By this time, *Howl* had been published, eulogized and banned. Ginsberg had moved with his partner Peter Orlovsky first to Morocco, and then they had spent time in India staying mostly in Calcutta and Benaras, and befriending Bengali poets Sunil Gangopadhyay and Shakti Chattopadhyay, and cultural aficionado Pupul Jayakar. It was in Benaras and Calcutta that Ginsberg had first heard the Hare Krishna chant, and the sound of the cymbals and the harmonium.

When he first came to one of A.C. Bhaktivedanta's sessions, what he had seen in India, in Calcutta and Benaras, the sight was the same, the music, that music, was the same. Here he was, once again, in the presence of a sadhu.

Later, when asked, Ginsberg recalled this connection at an event.

'Question: Where do the East Indian traditions fit in to what was happening in 1967?

'Allen Ginsberg: First of all, on a very basic level, you have the notion from Plato, "when the mode of music changes, the walls of the city shake". If you remember around the middle of the 1960s, Charlie Mingus and Ornette Coleman began experimenting with monochordal music and began listening to Indian music. It was also about the same time that the Hare Krishna movement settled in the Lower East Side where I was working with them for a while and then settled with Prabhupada (A.C. Bhaktivedanta Swami) in San Francisco right after the Be-in in Haight-Ashbury. Prabhupada was living there for some time, right off Haight-Ashbury on Frederick Street, I think. Then there was the singing in the street of the Hare Krishna people, the part of the street action or the notion of the street: street-fighting man or street smarts or street people.'[2]

What impressed Ginsberg was that this sadhu, this elderly monastic, of the kind that he had met in India, was, in America, living among the poor, among the destitute, among drugs users, and peddlers, around people who were looking to 'get high' using psychedelic substances whether to escape life, or at least to get a different perspective to it. A saint had come to live among the destitute, saw Ginsberg.

One of the first things that Ginsberg tried to help A.C. Bhaktivedanta was with staying for a longer period in America. The monk had come on a two-month visa and then got it extended for short periods several times. But after about a year, the authorities were refusing to quickly accommodate any extension. So, Ginsberg offered monetary help to get the right legal intervention.

As Ginsberg recalled: 'Swami Bhaktivedanta was having difficulty getting a permanent visa. He had a lawyer whom I met. He seemed like a naive local lawyer. Maybe somebody he'd (Srila Prabhupada)* met from Ananda (Ashram). I couldn't figure the guy out. I met him in the Jewish vegetarian restaurant a couple of times and talked with him on Second Avenue. At that time I was having problems with the narcotics bureau, which was trying to set me up for a bust, and that year, J. Edgar Hoover[†] put me on the dangerous security list, and the narcs made several attempts to frame me. So, I went to Robert Kennedy's[‡] office in Washington to put counterpressure and complain, and to warn them that someone might bring marijuana into my apartment, bust the door down, and accuse me of having it. I had a long talk about this with Kennedy. Later, I'd gone back to see his secretary, and he came back into the office in his shirt sleeves to see one of the secretaries. I said, "Oh, there's something I forgot. I was going to sing you

---

* Srila Prabhupada.
[†] First director of the Federal Bureau of Investigations (FBI).
[‡] United States Attorney General from January 1961–September 1964; brother of President John F. Kennedy.

Congregational chanting of the holy names—a process of worship introduced by Sri Chaitanya Mahaprabhu in Bengal in the fifteenth century.

Srila Bhaktivinoda Thakura (1838–1914), a prominent Gaudiya Vaishnava reformer and spiritual leader of his time.

Srila Bhaktisiddhanta Saraswati
(1874–1937), son of Srila Bhaktivinoda
Thakura and spiritiual master of A.C.
Bhaktivedanta Swami Prabhupada.
He founded the Gaudiya Matha in 1918
in Calcutta.

Abhay Charan De
studied at the Scottish
Church College,
Calcutta (1916–1920).
He was a member of the
English as well as the
Sanskrit Societies and
most of his professors
were Europeans.

Abhay Charan De met a revered
teacher, Bhaktisiddhanta Saraswati,
who he thought was very different
from the many sadhus he'd met
while growing up. Calcutta, 1922.

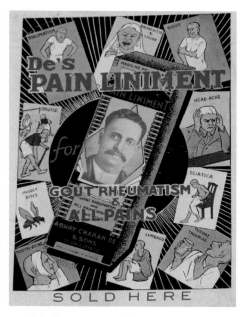

An advertisement of Abhay Charan De's
pharmaceutical product De's PAIN LINIMENT.
Calcutta, 1938.

Abhay Charan De with his son Prayag Raj, wife Radharani, father
Gour Mohan De (centre) and eldest sister Rajeshwari (with her
daughter Sulakshman). His nephew Tulasi and brother Krishna
Charan are standing behind. Calcutta, 1942.

Abhay Charanaravinda Bhaktivedanta first started to shape the movement for Krishna in the way he had dreamt of, under the name 'League of Devotees', in Jhansi, 1953.

A.C. Bhaktivedanta Swami started printing and distributing *Back to Godhead* magazine personally. Delhi, 1956.

Abhay Charanaravinda Bhaktivedanta accepted the order of sannyasa from Sri Srimad Bhakti Prajnana Keshava Maharaja, thereby receiving the title 'Swami'. Keshavaji Gaudiya Matha, Mathura, 17 September 1959. In the picture (*from left to right*): Muni Maharaja, Bhakti Prajnana Keshava Maharaja, A.C. Bhaktivedanta Swami.

Srila Prabhupada presenting Srimad Bhagavatam
to Prime Minister Lal Bahadur Shastri, Delhi, June
1964. Shastri acknowledged: 'His books are significant
contributions to the salvation of mankind.'

A.C. Bhaktivedanta Swami's quarters in Radha Damodar
temple, Vrindavan, before he embarked on his voyage to
America. 1959–1965

Swami Bhaktivedanta at the Chippiwada
temple, Delhi, with three volumes of the
newly published Srimad Bhagavatam,
Canto 1, 1965.

THE SCINDIA STEAM NAVIGATION CO. LTD.
BOMBAY

Nº 774 ·   Place of issue (CALCUTTA) Date 4. 8. 19 65

CABIN CLASS
NON-TRANSFERABLE PASSAGE TICKET

PER Regular Cargo Carrier S.S. JALADUTA embarking about _____ 10
m.v.

From the port of CALCUTTA Back   to the port of _____

Names	AGE Yrs.	Mths.	Cabin No.	Berth No.	Passage Fare	Taxes
1 Dr. ABHEY CHARAN ARAVINDA BHAKTIVEDANTA 69						
SWAMI.						
2						
3						
4						
5 (Complimentary Ticket with Food)						
6						
7						

Adults 1   Children ,   Infants ,   TOTAL one .

IT IS MUTUALLY AGREED that this contract ticket is issued by or on
behalf of THE SCINDIA STEAM NAVIGATION CO. LTD. and is accepted by the
passenger(s) on the terms and conditions printed or endorsed on the face and back
of this ticket.

For The Scindia Steam Navigation Co. Ltd.

(K. B. Mehta)
Senior Deputy Manager

Ticket for Srila Prabhupada's voyage in the cargo ship, *Jaladuta*.
He was provided free passage by Sumati Morarji, proprietor of
Scindia Shipping Company. August 1965.

In August 1965, Swami Bhaktivedanta set out in a cargo ship, *Jaladuta*, to spread the divine message of Lord Sri Krishna in the West.

In 1965 Swami Bhaktivedanta walked the streets of New York, chanting the holy names of Krishna, hoping to attract and convince Americans of the power of the holy names.

An important article on the Hare Krishna movement in the *East Village Other*, October 1966. The cover page carried a photograph of Swami Bhaktivedanta at Tompkins Square Park, Lower East Side, New York.

Srila Prabhupada with American poet and writer Allen Ginsberg, who was impressed that a saint had come to live among the destitute to spread love. San Francisco, 1967.

Swami Bhaktivedanta willingly went to one of the most unlikely places to spread the message of Krishna— Mantra-Rock Dance, a counterculture event in San Francisco, 1967.

Bay Group

Krishna Chants Startle London

By Philip Oakes
London Sunday Times

London

Hare Krishna is good for you. What it means, more or less, is "take heed of Krishna." Innocuous, you may think. But say it sincerely and wonderful things can happen according to believers.

It helps to cure insomnia. It aids concentration. It takes your mind off sex. "It is a chant which sets God dancing on your tongue," says Guru Das, of the Society for Krishna Consciousness Inc. — a missionary group from America which has lately arrived in London. "It has a cleansing effect."

Extravagant claims, maybe, but the Krishna people are walking, talking testimonials.

FROM S.F.

There are six of them, three husbands and their wives, all from San Francisco. The men have shaven heads — a sign of renunciation — with a scalp lock dangling at the back. Their foreheads and noses are daubed with white paint, signifying the footprint of Vishnu, and the banyan leaf — a symbol of strength and spirituality. They wear yellow dhotis, and around their necks they have slung a bag containing beads of tulsi-wood.

At present they all live in an old newspaper office in Covent Garden, where they've turned one room into a temple.

The locals, says Guru Das, don't object to the way they look. "Their only reaction seems to be just 'Wow!'"

gram which differs vastly from that of the Beatles' old Maharishi.

What's likely to earn them a public is their chanting. What they chant are mantras — incantatory prayers accompanied by harmonium, drum, conch shell, finger cymbals — which can last from 30 minutes to 24 hours.

They'll chant whenever and wherever they're invited, but already the police have turned them out of Trafalgar Square and Hyde Park, where the playing of musical instruments are forbidden.

HELL'S ANGELS

Guru Das is negotiating with the Ministry of Works for permission to perform in the streets, and it's possible that his application will succeed. "I hope it does, because our chanting can bring nothing but good," he said.

"At the time of the Grosvenor Square demonstrations we went along there and gave a couple of short chants which may have helped the situation.

"But the most striking example was in Oakland, Calif., when a group of Hell's Angels was all set to beat up a number of anti-Vietnam demonstrators. Alan Ginsberg, the poet, asked everyone to chant a mantra, and the mood of the crowd changed totally.

"When some of the Hell's Angels came to London the other week we asked them if they remembered that day. They said yes, they did, but they'd like to forget it. It wasn't good for their reputa-

Srila Prabhupada sent his three young American disciple couples to London. Their street *sankirtana* charmed Londoners. This was published in the *Evening Standard* which ran the headline 'Krishna Chants Startle London', 1969.

Prabhupada's indefatigable energy was evident in his constant travel.
He circled the globe fourteen times, while establishing over 108 Krishna temples worldwide. London Airport, 1969.

From left to right: Srila Prabhupada, Pattie Boyd, George Harrison and Dhananjaya Das. London, 1969.

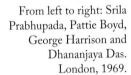

After several attempts to enter the USSR, Prabhupada was able to stay for five days. He successfully planted the seed of devotion in the heart of young Ivan and initiated him as Ananta Shanti Das. Moscow, 1971.

Srila Prabhupada meeting Dr Sarvepalli Radhakrishnan, the former President of India. Madras, February 1972.

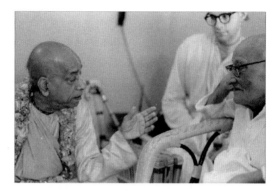

Srila Prabhupada with C. Rajagopalachari (Rajaji), the last Governor General of India. Rajaji acknowledged: 'I am not presumptuous enough to comment on one who has actually taken up the work. That is the difference between thinking and doing. Thinking is easy. Doing requires inspiration, and you [Srila Prabhupada] have taken it up.' Madras, 1972.

'I am just trying to disseminate this message of my spiritual master and if there's any credit for this service, everything goes to him.' At Radha Damodar Temple, Vrindavan, 1972.

Srila Prabhupada on a morning walk with his disciples. Los Angeles, 1973.

Srila Prabhupada with his disciples. New York, 1973.

Srila Prabhupada lands in Switzerland. 30 May 1974.

Srila Prabhupada with Professor Dürckheim, a German diplomat, psychotherapist and Zen master. Frankfurt, 21 June 1974.

Srila Prabhupada (on the top-most balcony) with his disciples at the ISKCON Paris Temple. June 1974.

Srila Prabhupada at Juhu, Mumbai, 1974. Srila signifies one who is invested with both beauty and the power to understand the *lila* of Lord Krishna. Prabhupada is the pure devotee who is surrendered at the lotus feet of the Lord.

Srila Prabhupada affectionately hands out *prasadam* to a child of one of his disciples. Paris, June 1974.

Srila Prabhupada leads a large gathering of 30,000 in a joyful kirtan at the Ratha Yatra festival. San Francisco, 1974.

Srila Prabhupada went to bed at 10 p.m. and woke up at midnight to write his books until morning. This was his routine every day since he incorporated ISKCON in 1965. At ISKCON, Dallas, 1975.

Srila Prabhupada with his disciples on the rooftop of the Manhattan temple. New York, June 1976.

Prabhupada's disciples in Mayapur, West Bengal, early 1970s.
With this, Srila Bhaktivinoda Thakura's desire came true, 'When in England,
France, Russia, Prussia and America, all fortunate persons, by taking up *kholas* and
karatalas, will take the name of Chaitanya Mahaprabhu again and again!'

a little song." He said, "Okay, I got a minute." So I sang about eight verses of Hare Krishna* mantra and he said, "What's that?" And I said, "When you hear this, it's supposed to bring immediate liberation." So he said, "Well, the guy up the block needs it more than I do," pointing up to the White House when Johnson was running the Vietnam war. That was Kennedy's introduction to Hare Krishna . . . Later on, when the Swami was having trouble, he asked around everybody who could help, and I said, "Well, let's see now. We could write to Kennedy." It's just a normal thing, you know. That's what senators are for. In this case Kennedy knew who I was and I knew Kennedy's people, or I was somewhat a celebrated literary figure, so if I wrote a letter saying this swami was good it would be taken seriously. So I wrote Kennedy a letter saying here was this nice swami who was really doing something interesting, bringing Hare Krishna, and his work could only be good; and if he was having trouble, that could only be bad. Is there anything they could do to facilitate and make sure that he didn't have any difficulties? That he really was a legitimate swami, and was doing something great. I don't know if it helped or not.'

Some of the first gifts that Allen Ginsberg left for Prabhupada at that Second Avenue temple were two harmoniums and a cheque for $200 to help with the legal fees.

This would begin a journey of collaborations over many years and not just in Manhattan but in other places in America—Ohio, California. The lessons and songs of A.C. Bhaktivedanta would come up in poetry readings and even television appearances of Allen Ginsberg. But for that story to unfold, one must first finish the story of what A.C. Bhaktivedanta did next in Manhattan—which was to create a real stir among its drug users and in its parks.

Perhaps the most testing part of that period in the Lower East Side of Manhattan for A.C. Bhaktivedanta, a man who refused to

---

* Hare Krishna.

touch even tea or coffee as they were stimulants, was dealing with groups of people who were addicted to the idea that the use of drugs was a window to an alternative reality.

In 1969, the first year that Gallup polling services ran a survey question asking people about their concern on drug use, about half of all Americans surveyed, or 48 per cent to be precise, told the poll that drug use 'was a serious problem in their community'.[3]

As we have noted earlier, the 1960s in America was a time of great social and political upheaval, of intense questioning of 'the mainstream', and its legitimacy by large sections of the population, especially the young who mostly made up the hippie crowd. It was a time of 'social upheaval, wars, vibrant creativity and missed opportunity. Mainstream culture and a psychedelic drug-using counterculture shared a belief in "better living through chemistry" . . . political activists clearly believed they could change the beliefs, attitudes and behavior (sic) of mainstream culture; and they did. Hippie counterculture on the other hand was largely alienated and strove primarily to develop a separate culture with its own mores, beliefs and lifestyles. Although there was some overlap between hippies and activists, hippies didn't generally have the same sense of political empowerment. Hippie enclaves developed in New York; Boston; Seattle; Austin, Texas and elsewhere . . .'[4]

The widespread drug use was not only about culture but it was also about the advancement of chemistry. Lysergic acid diethylamide (LSD) was discovered as a chemical in 1943 by the Swiss chemist Albert Hofmann. It was soon apparent that its consumption gave people a very different psychological experience, often putting them in a trance. So, for people looking to look at life, including their own, and society around them differently, the 1960s zeitgeist in America provided an easy escape.

'In fact, the drug's after-effects have seeped through much of Western culture, from art to literature to, most obviously, music, which was never the same after Bob Dylan, The Beatles and Jimi

Hendrix dropped acid. Whole genres have since flagged their debt to mind-altering substances: psychedelic rock, psytrance, acid house . . . the latter hailing from that other spike in psych: (19)80s and (19)90s rave culture. Although ecstasy is the drug most associated with the second summer of love, LSD also saw a resurgence in the UK at that time.'[5]

Along with LSD, of course, there was widespread use of marijuana and cannabis. And the influence of these substances and their use followed through the western world, especially the US and the UK, where A.C. Bhaktivedanta did most of his work in his last but most productive decade. Some of their legitimacy came from activism, culture and also elite academia.

The most famous case is worth retelling since it had a massive influence in America. The story is about two psychologists at America's most elite university—Harvard. Their names were Timothy Leary and Richard Alpert. In 1960, the duo started to examine the impact of 'psychotropic substances on the human mind.'[6] Alpert had a PhD from Stanford and Leary from Berkeley University. The two of them started the Harvard Psilocybin Project. 'Psilocybin is an entheogenic hallucinogen which naturally occurs in certain species of mushrooms; Leary and Alpert sought to document its effects on human consciousness by administering it to volunteer subjects and recording their real-time descriptions of the experience. At the time of Leary and Alpert's research at Harvard, neither LSD nor psilocybin was an illegal substance in the United States.'[7]

But within a couple of years, the powerful and influential Harvard academic community, namely its teachers and bureaucrats, turned against Leary and Alpert. They pointed out, it must be said not without reason, that the experiments that the two researchers were conducting violated many fundamental principles of research, especially the conditions in which it was conducted, and the selection of guinea pigs, in this case, many a time, students. Questions were asked about how informed their student 'volunteers' were about what they were being given. They were accused of not merely 'experimenting' on the effects of drugs, but actually promoting their use among students!

Even though regulations around the subject were lax at that time, their unconventional methods, and especially a case of using an undergraduate student as a test case, led to the duo being fired from Harvard.

But that wasn't the end of the careers of Leary and Alpert.

Leary went on to become a counterculture hero, promoting the use of psychedelic substances to ostensibly advance the limits of human experience and alter that experience. He even coined a famous hippie slogan—'Turn on, Tune in, Drop out'.

Alpert had an even more interesting turn. He returned to India and became a devotee at an ashram,* and was rechristened Ram Dass, becoming, over time, a well-known spiritual teacher in his own right with numerous books and even a Netflix show.[8] His most famous book is called *Be Here Now*.[9]

The story of A.C. Bhaktivedanta is, in a sense, a thread between these two journeys. He was successful in explaining to his followers the importance of an inner life, a spiritual life—and how to achieve this distance, this refusal to submit to merely the material aspect of life, and to achieve this without any substance abuse, but by chanting the mantra of Krishna.

This debate on drugs would reappear from time to time throughout the remaining period of A.C. Bhaktivedanta's life and work because it was so fundamental to so many of the people among whom he worked—from the most influential artistes to poverty-stricken hippies.

On this, the use of drugs to alter consciousness, he was challenged many times, but his answer never varied—any experience fuelled

---

* At the ashram of Neem Karoli Baba near Ranikhet in Uttarakhand.

by drugs could never be a true spiritual experience. In fact, when questioned by some followers of Timothy Leary, Bhaktivedanta threw at them the personal experience of one of his own followers. Hayagriva Dasa (Howard Wheeler before his initiation) proceeded to make the argument that would echo across the world, and does even today, quite simply, any 'high' is superficial and temporary. It is a 'high' which is inevitably followed by a 'low'.

To understand what or who was challenging A.C. Bhaktivedanta from the Leary camp, so to speak, a quick aside is relevant at this juncture on something called the Millbrook community. Such was the influence of Timothy Leary as an iconic, anti-establishment figure who claimed to want to awaken divinity in every person and preached the questioning of all authority, that three young heirs to the fortune of banker-politician Andrew Mellon (1855–1937) gave him control and access to one of their mansions, a sixty-four-room palace at Millbrook village, New York.[10] There Leary created a commune—a place full of 'endless parties, epiphanies and breakdowns, emotional dramas of all sizes'[11]—to run his experiments on an eclectic and eccentric bunch of young people, no doubt turned even more peculiar through the regular experimentation with drugs.

It must be remembered that little was known about the immense damage that use of drugs like LSD do physically and psychologically. It was still 1966 where many felt that LSD was only a little more intense than some weed.

But in that debate Hayagriva argued that all this was useless, transient, an illusion. He said: 'On LSD, we experience going up, but we always have to come down again. That's not spiritual consciousness. When you actually attain Krishna consciousness, you stay high. Because you go to Krishna, you don't have to come down. You can stay high forever.'[12]

No more coming down—as ISKCON's pamphlets of that period began to say.

What had A.C. Bhaktivedanta done through this process? He had taken what might have seemed like an impossible situation—living and preaching among (many) drug addicts in a foreign land, and using the language of his followers, their idiom, their worldview and telling his own story using these.

'Getting high', 'altering reality', all of this was integral to the lives of many of his followers. But how could they understand Krishna consciousness then? By preaching to them in terms that they understood easily—getting high and never coming down!

This is the spirit that had inspired Ginsberg about A.C. Bhaktivedanta, his ability to work among those who had little, or, seemingly, had little potential to understand what this monk from India might be preaching. But even with such an impossible audience, he had crafted a connection, a language and tune which they could comprehend, which could, and did, bring change to their lives. Bhaktivedanta's immersion into the world of the hippies and his undaunted understanding of this community shows up in his correspondence. For instance, writing in 1971 from Delhi, he advised one of his disciples, '. . . why not open a hostel for the hippies? I want that all the hippies should come to me and I shall solve their problems. Actually all these hippies should join us. I am seeing that in this Delhi city many hippies from your country are coming, but they are simply hungry and dirty and being cheated. During our pandal program some of them came to me and became my disciples. So we must look out for them and take interest that they should be delivered from this miserable condition. They are our best customers. If we give them place to sleep comfortably and nice prasadam, and if they agree to follow the four rules and attend our aratis* and classes, why not invite the hippies to live

---

* Prayer meetings.

with us? Gradually they will become devotees. The American Ambassador to India, Mr. Kenneth Keating, is very much in favor of our Movement, especially on this point of giving you people the right advice and saving them from intoxication and being hippies. If your government would give us some help I can save all of them. That would be a great blessing for your country. Otherwise this hippie class will simply spoil everything they have worked so hard for.' No doubt this understanding came straight from his early period in America. His first neighbours in New York could have, indeed, destroyed his mission in the country but he had changed many of them, they had become his 'best customers'.

Bhaktivedanta, thus, was undeterred by his circumstances. The only support one needed, he argued, was the Krishna mantra.

There is a particularly jovial, but illustrative, example of this from 1971. It comes from a letter A.C. Bhaktivedanta wrote that year: 'You mention ghosts (he wrote to his interlocutor). So far I have experience, the best way to remove them is to chant Hare Krishna very loudly and have jubilant kirtana until they leave. In England, on Mr John Lennon's* house where I was staying in 1969, there was one ghost. But as soon as the devotees began chanting very loudly, he† went away immediately.'[13]

This was the spirit A.C. Bhaktivedanta took to Tompkins Square Park. It was a park close to the Lower East Side neighbourhood where A.C. Bhaktivedanta lived and preached.

Tompkins Square Park had a history of rebellion. Police had attacked immigrants protesting food shortages in 1857 at this park, and in 1863, the blood-soaked Draft Riots had unfolded at this park and neighbouring areas as fighting on conscription for the American Civil War divided the Black people and the whites and spread across the Lower East Side.[14] These riots are

---

* Of The Beatles fame.
† The ghost, not Mr Lennon.

still considered the most racially divided and violent civil riots in American history, which caused a purge of the Black population from major parts of Manhattan.

By the 1960s, Tompkins Square was alive with numerous protests against the Vietnam war. It is in this melee that A.C. Bhaktivedanta arrived with his own radical message; the only answer was to sing of the love of Krishna.

They would have a motley bunch with their dhol,* tambourines and brass cymbals sitting, standing, even dancing under the billowing elm trees at Tompkins Square Park, singing the name of Krishna, the sixteen-word mantra, again and again:

Hare Krishna, Hare Krishna, Krishna Krishna, Hare Hare/ Hare Rama, Hare Rama, Rama Rama, Hare Hare.

On that day, 9 October 1966, curious onlookers watched as a white-bathroom-slipper-wearing elderly monk and his followers gathered to sing under the elm tree. What were they wearing? Were those bedroom pyjamas? What music was this?

Even though most could not understand the Sanskrit words or the chant, or even the spiritual background of A.C. Bhaktivedanta and his followers, they attracted attention. Something like this had never happened under the elms of Tompkins Square Park before. Even if people could not understand the words or even the moves, the palpable joy conveyed by the gestures seemed to have attracted many. In addition, the group was soon joined by Allen Ginsberg and his partner Peter Orlovsky.

This is one of the critical moments when Ginsberg changed the narrative for A.C. Bhaktivedanta and his followers. The appearance of Ginsberg connected the kirtan singers, around fifty of them, to the wider context of American life. Somehow, it would have seemed to many onlookers who recognized Ginsberg, that these singers and this old man in the middle had something to do

---

* Indian-style drum.

with the search for a new politics in America, a new voice, and a new way to live.

It would be the first time that Ginsberg would have sung the mantra of Krishna-love in public but as we shall see, this was only just the beginning for him.

For A.C. Bhaktivedanta this was the great emergence, now remembered as in a sense the inauguration of ISKCON in America. Under the elm tree, Bhaktivedanta and his followers were also rebels and protestors of a kind—they were protesting a life devoid of Krishna-bhakti. It was a demonstration demanding radical spirituality, to live a life for nothing but Krishna.

The *New York Times* found it worthy to report the incident, highlighting of course the presence of Allen Ginsberg and questioning him, in the article, on why he had been present at the gathering, and others on their lifestyle changes after meeting the swami. Ginsberg described Krishna as the Hindu god and 'bringer of light', and Rama as the 'prince of responsibility'.[15] Others explained, like Howard Wheeler né Hayagriva, that they had left all intoxicants under the influence of the Indian monk after years of experimenting with LSD.[16]

The swami, this is what A.C. Bhaktivedanta was increasingly being called at that time—the swami. The swami and his chanting were making a mark, noted the *New York Times*, while the more exuberant the *East Village Other* noted that the swami and his chanting was saving the earth, and that the mantra of Krishna has broken through to the 'world's toughest audience—Bohemians, acidheads, potheads and hippies'.[17]

In fact, these were the people, his 'toughest audience', who would give A.C. Bhaktivedanta's movement its first mass following, when the chants which his followers introduced at a Love Pageant Rally protested, of all things, the ban on possessing LSD. But then, all at once, the chant had spread and organically scores of people, who knew nothing about the Krishna cause or the septuagenarian monk, were chanting the mantra, without even knowing what it meant.

Hare Krishna, Hare Krishna, Krishna Krishna, Hare Hare/ Hare Rama, Hare Rama, Rama Rama, Hare Hare . . . it was breakthrough moment when word about the monk and his mission went, as it were, viral, even though in a relatively small place. *The Village Voice* described it as 'a sea of rhythmic chanting'.[18]

Word of the swami and his colourful disciples spread, more press reports followed, and so did the news of the Indian monk who cooked delicious food and served it for free and taught some of the wildest people in New York the joys of abstaining from the momentary pleasures of drugs and sex, all in the service of God. Two small presses were bought through the funds of the newly formed ISKCON to restart the *Back to Godhead* magazine, this time with the American pupils of the swami in charge. The stated dream of Swami Bhaktivedanta, as he was being called now, was to make it as big as *Time* magazine.[19]

Efforts continued to buy a building in Manhattan, and when an opportunity arose to record the music and chanting through a formal producer and a record label, Swami Bhaktivedanta embraced it—one more method to send out Krishna's word. Alan Kallman at the Adelphi Recording Studio was seeking a new sound and he had heard about this new group, this new chant— could it be the next big thing?

Listening to this recording today one can scarcely imagine how different and unique it might have sounded in 1966 to a producer sitting in downtown New York. Swami Bhaktivedanta's voice rises above the drums and cymbals, if one did not know that this was recorded in Manhattan, one could easily assume that this is a recording from a spiritual setting in India, Vrindavan or Mathura, the great Krishna-bhakti pilgrimage spots. In the recording, he sings unabashedly and seemingly unconcerned about any transmission losses of understanding due to language, mood, style and verve. But perhaps this is what made Swami Bhaktivedanta's style authentic and original, which is why it was noticed.

He had a small core flock in those days—about nineteen initiated disciples with varying levels of commitment. After his musical recording, using a dictaphone, rapid work was happening in translating the Srimad Bhagavatam too, the sixty-volume dream project.

There were many things to teach his pupils—how to wear their hair, how to behave in a bhakti congregation, how to eat, how to wash, how to pray. It had not been easy to teach vegetarianism, service, charity and giving up sex and meat-eating among the folks of the Lower East Side.

If, to counter the lure of drugs, the swami had promised a high from which one never needed to come down with Krishna consciousness, he had an explanation for sex too:

Madana–mohana, Madana–mohana. Madana means sex attraction. Madana, sex attraction, Cupid, and Krishna is called Madana–mohana. One can, I mean, neglect even sex attraction if one is attracted to Krishna. That is the test. Madana (is) attracting in this material world. Everyone is attracted by sex life. The whole material world is existing on sex life. This is the fact. Yan maithunadi-grhamedhi-sukham hi tuccham. Here, the happiness, the so-called happiness is maithuna, maithunadi. Maithunadi means here happiness begins from maithuna, sex intercourse. Generally, people . . . a man marries. The purpose is to satisfy sex desire. Then he begets children. Then again, when the children are grown up, they, the daughter is married with another boy and the boy is married with another daughter, another girl. That is also the same purpose: sex. Then again, grandchildren. In this way, this material happiness—

sriyaishvarya-prajepsavah. The other day we discussed. *Sri* means beauty, *aisvarya* means wealth, and *praja* means generation. So generally, people, they like it—good family, good bank balance and good wife, good daughter, daughter-in-law. If one family is consisting of beautiful women and riches . . ., many children, he is supposed to be successful. He's supposed to be most successful man. So *shastra** says, "What is this success? This success is beginning with sex intercourse. That's all. And maintaining them." So *Yan maithunadi-grhamedhi-sukham hi tuccham* (SB [†] 7.9.45). Here the happiness begins from sex life, *maithunadi*. We may polish it in a different way, but this *maithuna*, sex life happiness, is there in the hogs. The hogs also, they are eating whole day, here and there: "Where is stool? Where is stool?" and having sex life without any discrimination. The hogs do not discriminate whether mother, sister or daughter. So therefore *shastra* says, "Here, this material world, we are entangled, we are encaged (sic) in this material world only for this sex life." That is Cupid. Cupid is the god of sex life, Madana. Unless one is, what is called, induced by Madana, the Cupid, he cannot be, I mean to say, engladdened in sex life. And Krishna's name is *Madana–mohana*. *Madana–mohana* means that one who is attracted to Krishna, he'll forget the pleasure derived from sex life. This is the test. Therefore His name is *Madana–mohana*. Here is *Madana–mohana*. Sanatana Gosvami[‡] worshiped *Madana–mohana*. Madana or Madana. Madana means to become mad. And Madana, the Cupid.

So everyone is infuriated by the force of sex life. There are many places . . . In *Bhagavatam*[§] it is said, *pumsah striya mithuni-*

---

* Shastra or the scriptures.
† SB stands for Srimad Bhagavatam.
‡ One of the main disciples of Chaitanya Mahaprabhu.
§ Srimad Bhagavatam

bhavam etat tayor mitho hrdaya-granthim ahur. The whole
material world is going on: the man is attracted by woman,
the woman is attracted by man. And, seeking this attraction,
when they are united, their attachment for this material world
becomes more and more. And in this way, after being united, or
after being married, one woman and man, they seek nice home,
grha; *ksetra*, activities, business, factory, or agricultural field.
Because one has to earn money. So get food. *Grha-ksetra; suta,*
children; and *apta*, friends; *vitta*, wealth . . . *Atah grha-ksetra-
sutapta-vittair janasya moho 'yam* (SB 5.5.8). The attraction
for this material world becomes more and more tight. This is
called Madana, attraction by Madana. But our business is not
to be attracted by the glimmer of this material world, but to be
attracted by Krishna. That is Krishna consciousness movement.
Unless you become attracted by the beauty of Krishna, we must
have to be satisfied by beauty of this false beauty of this material
world. Therefore Sri Yamunacharya* said that *yadavadhi mama
cetah krishna-padaravindayor nava-nava-dhama rantum asit*:
"So long I have been attracted by the beauty of Krishna and I
have begun to serve at His lotus feet, and I am getting newer,
newer energy, since then, as soon as I think of sex intercourse, I
want to spite on it." That is *vitrsna*, no more attraction . . . The
central point of attraction of this material world is sex life, and
one, when one gets detached from sex life . . .

Tadavadhi mama cetah . . . ,
yadavadhi mama cetah krishna-padaravindayor
nava-nava-(rasa-)dham(anudyata) rantum asit
tadavadhi bata nari-sangame smarayamane
bhavati mukha-vikarah sustu nisthivanam ca

---

* Eleventh-century Vaishnava teacher; also known as Sri Alavandar and
Yamunaithuraivan.

"As soon as I think of sex intercourse, immediately my mouth becomes turned aside and I want to spite on it." So therefore Krishna is *Madana–mohana*. Madana is attracting everyone, sex life, and Krishna, when one is attracted by Krishna, then Madana also becomes defeated. So as soon as Madana becomes defeated, we conquer over this material world. Otherwise it is very difficult. The . . . *Daivi hy esha gunamayi mama maya duratyaya* (BG 7.14). *Duratyaya* means very, very difficult. *Mam eva ye prapadyante mayam etam taranti.* But if anyone surrenders unto Krishna, catches His lotus feet very strongly, "Krishna, save me," Krishna promises, "Yes, I'll save you".

As is perhaps obvious, such lessons, feelings, illustrations and moods of devotion were not easy to teach or absorb—at the heart of the hippie movement. Yet, Swami Bhaktivedanta had persisted, not least by serving generous quantities of tasty, hot vegetarian food of the kind most of his followers had not tasted before. If music was one of his paths to speak to them and get them to listen, food was equally vital—so much so that the morning porridge cooked at the temple on Second Avenue had come to be known as Heavenly Porridge![20] All of this had taken most of his time since he arrived in New York.

Now it was winter again, and his disciples had spread beyond New York. One of them, Michael Grant or Mukunda Goswami, had moved to the West Coast, to San Francisco to spread the good word about the movement there.

Towards the end of 1966, word arrived from Mukunda that a place—once again a storefront—had been discovered at a suitable location for an ISKCON temple in that region. All that remained was for Swami Bhaktivedanta to travel there and kickstart things in the correct manner.

This was astounding to his community at Lower East Side, but not perhaps to the swami who had always given the impression that he was ready to go where life, or more accurately for him, Krishna, took him.

The morning he left Lower East Side, it was again with just a suitcase, some clothes, some books, promising, perhaps even expecting, to return soon. But Krishna beckoned elsewhere.

13

'I Am Nobody's Guru.
I Am Everybody's Servant'

In January 1967, the San Francisco Bay Area was in a carnivalesque mood. Coming up in the city was an event called Human Be-In at the Golden Gate Park spread across more than one thousand acres. It was a giant coming together of everyone who believed in counterculture, and rebelled against the mindless materialism, soulless capitalism and the boundaries and restrictions of traditional society. These were the dropouts, the misfits, the protestors, the hippies and the students who wanted something different in their lives.

It was a special time to be in San Francisco. Far from the political glare of Washington DC or even the angry squalor of New York, San Francisco was awash with waves of peaceful rebellion.

It had all begun, as it were, on 6 October 1966, in this mass size and scale. It was the day that LSD was banned in San Francisco and, in protest, a giant Love Pageant Rally was held near the Golden Gate Park in a neighbourhood called the Haight-Ashbury district. The success of the Love Pageant Rally had led to an upscaling of plans. The Human Be-In programme was going to be much bigger. And all this was happening in the same neighbourhood, Haight-Ashbury, where the West Coast shop-front temple of ISKCON had opened.

So, when Swami Bhaktivedanta landed in San Francisco, with a nineteen-year-old secretary in tow, a recent addition to his list of Manhattan pupils, he had landed in what would swiftly become the pulsating centre of the counterculture movement.

Waiting to receive him at the airport, along with Mukunda and others, was Allen Ginsberg. Ginsberg was, naturally, headlining the Human Be-In. He was not alone. Others included Timothy Leary, who we have met earlier in this story, and it is at this Be-In that Leary would coin his most famous slogan 'Turn on, Tune in, Drop out'. Also attending was Alan Watts, the spiritual thinker and interpreter of *Eastern Wisdom*, who had written the influential book, *The Wisdom of Insecurity*, in 1951, and Richard Alpert, then in the process of becoming Ram Dass.

They were not the only ones. Some of San Francisco's most popular rock bands appeared at Human Be-In including The Grateful Dead, Jefferson Airplane and Quicksilver Messenger Service.

In what seemed astonishing to authorities, between twenty and thirty thousand people gathered in the area for this Be-In which began on 14 January 1967. Two days later, the United Airlines Flight 21 from New York carrying Swami Bhaktivedanta landed in San Francisco. Around fifty of the local hippie-cum-neo-Vaishnavas led by Mukunda and Allen Ginsberg were there at the airport, with flowers, to welcome him.

The swami would not have known during this, his first-ever flight, what he would be landing amidst. Already some of the local papers were anticipating his arrival. News of the Hare Krishna group from New York had travelled West, not least because a sort of functioning Sri Sri Radha Krishna temple had already been set up at Fredrick Street in Haight-Ashbury.

'The cultural studies theorist Stuart Hall once suggested that "hippies as a subculture constituted an American moment". In the first instance, hippies were a distinctive subcultural product of American society, a "moment" sustained by the economic boom, expanded leisure and political conflict at home and abroad. Perhaps more importantly, however (and never let us forget the importance of the local in American politics and society), hippies were a San Franciscan event. The city had captured the media imagination by 1966. Hundreds and then thousands of "flower children" had flocked to San Francisco in search of love, peace, community and self. They sought refuge from an American dream that was crumbling quickly in suburban wastelands and urban hothouses, as well as the jungles of Vietnam. The Haight-Ashbury district of San Francisco was the focus. Richard Alpert, the former Harvard colleague of acid guru Timothy Leary, observed at the time that: "The Haight-Ashbury is, as far as I can see, the purest reflection of what is happening in consciousness, at the leading edge of society. There is very little that I have seen in New York, Chicago, Los Angeles, that is giving me the hit that this place is because it has a softness that is absolutely exquisite".[1]

Swami Bhaktivedanta had landed in the middle of one of the great cultural moments of the twentieth century. Reporters asked him if his Krishna love was open and available for the twenty or thirty thousand people who had thronged the Human Be-In event, and he said yes, all were welcome. Only when they accept his message, and become his followers, explained Swami Bhaktivedanta, they transformed, they gave up meat, sex outside marriage, drugs and other intoxicants like gambling.[2]

And in order for this message to be heard Swami Bhaktivedanta was willing to go to the most unlikely of places—a Mantra-Rock Dance concert at a local ballroom. A place so wild that even the New York hippies objected to their master going there, a place of 'amplified guitars, pounding drums, wild light shows and hundreds of drugged hippies'.[3]

What convinced the swami to sing and chant at a concert alongside The Grateful Dead? There is evidence that he knew of the steady but growing acclaim of Ravi Shankar, the Indian classical sitarist, and that the swami thought such musical renderings by a renowned master, although Indian, classical and euphonious, since it was not directly about Krishna, it was *maya*.[4] So, Swami Bhaktivedanta would have known by that fateful January of 1967 that Shankar had not only received praise for his work in London and across Europe, but he had been building a significant American footprint with the jazz producer Richard Bock, founder of World Pacific Records. As we have seen with his expressed ambition of making *Back To Godhead* as significant and striking as the *Time* magazine, Swami Bhaktivedanta understood swiftly that if he had to win over the world, he would have to embrace its markers, its parameters without diluting his own message.

He had already been making these alterations and accommodations throughout his time in America. When described as conservative in San Francisco's biggest newspaper, the *San Francisco Chronicle*, he protested, 'We cannot depart from the Bhagavad Gita. But conservative we are not. Chaitanya Mahaprabhu was so strict that He (sic) would not even look on a woman, but we are accepting everyone into this movement, regardless of sex, caste, position, or whatever. Everyone is invited to come chant Hare Krishna. This is Chaitanya Mahaprabhu's munificence, His liberality. No, we are not conservative.' Though he may have preferred his pupils to be devoted only to Krishna, he had understood and accepted the need for men to be with women and put in place a format where the desire for sex could be fulfilled within the boundaries of marriage. And now, he was about to sing at a psychedelic rock concert.

That day before an audience, many of whom were devoted to the use of drugs, a seventy-one-year-old Indian monk in saffron robes urged the people who had paid $2.50 per person to attend the concert that they should try morning kirtan instead. The high was so much better than LSD.

And for more than two hours, in that ballroom, accompanied by Allen Ginsberg who had introduced the swami and played the harmonium, hundreds of people chanted the Krishna mantra again and again. The swami was fulfilling the prophecy of his guru, the kirtan of Krishna was ringing out in one more Western town.

Bonnie and Gary, two Texas students, had met and been impressed by the swami at Haight-Ashbury, and soon were initiated into the movement—Bonnie as Govinda Dasi and Gary as Gaurasundara.

Years later, Govinda Dasi noted in her reminiscences of the swami, the monk's reaction to listening to the music and chanting from that wild night in San Francisco.

Govinda Dasi wrote: 'One day while living with Srila Prabhupada at the New Jersey seashore, a tape arrived from the San Francisco temple; some devotees from New York brought it and Srila Prabhupada sat listening to the taped "San Francisco kirtan". Now, a bit of background: Gaurasundara and I had met Srila Prabhupada in San Francisco when he first arrived and had been initiated at the San Francisco temple, the Haight-Ashbury Frederick Street storefront, and then had followed him to New York when he returned in March of 1967. The San Francisco Haight-Ashbury district was quite wild, there was a hippie environment; Gaurasundara and I were students just prior to meeting Srila Prabhupada, were both in our senior year in the University of Texas; we found the more studious and sedate New York temple more to our liking. In New York, devotees were reading Srila

Prabhupada's books, chanting regularly, and following pretty strictly. In San Francisco, things were generally wilder, with lots of flamboyant kirtans and hardly anyone reading or following strictly. Because of this vast difference between New York mood and San Francisco mood, the natural tendency was for the New York devotees to look down upon the San Francisco temple, and to criticize and roll their eyes when talking about the San Francisco devotees. Yes, the politics had already begun. New York temple really did not take the San Francisco devotees seriously, and San Francisco did indeed have a mood of its own. Knowing all this, I was eager to see Srila Prabhupada's reaction to the San Francisco kirtan tape. As the old reel-to-reel tape player began blurring the new Hare Krishna chant, Srila Prabhupada began to wag his head in time to the music: Hare Krishna Hare Krishna Krishna Krishna Hare Hare. It was a new singsong chant, nothing at all like the morning and evening ragas that Srila Prabhupada had introduced. This was an American version for sure: horns blared, drums boomed, and cymbals clanged; it was a festive party sound. Some of the New York devotees were aghast; after hearing the tape through, Srila Prabhupada smiled broadly and expressed his appreciation: "Oh, they have done nicely. Very nice. They are chanting so enthusiastically." One of the tape bearers protested the modern unauthentic sound. Srila Prabhupada drowned him out. It was, in his opinion, wonderful. He sent a message to San Francisco to let them know he loved their kirtan tape and to go on chanting. Srila Prabhupada then said: "They are chanting Hare Krishna, that is the main thing. It may be this tune or that tune, doesn't matter—this way or that, but they are sincerely chanting. That is what Krishna wants."

'Please Srila Prabhupada, let me see your mercy and your incredible potency. By your divine presence you purified and inspired Westerners who were neither sattvic nor studious, neither austere nor conformists and made them into wonderful devotees of the Lord. You saw our hearts. If someone chanted with sincerity you didn't care for the outward trappings, you clearly saw the inner heart and you continue to see our hearts and lift us from wherever we are and whatever modes of nature we are enmeshed. No one has done this, Srila Prabhupada, only you. Thank you Srila Prabhupada for caring so much, foreseeing the glimmer of love sprouting in our dark hearts and fanning it with your mercy and grace. Even now, when I hear kirtans of various chants I am reminded of this incident and remember that different jivas like different types of music but the main thing is their chanting Hare Krishna, and although I may prefer Indian ragas, someone else may prefer Western chants, the important thing is "they are chanting Hare Krishna, that is the main thing".

Thank you, Srila Prabhupada.'[5]

This account is naturally redolent with the piety of a follower, but Govinda Dasi's account is important for other reasons too. It is an indication of what attracted some many so-called societal misfits into the shelter of ISKCON in its early days—the willingness of Swami Bhaktivedanta to accommodate them and his broad lack of judgement. In his book *Hare Krishna in America*, E. Burke Rochford Jr, a professor of sociology, anthropology and religion at Middlebury College, noted that while many of the early followers of ISKCON in America had experimented with drugs in some form or the other, a vast majority of such people did not stay within the movement for a long time. And once initiated within the movement, Swami Bhaktivedanta strictly prohibited substance abuse. So 'drug users' are only one part of the early ISKCON story. There is also the undoubted disillusionment from a purely materialistic life—and while the 1960s in America was a potent social and cultural period for people experiencing this to come together, the movement of Swami Bhaktivedanta continued to grow after this phase in history dimmed. Rochford analyses that the disenchantment with materialist values went much deeper than a momentary cultural outpouring and this is the trigger that continued to expand the ranks of ISKCON followers which found in the movement of the swami not merely lack of judgement for their failings or a connection with a cultural mood, but it filled something deeper, a more fundamental void that material pursuits had not been able to make complete.[6]

After the success of the rock-concert appearance, people started to pour into the tiny storefront temple at Fredrick Street in Haight-Ashbury, stragglers came, but so did serious seekers. Swami Bhaktivedanta was asked many questions, including, 'Are you the guru of Allen Ginsberg?', to which he responded, 'I am nobody's guru. I am everybody's servant.'[7]

It must be understood that the time that Swami Bhaktivedanta spent in San Francisco was one of the most radical in the city's history. The Human Be-In and its stunning success had a cascading impact. It led to one of the biggest civilian gatherings in America, a period that would come to be known as the Summer of Love which would stun the world.

Here's *Vanity Fair* magazine's description of what happened that year, that summer:

In a 25-square-block area of San Francisco, in the summer of 1967, an ecstatic, Dionysian mini-world sprang up like a mushroom, dividing American culture into a Before and After unparalleled since World War II. If you were between 15 and 30 that year, it was almost impossible to resist the lure of that transcendent, peer-driven season of glamour, ecstasy, and Utopianism. It was billed as the Summer of Love, and its creators did not employ a single publicist or craft a media plan. Yet the phenomenon washed over America like a tidal wave, erasing the last dregs of the martini-sipping Mad Men era and ushering in a series of liberations and awakenings that irreversibly changed our way of life.

The Summer of Love also thrust a new kind of music—
acid rock—across the airwaves, nearly put barbers out of
business, traded clothes for costumes, turned psychedelic drugs
into sacred door keys, and revived the outdoor gatherings of
the Messianic Age, making everyone an acolyte and a priest.
It turned sex with strangers into a mode of generosity, made
'uptight' an epithet on a par with 'racist,' refashioned the
notion of earnest Peace Corps idealism into a bacchanalian
rhapsody, and set that favorite (*sic)* American adjective, 'free,'
on a fresh altar.[8]

In a world where 'everyone' was 'an acolyte and a priest', amidst
waves of 'disaffected student groups,'[9] the movement of Swami
Bhaktivedanta stood out because it was in a sense the real deal—
with a real devout, spiritual leader at the helm of it all, unaffected
by the affectations of counterculture.

The ISKCON movement also delivered the other element
which placed it within this wild, alternative summer: a new kind
of music. This was a time when psychedelic music creating its
own ripples—that summer everything from the Doors eponymous
album to Pink Floyd's *Piper at the Gates of Dawn*, Jimi Hendrix's
Are You Experienced?, Cream's *Disraeli Gears* and *Sgt. Pepper's
Lonely Hearts Club Band* released amidst great fanfare.

In San Francisco, as his fame grew, Swami Bhaktivedanta even
procured clay-made mridangams from Calcutta to give his pupils
and followers an authentic feel of the kirtan. He spoke to adults,
he spoke to children, he spoke at open doors, at temples and in
rooms suffused with the smoke of marijuana and cannabis. Before
he left San Francisco to return to New York, he even prayed, and
preached, and chanted at a nudist colony, handing out rossogullas[*]
to participants in his programme. The man who invited him was

---

[*] Cottage cheese balls drenched in sugar syrup.

Lou Gottlieb, a bassist and counterculture intellectual and founder of the Morningstar Ranch, a free love, free-for-all, kind of place where hippies grew organic food and soaked in the sun, naked.

This is the same swami who introduced through murtis* of Jagannath, Balabhadra and Subhadra the rath yatra, famous in India at the ancient Jagannath temple in Odisha and in other places, all the way in San Francisco. It was the swami who organized the first rath yatra outside India ever, in the Bay Area.

This combination of piety and sticking to customs which were completely unfamiliar to his American audience fits in awkwardly with his outreach among drug addicts and nudists but perhaps the thing to notice about Swami Bhaktivedanta is his effort to bring every element of the devotional practice that he knew and loved in India to every arena where he appears in America. The words of Sanskrit and old Bengali are intact. He is happy to explain them, but he does not change them. And he does not see a contradiction: even when he speaks among the billowing smoke of marijuana, Swami Bhaktivedanta only speaks of Krishna.

As he had explained in 1967 to a TV interviewer, Allen Burke:

> He (Burke) said, "Well, if this movement is spiritual, why do you have a car? How is that spiritual?" Prabhupada said, "If a car is used in Krishna consciousness, then it is a spiritual car."[10]

In those early months of 1967 in San Francisco, Swami Bhaktivedanta dropped all barriers of access, in the name of Krishna, he was willing to go anywhere, talk to anyone, Krishna had brought him here, among these people of free love and alternate living, and he was determined to spread the word of Krishna among them.

---

* Wooden idols.

Back in New York, the disciples of Swami Bhaktivedanta were keeping alive the instructions of their master—the cooking, the instructions and the search for the right building for a grand temple in the city.

But fulfilling this dream would become fraught with peril. The people, including a property dealer, that the relatively new disciples of Lower East Side were dealing with had been trying to get money out of them. Swami Bhaktivedanta had been monitoring the proceedings through a flurry of letter exchange between him and his New York pupils.

Despite his stern advice, his disciples in New York ended up giving money to a real-estate broker, realizing soon enough that they had been duped. It was through the swami's legal advice and firm admonishments that they would be able to recover most of the lost cash. The dream of a grand temple in New York would have to wait.

In New York, where Swami Bhaktivedanta was back among his old pupils, he was soon confronted with a new problem—his own failing health.

The strain of the new country, new people and a punishing schedule finally took a toll on the seventy-two-year-old monk. He had a heart attack. He had already suffered a couple of heart attacks on his way via the ship *Jaladuta* from India to America. But once there, he always insisted that one must not identify too much with the body.

Now his body—after months of being pushed to its limits—collapsed, and he had to be hospitalized.

His devotees prayed incessantly, his disciples crowded the hospital room to take care of him, and when slightly better, Swami Bhaktivedanta wrote to his old associates in India asking if any Ayurvedic help could be taken. His visa troubles had begun again, and a return to India seemed imminent.

After days at the hospital, and against strict instructions from the doctors, Swami Bhaktivedanta left the hospital in New York when he felt a little better, refusing further injections or treatment, and moved to a cottage by the seaside in Long Branch, New Jersey, to recuperate.

Swami Bhaktivedanta spent about three weeks recovering from his near-death experience at the cottage by the sea. During this time, his main caregiver was Govinda Dasi, whom we have met earlier in our story. One of the most insightful instances during this period, recorded by Govinda Dasi, is how her partner Gaurasundara escaped being conscripted into the Vietnam War.

The upheaval of the [19]60s and the war in Vietnam was a fearful reality to many. Gaurasundara, my husband had lived in constant anxiety and fear that the draft board would call him to war. Though he was raised in a military family who fully supported the Vietnam war and they wanted him to become an air force pilot, Gaurasundara had other ideas about his destiny. Until late November, Gaurasundara was an art student at the University of Texas, and due to his student status, he was not likely to be drafted but in late November, Gaurasundara and I had left the university in our search for truth, and in December of 1967 we had become students of Srila Prabhupada. Even in Gaurasundara's first meeting with Swamiji in San Francisco, he had expressed his anxiety about being drafted to fight in a war he did not believe in. Only about six months later, his fear became a reality. He had received a notice from the New York draft board to appear. The fateful day had arrived. We were then staying in New Jersey with Srila Prabhupada at his seashore retreat, and Gaurasundara had to travel to New York for his draft board appointment. He would receive a physical exam and very likely be drafted into the army. We expressed our severe anxiety to Srila Prabhupada who also did not endorse the war in Vietnam. Srila Prabhupada reassured us that Krsna would take care of everything. The day came for Gaurasundara's

appointment and he almost tearfully bid good-bye to Srila
Prabhupada and me. He did not know what lay ahead; his future
was uncertain. On a silk rope around his neck he wore a small
murti of Lord Jagannath, and also along with that his huge red
wooden chanting beads, the beads given at his initiation. He
was full of anxiety yet calmly bowed down to say good-bye to
Srila Prabhupada. Srila Prabhupada stood calmly in the hallway
as Gaurasundara offered his last obeisances (sic) and prepared
to leave. Srila Prabhupada raised his right hand in blessing and
said to Gaurasundara: "Krishna* will protect you. I will request
him. Do not be afraid. Krishna will take care of everything." His
voice was sure and strong. He smiled compassionately. He knew
that everything would be all right and he conveyed that feeling
of faith to us in that fragile moment. Then, Gaurasundara left
for New York by train. Gaurasundara was gone the whole day.
Everything went on schedule at home. Srila Prabhupada had his
noon meal after Kirtanananda gave him massage and I did my
usual duties of cleaning & washing Prabhupada's clothes and
tried to do some art work. I was unable to concentrate, as my
mind was full of thoughts of Gaurasundara. I prayed to Krsna
constantly. Srila Prabhupada mentioned Gaurasundara several
times, so I knew that he was also thinking of him. Evening came
and he still had not returned from the city, so we were worried.
Suddenly we heard him chanting as he climbed the stairs. I
rushed to the door to greet him, giving him a big hug and noting
the big smile on his face. Srila Prabhupada called him into his
room and asked: "So, what happened?" Gaurasundara described
the visit, that because of his strange appearance, sporting big red
neck beads and a colorful Lord Jagannath on his chest he was
sent to a psychiatric doctor. The doctor asked Gaurasundara
questions and Gaurasundara answered as simply as possible,

---

* Krishna.

continually chanting Hare Krishna out loud on his wooden beads, and rolling his eyes upward in yogic fashion, focusing on Krishna's form in his mind. The psychiatric doctor had not seen this before and he apparently concluded that Gaurasundara was not suitable for military service. He gave him a 3-Y status, not as good as 4-F, but it certainly reduced his chances of being drafted, and Gaurasundara was never drafted. I wept for joy as Srila Prabhupada chuckled and wagged his head side to side. "Just see, Krishna has protected you. If we are sincere, Krishna will always protect. He sees everything. You have chosen his service, not the army service, so he has arranged everything." It was a joyful evening. So much stress that had been there for so long was no more and Gaurasundara could concentrate now more fully on service to Krishna and Srila Prabhupada. Krishna had saved him from a great danger, perhaps from his destiny to go to war and he was deeply grateful. Thank you, Srila Prabhupada for continuously saving us from the great dangers of the material world, the cycle of samsara. You are called the military general of Lord Caitanya. Indeed, you led an army. Like Rama led an army of monkeys, you led an army of American youth. You had your mission and we were drafted into your army, Lord Chaitanya's army. That was our greatest good fortune. We were unqualified, yet you so kindly protected us, infused us with your shakti and sent us out to do your work. May we always remember and be grateful for the opportunity to serve in your army and may we never forget that you are the commander in chief and always be obedient to you.

Srila Prabhupada, you changed our destinies. Perhaps Gaurasundara had been destined for Vietnam as so many other American youths, but you "requested Krishna" and He re-arranged our lives. Often Srila Prabhupada would say to me when I had a cold or flue (sic): "Yes, Krishna is checking off your account. He sees you sincerely desire to serve. You may deserve

to die at this moment but instead he is giving you little cold." He
would often say: "Krishna is watching us. When we are sincere
to serve him he begins closing our account or checking off our
account, meaning that he reduces our karmas from our stay in
the material world." You, Srila Prabhupada, would remind me
of this and still when I catch a cold I remember that maybe
Krishna is checking off my account. May we always remember
our precarious situation and constantly remember that you are
watching us and checking off our account.[11]

We have mentioned earlier that Swami Bhaktivedanta, who would
have known little, if anything, about America, its social or cultural
milieu or its politics before arriving in the country, had within
barely a little more than a year managed to fuse his teachings,
placing them deep into the American context. The loyalty that the
swami was able to generate came at least in part from his ability
to bring to life what to his pupils would have been highly esoteric
messages and characters from Hindu scriptures and medieval
Bengal, using American idioms and within the scope of everyday
American life in the 1960s.

Before returning to India as his health and visa both required,
Swami Bhaktivedanta had one last task in San Francisco. After he
brought the murtis of Lord Jagannath, Balabhadra and Subhadra
to the Bay Area, it had occurred to the monk that a rath yatra
on flatbed trucks would be perfect for the region. And he had
instructed his devotees to find out if this might be possible.

It was, and so it was that in 1967, the first-ever rath yatra
outside India was organized in the San Francisco Bay Area by
the disciples of Swami Bhaktivedanta—carrying the murtis on
flatbed trucks! The design for the chariots of the gods had been
hand-sketched by the swami—colourful canopies atop the flatbed
trucks. More than five hundred people joined the procession which
distributed chapatis and fruits as prasad along the way. This would

be the beginning of ISKCON organizing rath yatras in different parts of the world, but the very first one introduced yet another seemingly esoteric practice to the West. One of the black-and-white photos shows Swami Bhaktivedanta at Sharon Meadow in Golden Gate Park sitting cross-legged before a microphone and a giant speaker, and with a murti of Lord Jagannath beside him, preaching and chanting and praying, in his usual furrowed brow style, to all who would care to hear him.

Days later in an Air India flight, nearly two years after he had stepped off the *Jaladuta*, Swami Bhaktivedanta was off, back to the land of Chaitanya Mahaprabhu. Even at the airport, one of the last things his weeping disciples did was to sing a kirtan.

14

Ginsberg and George

How do we know that Swami Bhaktivedanta's name, and the fame of his movement, had spread far and wide within the span of less than two years since he landed on the *Jaladuta* in America?

We know this from a single, illustrative sentence that he wrote on 24 July 1967, en route to India from San Francisco by plane. It was from an airport hotel in London where he had his stopover during the long flight. In the letter, Bhaktivedanta Swami mentioned that the 'attention of Mr B.K. Nehru, the Ambassador of India (to London), was drawn to me the other day. I have told him about my Permanent Visa and he has promised to help me when I come back.'[1]

What a difference the months in America had made. When he had left India he could barely manage to get a visa, and once he reached New York, he struggled to keep extending his stay. But the fame of his small but resonant movement appeared to have had an impact—and now the Indian ambassador in London, no less, seemed to be paying attention.

Back in India and in his beloved Vrindavan, Swami Bhaktivedanta received news that publishing giant Macmillan was interested in publishing some of his books and he also initiated one of his first American disciples to the vows of sannyasa—Keith

Gordon Ham who was already known as Kirtanananda Dasa
became Kirtanananda Swami.

India was hot and dirty and chaotic. The swami thrived in this,
but his American disciples did not. What they did understand was
where—in spite of all the difficulties—their guru's devotion came
from. They were finally in a place where everyone understood
immediately what they were trying to do, and everyone seemed to
be immersed, no matter how haphazardly, in the same devotional
universe.

For all the activity, going from Delhi to Calcutta, and
renewed efforts to publish his books, this was a time when it was
increasingly apparent that Swami Bhaktivedanta was an aged,
unwell man. The repeated heart attacks had taken their toll, as had
the time spent in America in hectic activity. He was often unwell,
though unwilling to take even the advice of his preferred Ayurveda
doctors who suggested greater rest.

New ISKCON centres were opening—there was already one
at Montreal in Canada and another new one was coming up in
Boston. A visitor's visa was procured on the strength of the various
American branches of ISKCON inviting him and soon, through
the efforts of his disciples, a window opened for him to speak at
Harvard University. An Ivy League invitation could potentially
open the doors to his permanent visa in the US.

But before returning to the US, Swami Bhaktivedanta
travelled with his American pupil to Nabadwip, the birthplace of
Chaitanya Mahaprabhu, where he spoke to a large gathering of
more than seven hundred sannyasis and general devotees.* Less
joyfully, he returned to his childhood Radha Govinda temple in
the home of the Mullicks, only to see that the deities had fallen
to hard times and their old finery was absent, as was popular
devotion for them.[2]

---

* Junior monks in the process of becoming sannyasis.

As news came of the seriousness of Macmillan's intent to publish the books, and more centres opening in Los Angeles and Santa Fe, questions arose whether the fledging ISKCON had the capacity for such expansion.

But the swami was confident—even one devoted person could open and take care of a temple. He was keen to return to America as 1967 drew to a close, the air and the water, he noted, was perhaps much better for him in the country where he had started his movement, his spiritual home. The condition of his heart was highly suspect, but caution by disciples or doctors did not stop him—he knew that time was limited, often warning his pupils of his imminent passing, but exuding confidence that nothing would stop in his absence.

When he returned, to San Francisco and then to New York, to the arms of fervent devotees gathered to welcome him, he was, in a sense, no longer Swami Bhaktivedanta.

He was now Srila Prabhupada, the name meant he who has devoted his life at the lotus feet of the Lord (Krishna), the founder of a bona fide global religious movement.

His devotees even published an explanation of the term in the *Back to Godhead* magazine:

'The word Prabhupada is a term of utmost reverence in Vedic religious circles, and it signifies a great saint even amongst saints. The word actually has two meanings: first, one at whose feet (*pada*) there are many Prabhus (a term meaning "master" which the disciples of a guru use in addressing each other). The second meaning is one who is always found at the lotus feet of Krishna (the supreme master). In the line of disciplic (sic) succession through which Krishna consciousness is conveyed to mankind there have been a number of figures of such spiritual importance as to be called Prabhupada. Srila Rupa Gosvami Prabhupada executed the will of his master, Sri Chaitanya Mahaprabhu, and therefore he and his associate Gosvamis are called Prabhupada. Srila Bhaktisiddhanta Sarasvati Gosvami Thakura executed the will of Srila Bhaktivinoda Thakura, and therefore he is also addressed as Prabhupada. Our spiritual master, Om Vishnupada[108] Sri Srimad Bhaktivedanta Swami Maharaj, has in the same way executed the will of Srila Bhaktisiddhanta Sarasvati Gosvami Prabhupada in carrying the message of love of Krishna to the western world, and therefore the humble servants of His Divine Grace, from all the different centers of the sankirtana movement, are following in the footsteps of Srila Rupa Gosvami Prabhupada and prefer to address his grace our spiritual master as Prabhupada. And he has kindly said, "Yes".[3]

Where so many before him had failed, he, despite all odds, had made a successful beginning. There were different chapters in the Western world, there were committed devotees. The name of Krishna was being chanted in the West, if not yet in every street, town and village.

But his message to the West would not be complete until he had one critical destination—London.

In the summer of 1968, Swami Bhaktivedanta, now known more popularly as Srila Prabhupada, sent three disciple couples— Mukunda and Janaki, Syamasundara and Malati, and Guru Dasa and Yamuna—to London. Could this be the place where the next phase of ISKCON would flourish?

There were two rather unconventional directions that he offered them to spread the word in the British capital—first, to keep intact their dress and their preaching style. Prabhupada knew that Bhaktisiddhanta Saraswati had, too, sent his disciples to make a mark in London, and these preachers had tried, not least by adopting British dress and customs.

But they had failed. This time, Prabhupada explained to his disciples that in order to give a new message and get people to follow that message, one has to bring something unique to the table, and showcase confidence in its worthiness. As he argued— why not many British people adopt the Vaishnava way of dressing and living instead? The idea, also, was to preach mainly to the British people, and not Indians living in England. This second idea, no doubt, was driven by Prabhupada's own experience of years of trying to make a mark as a preacher in India and his disdain for the internecine battles he had seen even among the Vaishnavas there. His experience was that it was once he landed in America that he found devoted disciples who were Americans, and therefore his advice to his pupils going to preach in London was that they focus their attention on non-Indians.

Of course, even he could not have predicted the particularly special 'non-Indian' that his pupils would manage to attract with their devotion.

The England that these disciples landed in was going through turbulent times. The anti-Vietnam war protests had crossed the pond, as it were, and were now flooding the streets of London. But that was not all.

The year 1968 was when Indians and Pakistanis from Kenya, turned out by authoritarian laws in that country, began to move to Britain, and soon afterwards, Enoch Powell, the Cambridge-trained classicist-turned-politician, delivered his infamous 'River of Blood' speech, outlining extreme xenophobia against immigrants, especially from the Commonwealth countries.

In that incendiary speech, Powell said, among other things, 'We must be mad, literally mad, as a nation to be permitting the annual inflow of some 50,000 dependents, who are for the most part the material of the future growth of the immigrant descended population. It is like watching a nation busily engaged in heaping up its own funeral pyre . . . As I look ahead, I am filled with foreboding. Like the Roman, I seem to see the River Tiber foaming with much blood.'[4]

By all historical assessment, this would have not been the right year for a crowd of shaved head preachers, some in saffron robes, some in white, and some women wearing saris, singing in Sanskrit, and dancing with harmoniums, mridangams and cymbals to try and make an impact in London.

It was also the year when the biggest musical act of its time, The Beatles, took time off from their relentless touring and music-making schedule to travel to India and live in the ashram of Maharishi Mahesh Yogi who taught a form of spiritual practice called 'transcendental meditation'.

All these elements were about to come together in the most curious way for ISKCON and its preachers in London, even though through 1968 they would have little success.

In North America, though, the movement was growing swiftly. Srila Prabhupada had been featured in the famous *Life* magazine, and from San Francisco to Boston, Montreal to New York, and Los Angeles, ISKCON was steadily gaining ground, and his group of 'happies', as he termed his followers, a play on the word 'hippies', was growing steadily. In West Virginia, a forested haven commune had also come up which ISKCON called New Vrindavan, complete with organic agriculture and dirt floors settled with cow dung (just like in an Indian village).

In the early summer of 1969, Srila Prabhupada appeared on stage at Columbus, Ohio, with his old fan Allen Ginsberg to have some of the most candid conversations on his spiritual mission and what he was trying to achieve in the West. Ginsberg had been associated with ISKCON for a while at that time. In September 1968, he had made the maha-mantra of ISKCON famous across America when he sang it in his famous encounter on television with one of the most famous conservative intellectuals in the country, William F. Buckley Jr. Buckley invited Ginsberg on his TV interview show, *Firing Line*.

The recording on this clash of intellectuals, on opposite sides of the political divide, one, the icon of counterculture and the other, perhaps the sharpest conservative intellectual of the time in America, is still available. On YouTube, the video shows Ginsberg arguing with Buckley about the Vietnam war and the use of chemical weapons, especially napalm, by the United States in the war. He argued that the Chinese paranoia for America, and the American fear of communist China, were feeding off one another, mirror-images of one another, and escalating like a 'bar-room brawl'.[5] Buckley replied that Ginsberg was naïve about politics. At which point, the question of Ginsberg reading one of his poems was suggested by Buckley and, instead, Ginsberg picked up a small harmonium from the floor and proceeded to sing.

Before he started to sing, Ginsberg said: 'For the preservation of the universe, instead of its destruction, Krishna returns in Bhagavad Gita every time there's a flood, fire, original sin leading to atom bombs.'[6] Then, Ginsberg began to sing, 'Hare Krishna, Hare Krishna . . .'[7]

There is one more thing to notice in the conversation which is relevant to Ginsberg's association with ISKCON. In his argument with Buckley, Ginsberg chastised the Archbishop Francis Joseph Spellman, widely regarded as the most powerful Catholic in America, and who had died in 1967, for his support of the Vietnam war. He also criticized the Christian notion of the 'original sin' or the Biblical logic that because Adam and Eve disobeyed God, all human beings were born sinners. Ginsberg said that he was part of a much older tradition—referring to his association with ISKCON and Hinduism—where there was no original sin, and Krishna appeared again and again to protect mankind from disaster.

This was as powerful an endorsement that American counterculture could have ever given Srila Prabhupada's movement. The name of Krishna had appeared, as had the maha-mantra, at one of the most influential TV programmes of the time.

This, then, is the backdrop against which Ginsberg sat down to speak to Srila Prabhupada before scores of students in Ohio. The content of these conversations throw light on one critical aspect of Srila Prabhupada's mission—how was he able to convince some very influential and intellectual people about the honesty and integrity of his cause and get them to support it.

Consider the two extracts from their conversations below.

First:

Allen: Do you remember a man named Richard Alpert?

Prabhupada: No.

Allen: He used to work with Timothy Leary in Harvard many years ago. Then he worked in India and found a teacher and is now a disciple of Hanumanji, a devotee of Hanuman. We were talking about maya and the present condition of America and he said that his teacher in India told him that LSD was a Christ of the Kali Yuga for westerners, in that as the Kali Yuga got thicker and thicker that also salvation would have to be easier and easier and . . .

Prabhupada: That is a very nice testament, that in the Kali Yuga salvation is very easier. That is the version of Srimad Bhagavatam also. But that process is this kirtan, not LSD.

Allen: Well, the reasoning there was that for those who would only accept salvation in purely material form, in chemical form finally, completely material form, Krishna had the humour (sic) to emerge as a pill.

Prabhupada: The thing is that when it is material form, then where is the salvation? It is illusion.

Allen: The subjective effect is to cut out attachment. During the . . .

Prabhupada: If you have attachment for something material, then where is this cutting attachment? LSD is a material chemical. So, if you have to take shelter of LSD, then you take help from matter. So how are you free from matter?

Allen: The subjective experience is that while in the state of
    intoxication of LSD, you realize that LSD is a material
    pill, and that it does not really matter.

Prabhupada: That is risky. That is risky.

Allen: Do you take rebirth literally?

Prabhupada: Yes. What is the difficulty?

Allen: I just don't remember having been born before.

Prabhupada: You don't remember your childhood? That does
    not mean you had no childhood. Do you remember when
    you were a small boy? What did you do?

Allen: Certain things. Not very small, but . . .

Prabhupada: Or when you were in the womb of your mother?
    Do you remember?

Allen: No.

Prabhupada: Does it mean that you were not?

Allen: No, it does not mean that I was not.

Prabhupada: Then that you do not remember is not a reason.
    That is explained in Bhagavad Gita:

dehino 'smin yatha dehe
kaumaram yauvanam jara
tatha dehantara-praptir
dhiras tatra na muhyati
(BG 2.13)

Although I do not remember what I did in my mother's womb,
it does not mean that I had no little body. The body changes. I
am there. Therefore I change this body, I remain. That is just
common-sense reasoning. I'm changing my body every day,
every moment. Your childhood body and this body are not the
same. You have changed this body. But that does not mean you
are a different person.

Allen: But I have really never seen or heard anything but what
   I see and hear now. What I see and hear is what I can
   remember. I have never heard any reasonable or even
   thrilling description of previous incarnation or previous
   births.

Prabhupada: You have never heard?

Allen: I have never heard anything sensible sounding about
   it, anything that actually makes me think, "Ah, that must
   be."

Prabhupada: And why not? Your body in the mother's
   womb from the first day of the father and mother's sex
   life comes just like a pea. Then it develops. So from the
   pea you have come to this point. The body is changing,
   so what is the astonishment if you change this body and
   again take another pea body? What is the difficulty to
   understand?

Allen: Well, the difficulty to understand would be to
   understand that there is any permanent being, or any
   continuity of any form of consciousness from one body
   to another.

Prabhupada: Then you have to consult. Just like when you
   cannot understand something, you consult some great
   authority. Is it not?

Allen: Not enough to make me dream of it at night. No.
   Not enough to make me love it. Words are not enough.
   Authority is not enough to make me love it.

Prabhupada: You do not accept authority?

Allen: (Emphatically) Not enough to love.

Prabhupada: No . . . love, apart from love consult, consult.

Allen: No, it's not that I don't accept authority it's just that
   I can't even understand an authority that says that I am
   there when I don't feel myself there.

Prabhupada: Suppose when you are in some legal trouble you
   go to a lawyer. Why do you say you cannot understand?
   When you are diseased, you go to a physician. The
   authority you accept.
Allen: In America we have had a great deal of difficulty with
   authority. Here it is a special problem.[8]

And the next:

Allen: I have been learning to write music. My guru was a poet
   named William Blake. You know Blake?
Prabhupada: Yes, I know Blake.
Allen: So, I have been writing music. He is a lot like Kabir. I
   have been learning to meditate music in singing songs by
   William Blake, which I have written music to. So those
   are in the wind.
Prabhupada: I can give you so many songs.
Allen: Would you like to hear one of the Blake songs?
Prabhupada: Yes.
(Allen and Peter harmonize and sing Blake's 'To Tirzah'.
   Prabhupada listens with open-eyed amusement and
   delight.)
Allen and Peter:

Whate'er is born of mortal birth
Must be consumed with the earth,
To rise from generation free;
Then what have I to do with thee?
Thou, Mother of my mortal part,
With cruelty didst mould my heart,
And with false self-deceiving tears
Didst bind my nostrils, eyes and ears,

Didst close my tongue in senseless clay,

And me to mortal life betray.

The death of Jesus set me free:

Then what have I to do with thee?

It is raised—a spiritual body!

Prabhupada: He believed in spiritual body. That is nice. That
is Krishna consciousness.

Allen: He apparently fits into the West into what is called the
Gnostic tradition, which has similar bhakti ideas related
to the Buddhist and Hindu traditions. Similar cosmology.
He was my teacher.

Prabhupada: He did not give much stress to this material
body?

Allen: No, at the end of his life he didn't.[9]

What is really happening here? Srila Prabhupada is fitting the
questions, context and knowledge of Allen Ginsberg within—
rather than outside—the framework of Krishna consciousness.
Ginsberg mentions through references of things he has read, and
experienced, in India and outside, about Hindu spirituality, while
Prabhupada bridges these examples with the prescribed practices
of ISKCON. Prabhupada even takes a line from a William Blake
poem and connects to his own Vaishnava ideals.

The point Ginsberg makes about accepting authority is
illustrative. While being part of the counterculture movement, and
the desire of many Americans to look towards alternative ways to
live at the time, assisted the growth of ISKCON, it also meant
that Srila Prabhupada's fledgling organization had to establish
ideological hierarchy among people who were rebelling against
any notion of the establishment. This would have been particularly
difficult because the entire idea of a Krishna consciousness

movement was alien to America, it was being taken from India and applied in the United States. Its very grammar and idiom were foreign.

The success of the sagacious Prabhupada was to apply this foreign framework among his American pupils using the display of devoutness, but also the language of practicality. As he explained to Ginsberg, if one goes to a doctor when one is physically unwell, what could be the problem in seeking spiritual solace, medication for inner needs from a spiritual guru?

This logic and colour of ISKCON worship had begun to attract serious numbers of people. At the rath yatra in San Francisco in 1969, five thousand people marched with the procession of Lord Jagannath, Balabhadra and Subhadra.

By the end of 1968, something serious was brewing in London too. After several failures, one of Srila Prabhupada's disciples managed to do what the group had been trying for some time—meet one of The Beatles. It was perhaps not surprising that the pupils of Prabhupada were trying to approach The Beatles.

The still-new ISKCON had learnt, undoubtedly, the power of influencers through their experience with Ginsberg. In Britain, there was at that time perhaps no more potent cultural force than the all-male band, The Beatles, who had also recently started their own record label, Apple Records.

Also, Srila Prabhupada, having heard about The Beatles, explicitly instructed his students in London to reach out to George Harrison. He had heard that Harrison had—unbeknownst at that time to Prabhupada's nascent group at Haight-Ashbury—in 1967 observed ISKCON's work in San Francisco and found some solace in the chanting of the holy names of Krishna. This had happened even before he saw Srila Prabhupada's group in San Francisco.

In 1982, in a conversation with an ISKCON preacher, Harrison explained that the interest in Vaishnavism had come from his visits to India:

> Mukunda Goswami: Oftentimes you speak of yourself as a plainclothes devotee, a closet yogi or "closet Krishna," and millions of people all over the world have been introduced to the chanting by your songs. But what about you? How did you first come in contact with Krishna?
>
> George Harrison: Through my visits to India. So by the time the Hare Krishna movement first came to England in 1969, John and I had already gotten a hold of Prabhupada's first album, *Krishna Consciousness.(SIDE A/SIDE B)* We had played it a lot and liked it. That was the first time I'd ever heard the chanting of the maha-mantra.[10]

That Prabhupada already knew something about the London scene and The Beatles is noted by Syamasundara, the devotee who would take the lead in reaching out to The Beatles: '(In 1968) our spiritual master asked us to go to London . . . The scene, the centre of activity, was shifting from San Francisco to London . . . There were the Carnaby Street fashions and the Beatles and the Rolling Stones . . . Prabhupada had always wanted to have a centre in London because he was an Indian in the British Empire. He always thought about London as (a) Wizard of Oz type of city that should have a Krishna temple. So we took off!'[11]

The combination of stardom, music and, as we have noted before, an interest in Eastern religion, made The Beatles a natural candidate for outreach. But all initial methods, including sending an apple pie with Hare Krishna written on it, a wind-up, walking apple toy inscribed with Hare Krishna and even a record of

ISKCON with the kirtans, to the office of Apple Records had failed.[12]

Until one day, Syamasundara bumped into George Harrison at an event, and it turned out that Harrison had been looking to meet people from ISKCON as he had procured and had been incessantly listening to the music and chanting of ISKCON on a record.

By the time the preachers of ISKCON met Harrison, at the time one of the most famous musicians in the world, The Beatles had been going through what could only be described as an existential crisis.

The unprecedented fame and money of the group had still—it seemed to Harrison—left a certain void, at least in him. The group had travelled to India to find answers but that experiment, while interesting, hadn't really provided any long-term solutions.

So, when George Harrison met Syamasundara, his interest was immediately piqued and he asked the group to visit him at his home where he introduced the ISKCON people to the rest of the band: John Lennon, Paul McCartney and Ringo Starr.

From that point things moved very swiftly, as seen in the letter Prabhupada wrote to his London disciples at the end of 1968, 'It is understood from your letter that Mr George Harrison has a little sympathy for our movement and if Krishna is actually satisfied on him surely he will be able to join with us in pushing on the Sankirtana Movement throughout the world. Somehow or other the Beatles have become the cynosure of the neighboring European countries and America also. He is attracted by our Sankirtana Party and if Mr George Harrison takes the leading part in organizing a huge Sankirtana Party consisting of the Beatles and our Iskcon Boys surely we shall change the face of the world so much politically harassed by the maneuvers of the politicians. The people in general are in need of such movement. If Mr George Harrison wants to benefit himself, his country and the people of the world I think that he must join this Krishna Consciousness movement with no hesitation. His proposal to offer us a five story [sic] building is very welcome. Actually we need such a nice building is very welcome. Actually we need such a nice building in London. People of the world take it very seriously. During the British period in India, anything which was trademarked, "made in London" was sold very quickly, so try to make your London Yatra equally important so that when the young boys and girls of England and America combine together in Sankirtana Party it will be a great revolution in the world, even in Russia and China. I shall be glad to hear from you further on this matter.'[13]

'One can note from the reference to 'during the British period . . .' that Syamasundara's assessment of one of the sources of his master's interest in London was absolutely accurate.

George Harrison was self-confessedly urgently seeking spiritual succour when he first met the ISKCON folks. His lyrics for 'Within You Without You', the song Harrison contributed to the band's successful 1967 album *Sgt. Pepper's Lonely Hearts Club Band*, ached with this feeling:

We were talking about the space between us all
And the people who hide themselves behind a wall of illusion
Never glimpse the truth
Then it's far too late
When they pass away
We were talking about the love we all could share
When we find it, to try our best to hold it there with our love
With our love, we could save the world, if they only knew . . .[14]

But perhaps neither expected as rapid a progress as to the offer of a major building months after Syamasundara and others first met The Beatles—or for that matter the impact that would soon show in Harrison's music.

By 1970, the long-speculated break-up of The Beatles came to pass, as George Harrison and John Lennon, left to pursue independent careers as singer-songwriters. In the context of Harrison's spiritual hunger, the lyrics of two important songs he wrote, one with The Beatles, and one in his post-Beatles career, 'I Me Mine' and 'All Things Must Pass', are important to consider:

> I Me Mine
> All through' the day
> I me mine, I me mine, I me mine.
> All through' the night
> I me mine, I me mine, I me mine.
> Now they're frightened of leaving it
> Ev'ryone's weaving it,
> Coming on strong all the time,
> All through' the day I me mine . . .[15]

And, 'All Things Must Pass':

> Sunrise doesn't last all morning
> A cloudburst doesn't last all day
> Seems my love is up
> And has left you with no warning
> But it's not always going
> To be this grey
> All things must pass
> All things must pass away . . .[16]

These songs and their lyrics are crucial to keep in mind to understand what happened next, and how after barely meeting the ISKCON group for a few weeks, George Harrison seemed to have suggested to Srila Prabhupada's followers that he may be able to procure them a London building.

He would swiftly do something even better—record ISKCON's first album at the famous Abbey Road studio. It contained the ISKCON devotees singing the Hare Krishna maha-mantra on one side, and singing praises to Chaitanya Mahaprabhu, Srila Prabhupada and other sacred figures on the other side.

Titled the *Radha Krishna Temple*, the record was released by Apple Records in America and Britain in August 1969. Swiftly it climbed the charts to number twelve in Britain and rocked the bestseller charts in West Germany and Czechoslovakia. *Top of the Pops*, the most popular and long-running music show in Britain, invited the artistes of *Radha Krishna Temple* to come sing on the programme. This was an unprecedented success and money, so much in dire need for ISKCON in England, poured in. On the very first day of its release, the record sold seventy thousand copies.

During the course of 1970, George Harrison wrote and released his own triple album, *All Things Must Pass*, featuring his single 'My Sweet Lord'. The album was acclaimed as his best work ever, and both the album and the single were major hits.

The influence of 'My Sweet Lord' was impossible to miss in its lyrics. It reverberated with the name of Krishna.

. . . My, my, my Lord (Hare Krishna)
My sweet Lord (Hare Krishna)
My sweet Lord (Krishna Krishna)
My Lord (Hare Hare)
Hm, hm (Gurur Brahma)
Hm, hm (Gurur Vishnu)
Hm, hm (Gurur Devo)
Hm, hm (Maheshwara)

My sweet Lord (Gurur Sakshaat)
My sweet Lord (Parabrahma)
My, my, my, my Lord (Tasmayi Shree)
My, my, my, my Lord (Guruve Namah)
My sweet Lord (Hare Rama)
My sweet Lord (Hare Krishna)
My sweet Lord (Krishna Krishna)
My Lord (Hare Hare).[17]

Srila Prabhupada's dream had, to a great extent, been fulfilled. He had wanted to fulfil the prophecy of Bhaktivinoda Thakur, Chaitanya Mahaprabhu and the ancient *Padma Purana*—all of which had suggested the spread of the name of Krishna around the world. And here it was, being spread by one of the most popular singer-songwriters of all time.

Bhaktivinoda Thakur had written, 'In the world now, there are so many religious communities, and in their purest, mature form they are the religion of singing the praises of the Lord. At the present time there is a great spiritual quest going on in the world, and it seems that the one unalloyed religion which is the essence of all religions will soon emerge. What is that religion? It is plain to see that in western countries and in Asia, religions are engaged in conflicts. There is no doubt that these religions will not be able to endure. Therefore, many of the established religions which harbour prejudiced, conflicting beliefs have become fragmented. When all of these contradictory dogmas are removed, it is then and there that all religions will be united. Let us consider the specifications the Eternal Religion would have: (1) God is one and is the all-knowing source of knowledge. He is devoid of all limitations and is the reservoir of all good qualities, (2) All living entities are His infinitesimal parts and parcels of consciousness, and the eternal function of all living entities is to serve the Supreme Lord, and (3) To sing the glorious qualities of the Supreme Personality of Godhead and to establish the brotherhood of all men as pure religion.

'Gradually the established religions will then be removed of all specific contradictions, and the secular or "party spirit" will not remain. Then all castes, all creeds, and men of all countries will be united in coexistent brotherhood under the Supreme Personality of the Godhead, united in *nama-sankirtana*, the congregational chanting of the Lord's holy name.

'Very soon the unparalleled path of *Hari-nama-sankirtana* will be propagated all over the world. Already we are seeing the symptoms. Already many Christians have tasted the nectar of divine love of the holy name and are dancing with kartals (hand cymbals) and mridangas (drums). Educated Christians are ordering these instruments and shipping them to England. By the super-excellence of Lord Krishna's holy name and the grace of pure devotees, our consciousness gets purified . . . Oh, for that day when the fortunate English, French, Russian, German and American people will take up banners, mridangas and kartals and raise kirtana through their streets and towns. When will that day come? Oh, for that day when the fair-skinned men from their side will raise up the chanting of *Jai Sachinandana,** *Jai Sachinandana ki jai*, and join with the Bengali devotees . . . Soon a personality will appear who will preach the holy name of Hari all over the world.'[18]

No doubt Srila Prabhupada would have known of such utterances and prophecies—certainly his actions, his urgings to his own disciples show a desire to fulfil such proclamations.

With the support of Harrison and Apple Records, the devotees of ISKCON in London even found a suitable five-storey building at 7, Bury Place, near the British Museum. Srila Prabhupada had told his devotees in London that he would visit once they had a

---

* Another name for Sri Chaitanya Mahaprabhu, the son of Sachi Mata.

temple ready, in whatever shape or size. Now the arrangement for the temple had been made but civic clearances and refurbishment was pending. So where could Srila Prabhupada and his followers go in the meantime?

Why not a seventy-two-acre estate?

On the invitation of John Lennon, who had recently bought Tittenhurst Park, a Georgian country house near Ascot, the devotees and Srila Prabhupada were offered parts of it to stay in until their temple-residence was ready in London. When Prabhupada arrived in London, he was whisked to the Tittenhurst estate in Lennon's limousine.

When he met Harrison, Lennon and Lennon's partner Yoko Ono, Prabhupada tried to convince them to play a leading role in promoting ISKCON in the West and around the world. Newspaper articles on him and ISKCON started to appear in the British press too, as they had in America, as the movement's record sold in high numbers, and the association with The Beatles became better known. The Beatles did not immediately become ambassadors of ISKCON but support from Harrison and Lennon continued in some form or the other.

But the desired temple in London seemed to get tougher to acquire as it got mired in civic laws, and even local complaints about an office block being converted to a Hindu temple. Lacking a temple, Srila Prabhupada took to travelling across London, giving lectures, including at the five-hundred-seater Conway Hall and Oxford Town Hall.

The success of the record in England and Europe meant invitations to preach and sing, including in France and Holland. Prabhupada accepted them all, even if they were for only a few minutes. Every opportunity to spread the word of Krishna was welcome, as was every new town where His name could be proclaimed.

Even though Srila Prabhupada and his disciples were staying on the estate of John Lennon, the Beatle who engaged the most with them was George Harrison, who considered his introduction to ISKCON his 'karma'.[19]

George Harrison said about his association that, 'Prabhupada just looked like I thought he would. I had like a mixed feeling of fear and awe about meeting him. That's what I liked about later on after meeting him more—I felt that he was just more like a friend. I felt relaxed. It was much better than at first, because I hadn't been able to tell what he was saying and I wasn't sure if I was too worldly to even be there. But later I relaxed and felt much more at ease with him, and he was very warm towards me. He wouldn't talk differently to me than to anybody else. He was always just speaking about Krishna, and it was coincidental who happened to be there. Whenever you saw him, he would always be the same. It wasn't like one time he would tell you to chant the Hare Krishna mantra and then the next time say, "Oh, no, I made a mistake." He was always the same.

'Seeing him was always a pleasure. Sometimes I would drop by, thinking I wasn't planning to go but I better go because I ought to, and I would always come away just feeling so good I was conscious that he was taking a personal interest in me. It was always a pleasure . . . Prabhupada helped me to realize the multifaceted way to approach Krishna. Like the prasadam, for example. I think it is a very important thing, prasadam*, even if it's only a trick. Like they say, the way to a man's heart is through his stomach. Well, even if it's a way to a man's spirit soul, it works. Because there is nothing better than having been dancing and singing or just sitting and talking and then suddenly they give you some food.

---

* Prasad.

It's like it's a blessing. And then when you learn to touch Him or taste Him, it's important.

'Krishna is not limited. And just by Prabhupada's being there and pouring out all this information, I was moved. It's like the mind is stubborn, but it's all Krishna. That's all you need to know—it's all Krishna. This world is His material energy too—the universal form. And in Prabhupada's books there are these pictures showing Krishna in the heart of a dog and a cow and a human being. It helps you to realize that Krishna is within everybody.

'Although Prabhupada might have been teaching some higher aspect, what came through to me a lot was a greater understanding of how Krishna is everywhere and in everything. Prabhupada explained about the different aspects of Krishna, and he provided a meditation where you could see Krishna as a person everywhere. I mean, there isn't anything that isn't Krishna.'[20]

But while Harrison's connection with ISKCON would last, the engagement with John Lennon and Yoko Ono was about to come to an end. The finale was rather illustrative of the challenges of engaging with influential celebrities to spread Krishna consciousness. Yoko Ono suggested that two ISKCON devotees appear—barely clothed—at one of their presentation-concerts, and both Lennon and Ono asked Prabhupada to use his spiritual powers to ensure that the duo was reunited after death. This, Srila Prabhupada dismissed immediately as impossible. Prabhupada was also conscious of the overt sexuality that manifested all around John Lennon and Yoko Ono.[21]

Srila Prabhupada was always concerned, as we have noted earlier in the story, that what he described as 'mundane sex life' should not interfere with spiritual pursuits or indeed any aspect of ISKCON. To avoid this, he had allowed marriage between devotees, instead of the usual monastic norms of celibacy, and as the movement spread in the West, he was cautious about the depiction, also, of Radha-Krishna, the eternal celestial lovers.

In a letter written from Los Angeles on 31 December 1968, he advised a disciple, 'Regarding the article suggested by Rayarama,* you are correct in your doubts that Radha-Krishna *lila* should not be discussed in *Back To Godhead*. In the Srimad Bhagavatam there are so many philosophical discussions and we should concentrate on these philosophical aspects. Otherwise the less intelligent will surely understand Radha-Krishna *lila* as simply nonsense boy and girl sex life . . .

'Strictly we should avoid publishing these confidential topics in *Back To Godhead*. This is dangerous for the conditioned soul. Although such Krishna lila can do some good to the mundane people in the long run, to understand the philosophical aspects of Bhagavad Gita and Srimad Bhagavatam in the beginning is essential and will make for good stride in spiritual life. I do not know why Rayarama has asked you to send such article. It is not to my sanction. We shall be very careful about mundane sex life. That is the pivot center of conditioned life. You are intelligent enough and I hope that Krishna will help you in these matters.'[22]

And so, faced with blown-up sexual photos of John Lennon and Yoko Ono at Tittenhurst, Srila Prabhupada was increasingly convinced that the time was right to leave the estate, but the relationship with George Harrison continued. Harrison even paid for the initial publication cost of the first volume of Prabhupada's book, *KRISHNA—The Supreme Personality of Godhead*, and wrote its foreword. Harrison also donated money for building the marble altar of the temple at 7, Bury Place.

The deities—three feet high each of Radha and Krishna in pure white marble—were donated for the temple by a local devotee of Indian origin who had heard about the upcoming temple. They were the grandest deities ever established at an ISKCON temple till then.

---

* Another disciple.

By the end of 1969, the deities had been established at the Radha Krishna temple in London, and Srila Prabhupada, now seventy-three years old, had managed to create twenty-one temples around the world since he stepped off the *Jaladuta*.

Wherever he found disciples, he advised them to spread the word, critically, in the local language. For instance, in December 1968, he wrote to an interlocutor in Germany, 'I have seen your poetry and it is very nice. Try to write more and to have it published. If you like, I can send you more topics to write poetries about and to versify into the German language. Try to translate articles for a German edition of *Back To Godhead*, which you can arrange to be printed in Hamburg, as they are printing a French edition from our Montreal center (sic).

'Somehow or other you should dedicate your life for developing your Hamburg center. If you still like, you can marry in the future, but for the present continue with brahmachari life so far as you can. This brahmachari life can be continued only by deep absorption in Krishna Consciousness. Don't be disturbed in your mind. I have sent a letter to Sivananda to stay there and conjointly work with you and Krishna das in progressing the success of the Hamburg center.'[23]

The focus on localizing the work of ISKCON in the customs, culture and language of the places where it opened its centres contributed to its swift growth in the early years.

In England, for instance, among other people, Srila Prabhupada reached out to the Archbishop of Canterbury to seek a meeting and explain what ISKCON was trying to do. He instinctively understood that to operate in new geographies would mean building acceptance, even alliances so that ISKCON's path would be smooth. In this, Prabhupada was prescient as would be evident from some of the objections the movement faced in the conversion of the office building at 7, Bury Place into a temple. This kind of thing would recur. He had also recognized from various experiences that as his movement grew rapidly, pushbacks would come from local faiths. For instance, in Seattle, he was challenged by two local Christian ministers who had come disguised as reporters:

'When two men came to Prabhupada's apartment and presented themselves as reporters, Prabhupada's secretary allowed them in, thinking they also wanted an interview. But their interview became an interrogation. They challenged Prabhupada as to why he was not teaching that Jesus Christ was the only way to God. They were angry that Prabhupada was preaching on the campuses. When Prabhupada informed them that he accepted Jesus Christ as the son of God, they demanded, "But do you believe or not that Jesus is the only way?"

Prabhupada replied, "Do you believe that God is limited or unlimited?"

"Unlimited," they admitted.

"Then why are you limiting Him," said Prabhupada, "by saying that there is only one way to get to Him? Even an ordinary man can have twenty sons. Do you mean to say that God can have only one son? Why are you limiting Him?"

'Within a few minutes, the men were speaking to Prabhupada in loud voices. It became obvious they were not reporters, and they told him they were, in fact, local ministers. When they became blasphemous, the devotees asked them to leave the house. Prabhupada wrote in a letter to a disciple in New York, "The priestly class of Christian and Jewish churches are becoming envious of our movement. Because they are afraid of their own system of religiosity, because they see so many young boys and girls are taking interest in this system of Krishna consciousness. Naturally, they are not very satisfied. So we may be facing some difficulty by them in the future. So, we have to take some precaution. Of course, this priestly class could not do anything very nice till now, but the dogmatic way of thinking is going on. So anyway we shall have to depend on Krishna.'"[24]

Such experiences from the time he arrived in America reverberate in the letter he wrote in 1969 from Los Angeles to the Archbishop of Canterbury:

Your Holiness,

Please accept my respectful and humble obeisances (sic). I beg to introduce myself as an Indian monk, following the Vedic principles of religious life. At present, I am in the renounced order of sannyasa (age 73) and preaching God Consciousness all over the world. I came to America in 1965, and since then, I have many followers belonging to both Christian and Jewish faiths. Thus far I have established 17 centers for Krishna Conscious temples throughout the United States, Canada, Germany, London, and France.

My mission is in the line of Lord Chaitanya, Who advented (sic) Himself 482 years ago in India, and Who preached God consciousness all over the country. His mission is to revive God consciousness throughout the world, on the basis of Srimad Bhagavatam (Science of God). The basic principle of Srimad Bhagavatam is that any religious faith which helps a man to develop Love of God, without any other motive, is transcendental religion. And the easiest process for this age is to chant the Holy Names of God. From this definition of religion as we find in the Srimad Bhagavatam, the criterion test of religion is how it helps people to develop their dormant Love of God. This love is not artificially invoked, but it is aroused by association with devotees of the Lord and by hearing from the authorized scriptures.

The human form of life is especially meant for this purpose of reviving our God consciousness because the better development of consciousness is found only in the human body. Animal propensities are found both in animal life and human life, and unfortunately, people are nowadays more concerned with the principles of sense gratification, or the animalistic part of life. Thus, the world is gradually declining in God consciousness. This tendency is very much deteriorating, and because Your Holiness is the Head of a great religious sect, I would be very pleased to meet with you, and perhaps chalk out some program for helping to alleviate the present Godless situation.

The human society should not be allowed to continue in its present path at the risk of decreasing truthfulness, hygienic principles, forgiveness and mercifulness. Without proper instruction on these principles, the human society is gradually degrading in the matter of religiosity and justice. At present, "Might makes right" is gradually taking the place of morality and justice. There is practically no more family life, and the union of man and woman is gradually degrading to the standard of mere sexuality. Our Krishna Consciousness Movement is meant for overhauling the whole situation. We are creating man of character, and we are training our disciples to become lovers of God, or Krishna. From the very beginning, they are trained to refrain from the following four principles of degradation: 1) sex life outside marriage, 2) intoxication, 3) meat eating, and 4) gambling and idle sports. Our teaching are based on the authorized movement of Lord Chaitanya, the teaching of the Bhagavad Gita as the beginning, and the teaching of Srimad Bhagavatam as the graduate study.

I do not wish to prolong the body of this note further, but if you think that a meeting with you will be beneficial for the human society at large, I shall be very much pleased if You Holiness will grant me an interview. Thanking you in anticipation for an early reply.[25]

The point made in this letter about joint activity to activate the 'dormant love of God' hints at the way Prabhupada was thinking in terms of alliances in different countries to ensure that ISKCON's spread continued unimpeded.

This kind of outreach, the association, no doubt, with The Beatles and the positive press that the movement had been receiving with its hit record, led to the opening of the 7, Bury Place Radha–Krishna temple. ISKCON now had its grandest shrine in the world. But the story with George Harrison was not yet over.

In 1972, an ISKCON preacher, Dhananjaya Das, discovered in England the seventeen-acre Picot Manor in the Hertfordshire countryside, and convinced the movement's most famous English friend, George Harrison, to buy it as a new home of ISKCON. The popularity of the movement had outgrown the 7, Bury Place temple, and with Picot Manor, now renamed Bhaktivedanta Manor, it finally had space to grow.* Quarrels occurred soon enough as ISKCON started to host large gatherings at the Manor, choking the roads of the local village, and by the mid-1980s it seemed like the Manor might have to shut down.

But a massive global campaign, supported increasingly by British parliamentarians, pushed for, and won, a different alternative—an access road that bypasses the village entirely. This solution has over the years allowed the Bhaktivedanta Manor to host up to sixty thousand people at their biggest celebrations of the year, including Janmashtami, which marks the birth of Krishna. The Manor now regularly hosts British prime ministers.

When Harrison had gifted Picot Manor to ISKCON, Srila Prabhupada had told Harrison that as he had given them shelter, Krishna would give the musician shelter at His lotus feet.[26]

In 2001, when George Harrison lay dying at one of the homes of Paul McCartney at Beverly Hills in Los Angeles, apart from

---

* Today, it has expanded to seventy-seven acres.

his family, two ISKCON preachers, Shyamsundar Dasa and Mukunda Goswami, chanted verses from the Bhagavad Gita at his bedside. His final message as announced after his death by his family was: 'Everything else can wait, but the search for God cannot wait, and love one another.'[27]

15

'Dry Grass Catching Fire'

By 1970, Srila Prabhupada had established ISKCON in some of the most important centres in the Western world, including New York, San Francisco, Los Angeles and London.

There were, by the summer of 1970, twenty-six temples, including in Hamburg, Sydney and Toronto. The scale he had achieved in five short years would have been unimaginable when he left Bombay. But now, he worked to build in Los Angeles a definitive model which could be standardized and replicated at every ISKCON centre.

What had happened is what usually happens with organizations that grow rapidly and across geographies. How ISKCON needed to run every temple was decided by Srila Prabhupada but he could only focus on so many things at one time. Perhaps even more importantly, many of the disciples, even those in decision-making positions at various temples, were only relatively recent initiates into the movement. Their own understanding of Krishna consciousness often needed strengthening.

Questions were being asked by disciples even about what having a spiritual guru meant, or if they were to have only one. The tradition that Srila Prabhupada had followed had continued for centuries, and yet that tradition in India too was rife with problems. Therefore, it was perhaps inevitable that problems would surface in the West. Some of issues were, though, triggered through misunderstanding among his Western devotees who communicated with Vaishnavas in India. Srila Prabhupada had never had much support from India for his projects in the West; now even ideologically confusion was being created about the role of a guru—reserved solely for Prabhupada in ISKCON—and the relationship between the guru and God.

But what had begun by rules being broken and rituals ignored soon became a much bigger crisis, 'a fire',[1] as Srila Prabhupada described it, a persistent and growing feeling within him that various ISKCON centres and their heads were trying to push him in the background and take charge of the movement. What seemed to have underlined this feeling within him is an incident during the fourth year of the rath yatra at Los Angeles where his own disciples strongly advised him to not ride on the cart of the deities, thus not allowing him to, in a sense, 'front' the yatra. The ostensible reason was to keep him safe from unruly crowds but Prabhupada, as he saw other disciples take his place in the cart, felt that this was a thought-out plan: he was being replaced.[2]

That problems had been surfacing in several centres is apparent from a letter he wrote on 23 January 1969 to a disciple in San Francisco, 'I can understand from your letter that there has [sic] been some disagreements or misunderstandings in the temple, but I think that you should know that all such disturbances must be solved peacefully and with consideration of the entire situation. Chidananda[*] is the president there, and I think you understand rightly that everyone must cooperate with him in keeping the temple nicely and without any unnecessary tensions.

'Anyway, if you are feeling too much inconvenience staying in San Francisco, then you are welcome to come to Los Angeles

---

[*] Another senior disciple.

and stay here with me. But if you can help to smooth over the difficulties there that will be the best thing.' [3]

On his own, Srila Prabhupada would have preferred to leave the operational details to his disciples and leave them to expand the network of temples whereas he would focus on completing his elaborate writing and publishing plans. But this was not to be.

So Prabhupada, the founding leader of ISKCON and spiritual master to all his disciples, did the next best thing—he started creating structures for the global ISKCON movement. With thirty-four chapters or centres around the world, ISKCON was given a new Governing Body Commission made up of twelve handpicked pupils[*] of Prabhupada, and he announced that while he was alive (he was then seventy-five years old), these men would be his direct representatives and, after his death, they would be the governing body which would run ISKCON around the world.

One of Srila Prabhupada's biggest concerns was that his own pupils seemed to be differing in rituals and practices from centre to centre, and therefore this committee would ensure that the basic practices—sixteen rounds of daily chanting, hygiene and cleanliness, attending and organizing the mangal aarti at 4.30 a.m., taking Srimad Bhagavatam classes, reciting Sanskrit verses and distributing ISKCON literature would be mandatory. The fundamental principles to be part of the movement had to be regularized and established equally everywhere.

He also announced a three-member team[†] to take care of all publishing operations under the Bhaktivedanta Book Trust. But along with this he announced something else that was unexpected.

---

[*] Rupanuga Das Adhikary, Bhagavandas Adhikary, Syamsundar Das Adhikary, Satsvarupa Das Adhikary, Karandhar Das Adhikary, Hansadutta Das Adhikary, Tamala Krishna Das Adhikary, Sudama Das Adhikary, Bali Mardan Das Brahmacary, Jagadisa Das Adhikary, Hayagriva Das Adhikary, and Kåñëadas Adhikary.

[†] Rupanuga, Karandhara and Bhagavan.

He would return to India to build three major temples there—in Mayapur, the birthplace of Chaitanya Mahaprabhu; Vrindavan; and Jagannath Puri or, colloquially, Puri.

This was startling fare. We have seen earlier in the story that Srila Prabhupada had indicated that, in a sense, his real home and movement was not in India but in the West. After all, hadn't he struggled to spread the message in the manner that he wanted to for years in India without success?

But the times had changed. Perhaps Prabhupada now felt that for his movement to be rooted, it needed to be properly grounded at the heart of Vaishnavism. It must have a home in the land of Krishna and Chaitanya. This could be the way to save it from disintegrating into the one thing he disliked the most, a hodgepodge, to use one of his oft-used words of customs and practices. Localization was one thing but dilution was unacceptable.

If one reads his letters from this period, there is a constant emphasis on sannyasa and letting go of personal ambition. He had accommodated on the sannyasa point when he started in the West because he had seen that few could follow the life of the Indian sannyasi—but that had led to the flowering of ego in some cases, and personal ambition which had threatened the movement.

So Srila Prabhupada was going back to the core, to the source of Krishna consciousness—India.

Two letters he wrote explain his motivations explicitly, the first one was to two disciples in Boston:

'You are all my children, and I love my American boys and girls who are sent to me by my spiritual master and I have accepted them as my disciples. Before coming to your country I took sannyas in 1959. I was publishing B.T.G. *(Back To Godhead)* since 1944. After taking sannyas I was more engaged in writing my books without any attempt to construct temples or to make disciples like my other God-brothers in India.

'I was not very much interested in these matters because my Guru Maharaj* liked very much publication of books than constructing big, big temples and creating some neophyte disciples. As soon as He saw that His neophyte disciples were increasing in number, He immediately decided to leave this world. To accept disciples means to take up the responsibility of absorbing the sinful reaction of life of the disciple.

'At the present moment in our ISKCON campus politics and diplomacy has entered. Some of my beloved students on whom I counted very, very much have been involved in this matter influenced by Maya. As such there has been some activity which I consider as disrespectful. So I have decided to retire and divert attention to book writing and nothing more.'[4]

That he saw his move to India as 'retirement' would have come as a shock to his Western movement.

The second letter is even more melancholic, for it notes Srila Prabhupada saying that even though his health was indeterminate, he was still adding responsibilities of travel as he saw that the movement was not in good health and wished to set an example:

'In order to set example to my other Sannyasi students I am personally going to Japan with a party of three other Sannyasi students. Although it is beyond my physical condition, still I am going out so that you may learn the responsibility of Sannyas . . .

'I am fervently appealing to you all not to create fracture in the solid body of the Society. Please work conjointly, without any personal ambition. That will help the cause.

'It is the injunction of the Vedas that the Spiritual Master should not be treated as ordinary man, even sometimes the Spiritual Master behaves like ordinary man. It is the duty of the disciple to accept Him as a Superhuman Man. In the beginning of your letter your comparison of the soldier and the commander

---

* Bhaktisiddhanta Saraswati.

is very appropriate. We are on the battlefield of Kurukshetra—one side Maya, the other side Krishna. So the regulative principles of a battlefield, namely to abide by the order of the commander, must be followed. Otherwise it is impossible to direct the fighting capacity of the soldiers and thus defeat the opposing elements. Kindly therefore take courage. Let things be rightly done so that our mission may be correctly pushed forward to come out victorious.'[5]

That Srila Prabhupada's diagnosis was correct was apparent when he stopped in Hawaii en route to Japan and then India. He personally offered to install the deities at the ISKCON temple at Hawaii but received only an evasive response from the head of the centre, and no concrete invitation to stay and consecrate the deities appeared. Once again, it seemed that he was being replaced.

Some of the troubles that Srila Prabhupada had as his movement spread exponentially were deeply ideological, and to understand this we have to tackle some philosophical comparisons and the difference between the teachings of Advaita Vedanta and Dvaita Vedanta, two interrelated schools of philosophy in the broader universe of Hindu philosophies. To put it very simply, Adavita Vedanta teaches that all forms of the divine are paths to realizing the formless, infinite, impersonal divine, whereas Dvaita argues that finally God does have a non-material form and transcendental personality, and that is Krishna.

Prabhupada was sternly against Advaita philosophy, dismissing its proponents as 'mayawadis'. Many of his disciples had dabbled in different kinds of approaches to Hinduism, and the interweaving of these approaches in their minds, combined with the very rapid pace of the growth of the organization, sometimes diluted—to Prabhupada's distaste—some of the rigour that he wanted to see at every chapter of ISKCON in ritual and spirit. Further complication was added by the need to keep the peace in a sense with major religions of the West like Christianity and

Judaism as his own chapters grew rapidly in major centres of the
Western world. For instance, teaching at a school in Sydney, he
emphasized to the students, 'Don't think that it is a sectarian
religion. We are making people God conscious. It doesn't matter
what religion you may belong. If by following the principles of
religion one becomes advanced in God consciousness, that is
first-class religion.'[6] In the Soviet Union, trying to get permission
to preach in that country or distribute books, Srila Prabhupada
pitched Krishna consciousness in communist terms, telling his
Soviet interlocutor, 'I think the Vedic concept of socialism or
communism will much improve the idea of communism. For
example, in a socialistic state the idea is that no one should
starve; everyone must have his food. Similarly, in the Vedic
concept of grihastha (householder) life it is recommended that a
householder see that even a lizard or a snake living in his house
should not starve. Even these lower creatures should be given
food, and certainly all humans should. It is recommended that the
grihastha, before taking his lunch, stand on the road and declare,
"If anyone is still hungry, please come! Food is ready!" If there is
no response, then the proprietor of the household takes his lunch.
Modern society takes the people as a whole as the proprietor
of a certain state, but the Vedic conception is *ishavasyam idam
sarvam*—everything is owned by *isa*, the supreme controller. *Tena
tyaktena bhunjitha*—you may enjoy what is allotted to you by Him.
Ma grdah kasya svid dhanam: but do not encroach upon others'
property. This is the Isopanisad Veda. The same idea is explained
in the different Puranas. There are many good concepts in the
Vedic literature about communism. So I thought that these ideas
should be distributed to your most thoughtful men. Therefore I
was anxious to speak.'[7]

Balancing this dichotomy of the ideological underpinnings of the core of Vaishnavism and making space to accommodate local sensitivities created some cognitive dissonance among his students, which had to be addressed from time to time.

But some of these troubles would have started to recede in Srila Prabhupada's mind as he boarded the flight to Japan and then to India. In Japan, where he had tried so hard to go to earlier in his life, without any success, he was now welcomed as a major world religious teacher and managed to come to agreement with one of the biggest publishers in Japan, Dai Nippon, to publish his books.

His return this time to Calcutta was triumphant. Crowds gathered to see this seventy-year-old swami who had American disciples singing, dancing and speaking the Sanskrit verses of the Bhagavad Gita on the streets of communist, violence-torn Calcutta.

As Vivekananda was feted upon his return from Chicago, so was Prabhupada, the colour and gaiety of whose movement drew crowds wherever he went in Calcutta with his devotees. He even created a new Life Membership Program which would allow anyone to pay an upfront fee of Rs 1111 and become a member,* and get free access to all ISKCON publications and free stay at ISKCON centres around the world.

But his dream remained unfulfilled—land in Mayapur, the birthplace of Chaitanya Mahaprabhu, to build a temple. When one more attempt to acquire Mayapur land failed, Prabhupada turned his gaze towards Bombay, the city he had come to know before he left for America.

Bombay welcomed Prabhupada. It had some old, rich business families which provided the first hosts, and life members, to this ageing monk who seemed to have done the impossible—made the

---

* This programme still continues in ISKCON.

white man sing the kirtan! On his part, Prabhupada never tired of telling the absolutely true story that many of his disciples had every ill habit possible—from drug and alcohol abuse to illicit sexual relations—until they embraced the love of Krishna.

This had a lightning effect on the audience, not least at a Chowpatty beach session where Prabhupada and his followers set the gathering on fire by their fervent kirtans, getting the entire audience to their feet for hours.

What was happening?

Srila Prabhupada's movement was being embraced for having turned the colonial gaze—no longer was India the preaching and conversion ground of missionaries, but here were live examples in India of an Indian monk who had managed to do just the reverse! As one veteran journalist noted, 'Do you realize what is happening? Very soon Hinduism is going to sweep the West. The Hare Krishna movement will compensate for all our loss at the hands of padres* through the centuries.

Never before had Srila Prabhupada been invited to more homes and gatherings of India's wealthy across the country, from Bombay to Amritsar, Calcutta to New Delhi.

From Indore to Surat to Allahabad (at the Ardh-Kumbh Mela), hundreds gathered to listen to this monk who sang, danced and prayed, and all he asked of his audience was to say, and say again, the maha-mantra of Krishna:

Hare Krishna, Hare Krishna, Krishna Krishna, Hare Hare/
Hare Rama, Hare Rama, Rama Rama, Hare Hare!

In Surat, in December 1970, for instance, 'thousands lined the street for many blocks, while the devotees, playing karatalas† and

---

* Christian missionaries.
† Cymbals.

mridangas* and chanting Hare Krishna, made their way along. Spectators stood on rooftops or clustered at windows and doorways, while others joined the procession. The police had stopped traffic at the intersections, allowing only the kirtana procession to pass. The earthen road, freshly swept and sprinkled with water, had been decorated with rice flour designs of auspicious Vedic symbols. Green, freshly cut banana trees adorned either side of the way. Overhead, women's saris strung like bunting across the narrow roadway formed a brightly colored canopy over the kirtana party. Mr Bhagubhai Jariwala, Prabhupada's host in Surat, had advertised the daily parade routes in the local newspapers, and now, day after day, the devotees were holding a kirtana procession through various sections of the city. While more than twenty of Prabhupada's disciples led the daily procession, thousands of Indians chanted, cheered, and clamored (sic) to see, and women threw flower petals from the rooftops.

'Often the procession would have to stop as families came forward to garland the devotees. Sometimes the devotees would receive so many garlands that their blissful faces would be scarcely visible, and they would distribute the garlands to the people in the crowd. Never before had the devotees met with such a reception.

'"It is a city of devotees,"' Prabhupada said. He compared the people of Surat to dry grass catching fire. By nature they were Krishna conscious, but the arrival of Srila Prabhupada and his sankirtana† party had been like a torch, setting the city spiritually ablaze.

'The entire population of Surat seemed to turn out every morning, as tens of thousands flocked at seven A.M. to the

* Mridangas.
† Kirtan.

designated neighbor hood (sic). Men, women, laborers, merchants, professionals, the young, the old and all the children—everyone seemed to be taking part. Cramming the streets and buildings, they would wait for the kirtana party, and when the devotees arrived, everyone became joyous.'[8]

The reception that Srila Prabhupada and his party received in India had surprised and delighted them. In most places they had been cheered, celebrated and provided with the best hospitality, but there were also lessons for his American disciples on the hardships of the land of Krishna consciousness. Most were unaccustomed to the heat and the dust, and the crowds. Their guru insisted on putting them through the most chaotic experiences, whether it was to try and go by road to Mayapur from Calcutta or right after the luxurious reception in Surat, decide to go to the Ardh-Kumbh Mela at Allahabad, a gathering of tens of thousands of people in a rudimentary tented city on the banks of the sangam—a meeting point of three rivers.

As one of his pupils noted: 'Srila Prabhupada also started to notice that some of us were coming late to mangala aarti[*] and that some of us were not coming at all. Prabhupada became very upset about this, because he knew how important mangala aarti was for us. So one morning, although he was a little frail in health, he got up at four o'clock and came out in his *gamcha*,[†] sat down under the pump, and took that ice-cold bath early in the morning—just to encourage us to get up, bathe, and come to *mangala aarti*. That had a very profound effect on all of us, and we felt so ashamed that we just couldn't sleep late any more . . . Dawn came and the sky lightened—but only barely. A damp, heavy fog from the river, mingling with the smoke from the campfires, clung to everything. Rain began to fall. The devotees were unprepared for this weather.

---

[*] Mangal aarti, a prayer conducted very early in the morning.
[†] Towel.

With food hard to get and cook, and toilet facilities the crudest, the devotees wondered how they would last for the scheduled two weeks.

'Prabhupada, however, who shared with his disciples all these austerities, remained transcendental and apparently unaffected. If the sun peeked through the clouds, he would sit outside and take his massage. Then he would bathe himself, sitting in his gamcha, dipping his *lota** into warmed Ganges water, and pouring it over his body. He seemed so content, the devotees took heart. He wasn't complaining, so why should they?'[9]

In every place the troupe went, they seemed to have made a mark, including in Gorakhpur with Hanuman Prasad Poddar, the famous founder of Gita Press Gorakhpur, the biggest publisher of books on Hinduism, who had helped Srila Prabhupada get monetary support before he left for America. This time, it was a different kind of meeting—Prabhupada had books of his own to show, and his books were beautifully designed and printed. What Poddar had in sheer volume and scale, Prabhupada was building through the highest possible quality of colour image, and print and paper quality.[10]

The upgradation of ISKCON in India also started with the procurement of a rented flat in Bombay as a home for the movement. From that base, Srila Prabhupada and his handful of disciples, mostly non-Indians, organized the first eleven-day Hare Krishna Festival in the city, at Cross Maidan Exhibition Grounds, under a giant tented pandal seating more than thirty thousand people, serving prasadam food to thousands every day, and complete with a helium balloon to advertise the festival. Prabhupada himself appeared at the festival in a horse-drawn carriage chanting the holy mantra and followed by thousands. It was just the sort of thing that captivated Bombay, a real spectacle—but this one not

---

* A steel mug.

for mere entertainment. The newspapers called it a grand finale for ISKCON, but in fact Prabhupada was only just beginning his work in the city.

Prabhupada had successfully created the biggest Krishna fest the city had ever seen, drawing attention from some of its wealthiest patrons. But just when it seemed like the guru of ISKCON was about to dig deeper and spend more time spreading the word in his home country, Srila Prabhupada remembered his global dream again.

He explained: 'It is the duty of a mendicant to have experience of all varieties of God's creation as *Paribrajakacharya* or travelling alone through all forests, hills, towns, villages etc. to gain faith in God and strength of mind as well as to enlighten the inhabitants of the message of God. A sannyasi is duty bound to take all these risks without any fear and the most typical sannyasi of the present age is Lord Chaitanya Who travelled in the same manner through the central India jungles enlightening even the tigers, bears, snakes, deers, elephants and many other jungle animals.'[11]

There were perhaps two distinct reasons for Prabhupada's refusing to focus only on one geography—one, of course, was the desire to fulfil the prophecy of the name of Krishna to ring out from towns and villages in every part of the world, and the other was perhaps that he felt singular distaste for modernity as he experienced it. Long before he travelled to America, Srila Prabhupada had dreamt of a sort of a Gandhian spiritual and cultural 'conquest' around the world. He wrote, '(Certain Gandhian programmes) if systematically carried on will help very much in the spiritualising process. They can be given a real spiritual shape in accordance with the principles of Bhagavad Gita and other authentic scriptures. And by doing so India's original culture will not only be revived and re-established but also will foster India's indigenous culture in other parts of the world. That will be a sort of cultural conquest of all (the) world by India. By such conquest the people of the world will get relieved of the so-called material prosperity terrorised by atomic bombs.'[12]

This is one of the reasons why Srila Prabhupada and his earliest American disciples had something vital in common, despite their vast cultural gaps—they understood the ills of capitalist society trapped in cycles of violence, especially with the coming of the atomic bomb and nihilistic violence.

In the first volume of his initial self-published Srimad Bhagavatam, Prabhupada wrote, 'The human society, at the present moment, is not in the darkness of oblivion. It has made rapid progress in the field of material comforts of life, education and economic development of the entire world. But it suffers a pin-prick somewhere in the social body at large and therefore there is large scale quarrel even on less important issue(s). Therefore there is the want of a clue as to how they can become one in peace, friendship and prosperity by the common cause. Srimad Bhagavatam will fill this need, for it is a cultural presentation for re-spiritualization of the entire human society.'[13]

Like Gandhi, Srila Prabhupada believed that the machine age had taken human beings away from their innate spirituality, and that this could only be regained if people came closer to God and sought His divine benevolence instead of mere materialistic advancement and pleasure.

'Human prosperity flourishes by natural gifts and not by gigantic industrial enterprises. The gigantic industrial enterprises are products of Godless civilization and they are cause for destruction of noble aims of human life. The more we go on increasing such troublesome industries for squeezing out the vital energy of the human being, the more there will be unrest and dissatisfaction of the people in general although a few only can live lavishly on the exploitative means on other living beings. The

natural gifts such as grains and vegetables, fruits, the rivers full
with water, the hill full with jewels and minerals and the seas
full of pearls and stones. Such natural products are supplied
by the order of the Supreme and as He desires the material
nature produces them in abundance or restricts them at times.
The natural law is that human being may take advantage of
these Godly gifts by nature and satisfactorily flourish on them
without being captivated by the exploitative motive for lording
it over the material nature. This is not possible and the more we
attempt to exploit the material nature according to our whims of
enjoyment the more we shall become entrapped by the reaction
of such exploitative attempts. If we have sufficient grains, fruits,
vegetables and herbs then what is the necessity of running on
a slaughter house and kill the poor animals at the risk of being
killed by them again and again. A man cannot kill an animal if
he has sufficient grains and vegetables to eat. The flow of river
waters fertilize the fields and there is production more than what
we need. The minerals are produced in the hills and the jewels
in the ocean. If the human civilization has sufficient grains,
minerals, jewels, water, milk etc. then why should it hanker after
terrible industrial enterprises at the cost of the labour of some
unfortunate men. But all these natural gifts are dependant on the
mercy of the Lord. What we need, therefore, to become is to be
obedient to the laws of the Lord with an aim to achieve human
perfection of life by devotional service.'[14]

In both Gandhi and Prabhupada, the concern of nature,
and its bounties, is a recurring theme. The vegetarianism and
environmentalism both propagated was, at once, appropriate, and
ahead of its time. Like Gandhi, Prabhupada had seen war and its
ravages, and how technology could be used for mass destruction,
he lived under the shadow of absolute atomic carnage, and this
had convinced him that a better, more 'natural' way, was not only
possible, but it was divinely ordained as the duty of human beings.

But after his successes in his home country, it was an even more resolute and confident Srila Prabhupada who set out to preach in Australia, Malaysia, Paris and New York, and pushed to spread even in the (at that time) Soviet Union. Undeterred by threats of violence, including to his very life, which he received from communist Naxal extremists while organizing a ten-day Sankirtan Festival in Calcutta, Prabhupada continued to push for expanding the footprint of ISKCON. Even if that meant getting policemen to guard the organization's massive Calcutta festival attended by forty thousand people.[15]

From the Soviet Union (where, despite his strong pitch for 'Vedic socialism'), Srila Prabhupada could not get permission to preach to Paris where he fared much better with his books being translated into French, and appearances on television and radio, Prabhupada began a hectic tour to spread ISKCON. Upon his return to America, he visited new centres—Detroit, Chicago, across the Midwest. He spoke in Jacksonville, opened a new temple in Atlanta, addressed a gathering at the University of Florida—everywhere the same lesson: of devotion to Krishna, a life free from stimulants and, yes, no illicit sex and no eating meat.

Alongside all the travelling and preaching, the seventy-five-year-old Prabhupada kept on a punishing schedule of translating and publishing with ISKCON Press, selling greater numbers of volumes each year. But the intense stress showed as he fell ill consistently—his body had been ravaged by repeated occurrences of heart disease, and the strain of leading a life of constant international travel started to show.

It was around this time, in the middle of 1971, that Prabhupada received an invitation to recuperate in sunny Africa rather than chilly Europe or America. A lifelong lover of the sun, he went to Nairobi and Mombasa, though instead of just convalescing, of course, he proceeded to preach actively across the two cities, and especially drew a large following among the Indian community living in Nairobi by the autumn of 1971.

By the time he left Africa after staying for about five weeks, he had already organized the first outdoor kirtan in Nairobi under the biggest tree at Kamkunji Park, an emblem of Kenyan independence. Like the elm tree at Tompkins Square Park, here was Prabhupada once again recreating that mood of liberation and devotion under another iconic tree, in the same spirit of spiritual freedom.

Would he now be able to root this spirit into the soil where it was born? Land had, finally, been acquired in Mayapur, the promise of new centres had emerged in Bombay and Calcutta, but would Prabhupada be able to get his young ISKCON to fit in seamlessly with hundreds of years of tradition at home?

16

Krishna in War and Peace

In the many photographs of Srila Prabhupada, whether he is meditating with his eyes closed or singing or even walking, there is one curious common feature—more often than not, his face seems consistently slightly upturned, as if he is in conversation with someone above him.

This is perhaps a befitting pictorial representation of the life he sought to live—in the world, but with his mind upturned, as it were, towards the divine.

This was perhaps even necessary for Srila Prabhupada; as he approached his mid-seventies, he was mired in the management of a global movement that stretched his physical abilities to the point of exhaustion.

The Mayapur temple needed to be seminal, in his imagination, three-hundred-foot high, complete with a grand guest house and a planetarium of the universe according to the Srimad Bhagavatam. In his interviews, Srila Prabhupada used to be asked why so many in the West were turning away from Christianity and moving towards Eastern gurus and he would answer that Christian leaders could perhaps not make people very interested in their religion, and that's why churches were closing across the Western world.[1] This point about closing churches—a major topic of discussion today—was being pointed out by Prabhupada as early as the mid-1970s.

So Prabhupada's focus when creating his own temples for ISKCON, and even with his earliest publications, for instance when asked for *Back to Godhead* to compete in look and feel with *Time* magazine, was to make things as attractive as possible. After all, Krishna was radiance personified, so why should the worship be any less?

As the movement grew to a massive, tented festival in Delhi, a regal welcome for Srila Prabhupada in Vrindavan and ISKCON's quest for land to build a temple in Vrindavan, that holiest of Krishna towns, we hear again and again Prabhupada elucidating that this—his movement—was broad and free from sectarian boundaries.

He recognized perhaps that as movements spread, so do a sense of contradiction and localized resistance. Emphasizing the non-sectarian spirit of ISKCON also helped him explain, at home especially, how he had been able to do what others in the Vaishnava *sampradaya** could not—bring westerners into the fold of Krishna bhakti.

At Vrindavan he said, 'We should not consider that Krishna is Hindu or Indian. Krishna is for all. These foreigners are taking to Krishna consciousness by understanding that Krishna is for all. They are not accepting a form of religious principles, like Hindu or Muslim or Christian. These are designated religions. If I am calling myself a Hindu, this is not my religion—this is my designation. Because I happen to take birth in a Hindu family, therefore I call myself a Hindu. Or because I take birth in a particular land, I call myself Indian or American. But our Krishna consciousness movement is not for such designated personalities.

---

* Sect or community.

This Krishna consciousness is *sarvopadhi-vinirmuktam.*˙ When one becomes free from all designations, he can take to Krishna consciousness. As long as one is Hindu or Muslim or Christian, there is no question of Krishna consciousness.

'So these boys and girls, or ladies and gentlemen, who have joined me, they have given up their designations. They are no longer Americans or Canadians or Australians. They are thinking of themselves as eternal servants of Lord Krishna. Without this, there is no question of liberation from the material contamination.'[2]

In Tehran he would say, 'So our Krishna consciousness movement means to educate people how to become free from designations. Therefore, we accept from any group. If I think that he is under designation . . . But our business is to make him free from the designation. We therefore welcome anyone. He may come with designation, but if he lives with us, he follows our rules and regulations, he becomes free from designation. And this so-called designated religious system will not help us. If we keep ourself on the designated platform—I am American, I am Indian, I am Iranian, I am Hindu, I am Muslim, I am Christian, I am Buddhist—then we have to continue in that designation. There is no question of freedom.'[3]

There is one more vital factor to consider in Srila Prabhupada's non-sectarian pitch for ISKCON, if it allowed him to bypass inter-religion strife overseas, at home in India, it ensured that he could connect his movement to the anti-caste discrimination, anti-birth-based lineage hierarchy legacy of Bhaktisiddhanta Saraswati. The old world of the Vaishnavas was mired in the question of *adhikara*, the idea that only people born in certain caste, even families, were entitled to rise to positions of influence in the Vaishnava community. But Srila Prabhupada had created a movement where the senior-most monks after him were not

---

˙ Loosely translated, the removal of all designations or markers.

even Indians, therefore the propagation of a movement untied to such knots of tradition allowed Prabhupada the freedom to build ISKCON as the unambiguous home for anyone who had Krishna love, that alone was the criterion.

As he built ISKCON, the world was going through epic changes. For all of these, Srila Prabhupada provided what in his opinion seemed like the most honest reaction from a spiritual perspective. Asked about the spread of nuclear weapons after India's first nuclear tests in May 1974, Prabhupada said, 'What is this nuclear bomb? I will drop it on you and in turn you will drop it on me. What is the advancement over the dogs? This tearfulness of one nation for another with nuclear bombs is the dogs' mentality. Sometimes, even when chained by their respective masters, two dogs will fight as soon as they meet. Have you seen it? It's no better than that . . . there will be no nuclear war if they take to Krishna consciousness. And even if there is nuclear war, that is not going to end everything.'[4]

For Prabhupada, the answer was Krishna. As a devoted monk, he realized that superficial solutions—victory in war, banning certain weapons—could only take humankind so far. There was something much more fundamental that was missing. Until that was resolved, until the deepest quest of man was fulfilled, the anxiety and the fear would never recede. A potent glimpse of Prabhupada's argument emerges in an exchange from 1971 as India and Pakistan were at war over the Bangladesh independence movement. Here Prabhupada is talking to a journalist in New Delhi.

'I understand,' said the reporter, 'that by Krishna you mean some eternal principle.'

'I do not mean a principle,' Prabhupada replied. 'I mean a person like you and me.' Prabhupada was explaining Lord Krishna as the Supreme Person when suddenly sirens began sounding.

'Blackout! Blackout!' cried the reporter and others in the house. War between Pakistan and India had been imminent for weeks, and air raid drills and warnings were now commonplace in Delhi.

'Sir,' the reporter spoke tensely in the darkened room, 'this is the presence of reality. We are being threatened by this fight with Pakistan. The siren is the ugly reality coming for us.'

'We are always in the ugly reality,' Prabhupada said, 'twenty-four hours a day. Suppose there is no blackout? Still, if you go in the street, there is no guarantee that you will get home. In this way, you are always in the ugly reality. Why do you say only this blackout? This is just one of the features of this ugly reality. That's all.'

Reporter: 'Yes, but at the moment . . .'

Prabhupada: 'You do not realize that you are in ugly reality twenty-four hours a day? *Padam padam yad vipadam.* There is danger at every step.'

Reporter: 'I know, sir, but this is collective, national danger. Have you anything to offer us as a remedy?'

Prabhupada: 'Krishna consciousness is our only remedy. Take to this process, and you will be happy.'

Reporter: 'Sir, I think someone should go to Yahya Khan (the president of Pakistan).'

Prabhupada: 'What benefit will you derive by going to Yahya Khan?'

Reporter: 'Someone is out to kill me.'

Prabhupada: 'But suppose Yahya Khan does not kill you? Will you be safe? Then what is the use to go to Yahya Khan? You will die today or tomorrow. If you want to save yourself, then go to Krishna. That is our proposition. Even if you go to Yahya Khan, and he does not fight, then you mean to say that you will live forever? What is the use of flattering Yahya Khan? Flatter Krishna, so that you may be saved perpetually. Why don't you do that?'

Reporter: 'I was only thinking in terms of collective security. I can see your point . . .'

Prabhupada: 'You should know that you are always in danger.'

Reporter: 'Yes, sir, we agree. The late Einstein said the same thing . . .'

Prabhupada: 'That is our position, and Krishna says, "I will save you." Therefore, let us go to Krishna. Why go to Yahya Khan?'

Reporter: 'Simply because he is disturbing us, that's all.'

Prabhupada: 'Your mind is always disturbing you all the time, because it is always with you. Your body is always with you. Are you not suffering from bodily pains? Why don't you go to Yahya Khan to cure your pains? You are always in danger. Why don't you realize that?'

Reporter: 'We realize that this is a national disaster.'

Prabhupada: 'These are symptoms. People are trying to give a patchwork cure for the disease. We are giving the supreme cure. This is the difference. No patchwork cure will help you. You need a complete cure.

> *janma karma ca me divyam*
> *evam yo vetti tattvatah*
> *tyaktva deham punar janma*
> *naiti mam eti so'rjuna*

The cure is no more repetition of birth and death. That is what we want. That is the benefit of Krishna consciousness. *Yam prapya na nivartante / tad dhama paramam mama.* If you go to Krishna, then you don't come back again to this material world.'

Reporter: 'Sir, mine was a very hypothetical question. Suppose a hundred pure, saintly, Krishna conscious people are meditating or discussing together, and someone comes along and drops the bomb.'

Prabhupada: 'Those who are Krishna conscious are not afraid of bomb. When they see a bomb coming, they think that Krishna desired the bomb to come. A Krishna conscious person is never afraid of anything. *Bhayam dvitiyabhinivesatah syat*. One who has the conception that something can exist outside of Krishna is afraid. On the other hand, one who knows that everything is coming from Krishna has no reason to be afraid. The bomb is coming, he says, "Ah, Krishna is coming." That is the vision of the devotee. He thinks, "Krishna wants to kill me with a bomb. That is all right. I will be killed." That is Krishna consciousness.'[5]

Commenting on such subjects had become inevitable now in Srila Prabhupada's life: the once obscure monastic was now a public figure with a worldwide institution with significant resources and plans to acquire vast amounts of land to build marquee temples.

Within ISKCON, Prabhupada continued to struggle to find the right people for his elaborate expansion plans. He had been wanting to retire and hand over all day-to-day running of ISKCON to the twelve Governing Body Commission members he had selected. He wanted to retire and write for the remaining period of his life. But this proved challenging as issues kept cropping up which had to be tackled directly by Prabhupada.

Land had been found bordering the beach at Juhu in (what was then) the distant Bombay suburbs, and a grand temple had to be built there too. But Srila Prabhupada found himself, to his dismay, embroiled in even monetary conversations with contractors who would inevitably fleece his American disciples.

ISKCON was spreading to Australia and New Zealand where, again, its devotees, initially, were hippies. Space for temples had been found, deities established but who would take regular care of them? And, more importantly, how could he train his disciples to run ISKCON, organize their temples but remain ascetics and devotees, and not become managers?

In Australia, a man who called himself the Wizard, a former professor, appeared at an ISKCON gathering and declared he knew that he was God. 'I am the centre of the universe,' the man said. 'And I will prove sometime next year that I am the centre of the universe.' To this Prabhupada wryly remarked, 'That's all right. Everybody is thinking like that. What makes you different?'[6]

These interactions were sometimes fraught with tension. There is a video[7] of Prabhupada's visit to Sydney in 1971 and his appearance, riding a blue Volkswagen Kombi van, to another of his storefront temples at Paddington, Sydney. One of the new ISKCON disciples waiting there was Sheryl Zimmerer, a college graduate-turned-treasury employee-turned Krishna bhakt[*]— not only just Sheryl, but her mother and aunt, worried and flustered, were at the venue too. While her daughter participated in proceedings inside the temple, sitting cross-legged and chanting and being initiated into the fold by Prabhupada, her mother spoke to a TV reporter outside.

'Well, I'm not happy with it, I don't go along with it, but it's her life, it's what she wants. So, my husband and I make the best of it,' said her mother.

The reporter asked: 'What worries you about her?'
Sheryl's mother said: 'Her future. Her whole future and the fact that they are teaching them not to have sex. I came here last night, and the spiritual master was telling them that to have sex is like animals. Well, this isn't the way I've brought my children up. When I hear this sort of thing, I am wondering what her future is. She has given up university to do this, she's given up everything, she is not working, and I can't see any future in it at all. What's going to happen in ten years' time?'
Reporter: 'And what religion are you, can I ask?'
Mother: 'Church of England . . . She's been christened, she's been confirmed in our own church and she suddenly turned to this all in a matter of two months.'

---

[*] Devotee in Hindi.

Reporter: 'What do you think has attracted her most of all about this?'

Mother: 'Well, she's been looking for something. She's an introvert, and she's felt that she wants more out of life than what she's been getting. She's obviously been getting it, isn't she because she seems very happy since she has been here. Her ideas coincide with these peoples' ideas and I think they are very good living people. They are very sincere in their ideas, but they are not my ideas.'

Reporter: 'One of things you don't particularly appreciate is the prostrating . . .'

Mother: 'No, I can't see the point of doing this . . .'

At this point, the daughter Sheryl entered the frame. The reporter asked Sheryl, 'Sheryl, why do you in fact prostrate yourself like that?'

Sheryl: 'Well, it's a sign of humility. The spiritual master, he is a messenger from God, an associate of God, he's actually Krishna's friend, God's friend. That's why we bow down to the spiritual master because the spiritual master is giving us this knowledge, how to go back home, back to Godhead, back to Krishna. It's so potent in the world. We have fifty-two temples all over the world today.'

Reporter: 'Your mother is worried that all the things you are saying are largely due to brainwashing. Are you worried that she's worried?'

Sheryl: 'Well, yes I'm worried that she's worried but I don't think she should because you can see that there is peace and happiness there.'[8]

This conversation is a striking example of the kind of tensions that brewed within and outside ISKCON as, what came to be known colloquially as the Hare Krishna movement, it built new centres and found new followers around the world.

From Tokyo to Honolulu, from Bombay to Madras,* Srila Prabhupada travelled relentlessly to teach, preach, build and sometimes to even put out fires of clashing egos. One of the main things he focused on was his first love—writing, translating and publishing books. Prabhupada had always been steadfast in the belief that books were more important, and more potent, than even temples in telling millions of people about the love of Krishna. 'Our only hope is books and literature,'[9] he reiterated again and again. 'Practically, our Society is built on books.'[10]

The ISKCON publishing centre had, upon Srila Prabhupada's encouragement, rapidly increased its publishing programme, and one of the core activities of the preachers in the movement was to go out and sell its books at street corners or wherever else they could.

Whether living in a hut at the site of where his dream Mayapur temple would come up or being carried down from his quarters in a palanquin at dusk surrounded by disciples carrying flaming torches at the New Vrindavan temple complex in Virginia, or worrying about payments made for land in Juhu, or receiving George Harrison and Ravi Shankar at the ISKCON temple in London, Srila Prabhupada traversed many climates, conditions and audiences, by all accounts with a resolute sense of equanimity.

Among all his transcendental teachings, there were also some non-negotiables, like eating meat, which Prabhupada associated with 'rascals', his favourite invective reserved for those upon whom he felt most disdain.

In one of his classic declarations on the subject, he propounded, 'Our prohibited injunctions are that we should not eat meat. So I have seen when on the plane . . . Of course we never go to the hotel

---

* Chennai.

or restaurant, but on the plane we see so many European, American friends traveling. They are eating the meat, not very large quantity, very little quantity. Some of them are eating voraciously, no, but generally I see . . . But if they give up that little one piece of meat, say, one ounce or two ounce, immediately we can save ourself from so much sinful activities, so many slaughterhouses running on all over the world. If we simply control the tongue, what is that? You are eating a piece of meat. But they cannot. They cannot. *Jihva-vegam.* The tongue is dictating, "No, meat is very nice. Take it." A little. It is not much. He's not living on meat. There are loafs, there are vegetables. Actually he's living on that. Nobody takes two or three loaf, of the same weight meat. Meat, little quantity. But they take loaf, butter, rice, other things. Without vegetables, without food grains, you cannot live. It is simply for the tongue. *Ta'ra madhye jihva ati lobhamoy sudurmati.* Simply for this tongue, little only. He cannot live simply on meat unless he's an animal exactly. He has to take vegetable, food grains, butter. These are milk products. Otherwise he has no chance to live. But for the tongue's sake he's taking little piece of meat, and for that reason, we have to maintain thousands and thousands of slaughterhouse. This is our position.'[11]

For Prabhupada, meat-eating was among the four defining sins of the Kali Yuga, the age of darkness and the fall of humankind˙— along with gambling, intoxication and illicit sex, or sex outside marriage.

'So what is legal meat-eating? Legal meat-eating is that you sacrifice one animal before the goddess, deity Kali, Goddess Kali, and there are so many rules and regulation. Under regulative principle one was allowed to eat meat. Not that maintain big, big

---

˙ The Hindu conception of time is divided into four yugas: Satya, Treta, Dwapar, and Kali, a sort of virtuous to non-virtuous cycle of mankind with Satya being most virtuous, and Kali being the age of the fallen, and back again.

slaughterhouse and purchase from the butcher shop and eat meat. This is illegal.'[12]

Some of his toughest diatribes were against these activities, and he spent time and effort around the world and in India to preach against these. But these are not the only vital lessons that Srila Prabhupada had to teach his disciples—some of the most critical teachings were about handling money and land.

As had happened before in the process of trying to acquire a building for a temple in Manhattan, it occurred again in Juhu, Bombay. As the process of completion of sale of land got mired in bureaucratese and legal challenges, there was a strong sense that his followers might get cheated.

He wrote to his disciples about the Bombay case, suggesting that they were too timid to handle a situation where the other party was bullying them and taking advantage of their simplicity. They were being lied to, suggested Prabhupada, but once he dealt with the situation directly, he was convinced that it would not be easy to fool him and he would be a far tougher negotiator than his disciples.[13]

Wherever he went, from Honolulu to Vrindavan (where, too, Srila Prabhupada dreamt of a grand temple), the worry about his disciples living in makeshift arrangements, tents, mostly, on land near the seashore, failing to conclude negotiations and being threatened by the local owner plagued Prabhupada.

It finally landed on Prabhupada's doorstep to negotiate again and again with the owner of the land, as a monk, as someone conducting a transaction, in peaceable nuances and in rage.

In the final heated showdown between the owner, a man referred to in ISKCON documents as 'Mr N', things blew up to a point where the man threatened to demolish the makeshift shrine that had been built on the land and remove the deities himself.

Days after this heated quarrel and the threat against the deities, Mr N died of a heart attack. But the battle continued with his wife, who managed to get a municipality order to demolish the temple. This was almost completed until a plea to Bal Thackeray, the founder and chief ideologue of the Shiv Sena political party, stopped the sanctum sanctorum, where the deities were seated, from being disturbed.

The temple was rebuilt, and with it, the mission in Bombay rescued. In the last leg of the fight, the wife of Mr N would, in fact, fall at Srila Prabhupada's feet and ask for his forgiveness.

In Mayapur, the plans were even bigger. Srila Prabhupada was seeking to build not merely large temples, but mini townships— places where all the people he preached to could gather and praise the name of Krishna. This would echo, he believed, around the world.

How else, for instance, was a rath yatra happening in London in 1973 through Piccadilly and sweeping up Trafalgar Square? Prabhupada, a seventy-seven-year-old man, frequently unwell from his non-stop travelling and existing fragile heart condition, danced before wild crowds that stunned the British capital?

This time in England, Srila Prabhupada could stay at the expansive and relatively secluded Bhaktivedanta Manor, and his profile meant that he was invited to answer existential questions from scholars like the English historian and philosopher Arnold Toynbee. Their exchange gives us an understanding into the interest and uptake of Srila Prabhupada's ideas even among some of the most intellectual Western minds. Their interaction:

Prabhupada: So far I think that British people, they organized very nicely the British Empire, but some way or other, it is now lost. But still, the British prestige can be elevated if actually, according to the Vedic instruction, you try to make your social construction, the political institution and economic development . . . Every direction is there. So you are all great historians. And there are many politicians. If you take this instruction of the Vedas little seriously, you can make your state an ideal state, and people are still ready to follow you. Then the whole history of the world will change. And if you people agree, then I can help you. I can help.

Dr Arnold Toynbee: Yes, yes, yes. (pause)

Prabhupada: There must be ample production of food grains and milk product. Then the whole economic problem solved. And the formula is there. How to get ample agricultural production and milk, everything is there in Bhagavad Gita and *Srimad Bhagavatam* . . . We must be serious to accept this formula for practical application.

Dr Arnold Toynbee: Yes, yes. You would apply the teachings of the Gita to all human societies at all times. Yes, yes.

Prabhupada: Yes, yes. Yes, that is my ambition, that let the teachings of Bhagavad Gita be practically accepted by the human society, and surely they'll be happy. Surely. *Yada yada hi dharmasya glanir bhavati bharata* [BG 4.7]. That is stated in the Bhagavad Gita. So now everything is confused. And in your country, or western countries, they are very organized. So you are not feeling now so much confusion. But it is coming. But in India and countries like that, it is very confusion state. Yes. They have lost their own culture, and they could not assimilate the western type of civilization. So they are lost. They are lost.

Dr Arnold Toynbee: In India is everybody lost, the Indian culture . . .?

Prabhupada: No, not everybody.

Dr Arnold Toynbee: No, no.

Prabhupada: Not everybody. But general mass of people, at least, the so-called educated, five to ten per cent people, they are lost.

Dr Arnold Toynbee: Yes.

Prabhupada: Yes. And so-called educated, they practically guide. You'll be surprised to know that in 1950, one of my students, he was a government statistics officer. So he went to some village, and he gave me report that the villagers inquired from him that "*Babuji, agar angarej ko vote diya yai pasatela* (?)"

Dr Arnold Toynbee: Yes.

Prabhupada: You understand Hindi? No.

Dr Arnold Toynbee: No, I don't. No, no, no.

Prabhupada: No. The inquiry was that "If we again give votes to the Englishmen, will they come and do." (laughs)

Dr Arnold Toynbee: Yes, yes, yes.

Prabhupada: Yes. So they were feeling the . . . Actually, in India . . . In our childhood, we know. Every Indian felt very secure. They never expected that Britishers will go. They were so sympathetic. And now they . . . This is the pulse felt by that statistics officer. They are not very much satisfied with the present system of government. British administration was very much appreciated by the Indians. Even Bhaktivinoda Thakura appreciated. Bhaktivinoda Thakura, he has written in something, somewhere, that "The Britishers also very nice because they don't interfere with the religious affairs." So as soon as they changed their views and tried to divide the Hindus and Muslims, the British Empire lost. According to Queen's declaration, the Britishers pledged that "They will not interfere with your religious affairs." Later on, for political purposes, when they interfered with this Hindu–Muslim question, then the British Empire lost.

Dr Arnold Toynbee: Yes, yes. But the people who rule India now have a western education mostly. The Indians who . . .

Prabhupada: Yes. Perverted, converted. Just like Nehru. Nehru was western educated. He was educated in London . . .

Dr Arnold Toynbee: Yes.

Prabhupada: Yes. That was the res . . . Formerly, in our childhood we saw that any gentleman coming here in London and goes back to India, he no more mixes with the Indian soil. He . . . They were called "England-returned". So they made their own society. Then our Ram Mohan Raya,* he formed a Brahmo Society. And so many things changed. Again, they are now topsy-turvied (sic). So actually, India's position is that they have lost their own culture, and they could not assimilate the western culture. But in the western countries, if they accept this Vedic process of civilization, then they will again take it.

Dr Arnold Toynbee: Yes.

Prabhupada: Yes. (pause)

Syamasundara: "A Rival for Nelson."

Prabhupada: Hm?

Syamasundara: "A Rival for Nelson."

Prabhupada: Yes. There was newspaper photograph. You have seen that?

Syamasundara: Guardian.

Prabhupada: Guardian. "A Rival for Nelson." Yes.

Dr Arnold Toynbee: Well, the western countries are mostly concerned with economics, money, wealth . . .

---

* Raja Rammohun Roy.

Prabhupada: No, that is . . .

Dr Arnold Toynbee: It's about the same as . . .

Prabhupada: That they can continue. But the spirit of Vedic culture should be accepted. It is not that because one has to accept the Vedic culture, he has to stop industry or material progress. Not like that. Bhagavad Gita does not teach that. Simply to change the consciousness. Therefore, we have named the Society "Krishna Consciousness." One has to become Krishna conscious. Then everything will be adjusted. Not the mode of life should be changed. Little change. Just like we recommend that four things should be avoided: illicit sex, meat-eating, intoxication and gambling. So to give up these four kinds of activities, which are considered to be sinful, that is not very difficult. That is not very difficult. These English and, I mean to say, European and American boys, they are young men. They have given up. So in the society, if there is prevalence of sinful activities, then there will be reaction. So these four things are considered sinful activities: illicit sex, meat, unnecessarily killing of animals, and intoxication, and gambling. *Yatra papas chatur-vidhah.* These are four kinds of sinful activities. So Vedic civilization means they should be freed from the sinful activities. Then other things will automatically come.

Syamasundara: I think Mr Toynbee . . . I saw on television, I saw you once on a television programme in New York.

Dr Arnold Toynbee: Yes, yes.

Syamasundara: And you concluded that if men came out of this age who had developed a spirit of renunciation, true renunciation from material pursuit, that this would enable the world to rectify its present precarious position.

Dr Arnold Toynbee: Yes, yes, yes. Yes.

Syamasundara: So . . . Yes.

Dr Arnold Toynbee: Do you see any signs of change in the western world or not?

Prabhupada: Well, change can take place any moment, provided they will take this movement little seriously. Change for good.

Dr Arnold Toynbee: Change for good. Yes.

Prabhupada: Yes. And your article showed that you are also for change for good.

Dr Arnold Toynbee: Yes, yes.

Prabhupada: Yes. So our movement and your honor, we can cooperate for the good of the general people.

Dr Arnold Toynbee: Yes.

Syamasundara: How do you see this "spirit of true renunciation," as you call it, how do you see it . . .?

Dr Arnold Toynbee: Yes.

Syamasundara: How do you see that that is able to come about at this time in history?

Dr Arnold Toynbee: There are some signs in western countries, of people turning away from just money-making professions, I think. Small signs, but distinct signs perhaps. But it'll take a long time, and probably only through a great deal of suffering will people learn to change their attitude to life, I think. I think in Britain at the present, people of all classes are going for more wealth, more material standard of living, and so on, they're thinking almost entirely of this, which doesn't make for happiness and cannot really be achieved by everybody.

Syamasundara: Many young people, especially young people . . .

Dr Arnold Toynbee: Yes.

Syamasundara: Many people nowadays are finding this renunciation quite simple and easy . . .

Dr Arnold Toynbee: Yes, yes.

Syamasundara: . . . as Prabhupada was saying about the four rules and so many other activities. We may perform

something on the surface, but the renunciation is there
in our consciousness because we're giving everything to
Krishna as a service.

Dr Arnold Toynbee: Yes. What about America? (Sound of
water being poured into glasses)

Syamasundara: Oh yes.

Dr Arnold Toynbee: That's good.

Devotee: Some water, Dr Toynbee?

Dr Arnold Toynbee: No, thank you. And what about Japan?
She's an Asian country, but has been very successful in the
western way now.

Syamasundara: Well, we have two centers there also. Japan also,
we have centers.

Dr Arnold Toynbee: I get the impression the Japanese are not
very happy. They're very . . .

Prabhupada: Nobody can be happy with this materialistic way
of life. That is a fact.

Dr Arnold Toynbee: Yes, yes, yes, yes.[14]

Back in India, ISKCON's dream temples were coming up. In
Vrindavan, Srila Prabhupada envisaged a Krishna-Balaram temple
instead of the usual Radha-Krishna temple. The land they had
was on the soft sands where Krishna and Balaram had played,
and Prabhupada wanted his temple to stand out—unique, like his
multicultural global movement.

In Mayapur, an even bigger temple was coming up, and
alongside it, a full town of ISKCON, complete with foreigners
from distant lands who had embraced Vaishnavism—the prophecy
being fulfilled.

Every now and again, Srila Prabhupada would express a desire
to retire, so to speak, and not have to manage the multimillion-
dollar affairs of ISKCON, the massive constructions, the many
programmes in many parts of the world. He wanted to leave it

all to his disciples and find a peaceful corner for himself to write quietly. But that was not to be.

Not only did Prabhupada have to remain involved in managerial aspects of running ISKCON, but he also had to keep checking the books of accounts for the temples that were being built to ensure that money was being spent properly.

Side by side his own speaking engagements continued relentlessly—Rome, Paris, Geneva, Frankfurt, Melbourne—revelling in the sound of the mridangam even in distant German villages and ensuring a fusillade of kirtan drowns out miscommunication when he felt the audience wasn't quite getting his message. This part—drowning out miscommunication or acrimonious attacks at a preaching session through joyous kirtans—seemed to have almost always worked for Prabhupada.

In some places, though, the mood turned ugly. At a university in Paris, Prabhupada and his disciples had been booed and jeered at, and at a similar student gathering in Melbourne, they were attacked. Someone even pulled out a knife, and while leaving hastily, stones and ink had been thrown at their vehicles. Srila Prabhupada, who was always determined that the highest divine form was Krishna, had tried to defuse the situation by saying that he too was a 'servant of Jesus'[15] to the Melbourne students but to no avail. As the movement grew, and so did its finances, such attacks and criticism also seemed to mushroom from time to time. Prabhupada had maintained a deep sense of personal austerity but the movement, and his disciples, wanted the best for ISKCON, if they could afford it (including a controversial borrowed Rolls Royce to receive Prabhupada in). And the financial, and ideological, dissonance flared up periodically even as Srila Prabhupada grew older and frail—though not any less determined.

In Chicago and San Francisco, the rath yatras grew tremendously in size, sometimes frazzling local police and traffic, and in London, at one of the most successful rath yatra venues, the local authorities refused permission citing serious disruption in traffic. All of this was perhaps inevitable. Srila Prabhupada's movement had grown too large, too quickly. In barely five to six years since it started in New York, ISKCON was organizing some of the biggest religious gatherings in some of the world's most important cities.* As Prabhupada would often say, people weren't going to churches, but they were thronging the events of ISKCON. Some brickbats were impossible to avoid.

Meanwhile in India, building grand temples, that too with the daily management of construction led by American devotees, who had been translocated to India, was easier said than done.

At Vrindavan what was to be a grand opening of a beautiful temple with visitors and devotees from around the world failed spectacularly as the temple was not completed in time and then, having returned to Vrindavan and faced with this debacle, Srila Prabhupada fell seriously ill. By the time he recovered, it was clear that the deadlines he had in mind could not be kept. Similar problems were being faced in Bombay where municipal clearances were deadlocked.

But slowly, through ingenuity, and no doubt divine intervention, the blockades shifted and in Bombay, finally rooms could be built atop older buildings that stood on ISKCON land so that the devotees did not have to live in rat-plagued huts any more, and the land was freed for the temple to be constructed.

In Vrindavan, scarce cement was found and the tri-domed temple rose, its floors wrapped in marble. In many ways, this was a homecoming for Srila Prabhupada. This was the town where he had spent countless struggling days and nights, devoted but largely ignored, scholarly but unread. He had received little support from his gurubhais or brother monks with the same guru, Bhaktisiddhanta Saraswati. Undeterred, he had built something that seemed impossible—a global Vaishnava movement. But still, the path ahead would not be simple.

---

* About fifteen thousand people, for instance, had attended the ISKCON rath yatra at San Francisco in the summer of 1974.

17

The Great Liberation

'The entire and basic issue before this court,' ruled Judge John J. Leahy 'is whether or not the two alleged victims in this case and the defendants will be allowed to practice the religion of their choice—and this must be answered with a resounding affirmative.'

The judge, in 1977, was passing of the most infamous cases before him—a charge of brainwashing and mind control against ISKCON.

It was a price Srila Prabhupada and his now world-renowned movement was paying for the rapid expansion of the world's first global Vaishnava organization.

It was a bizarre case. A twenty-two-year-old girl complained that her mother had kidnapped her to 'deprogramme' her from her devotional allegiance to ISKCON. In turn, the mother and others filed a case on ISKCON for using mind control and brainwashing!

The surge to promote Krishna consciousness was facing its greatest challenge at its very birthplace—America. This sort of accusation, packed with orientalism, and racism, had been emerging in the West, in Europe, and now in America over the years as ISKCON's work grew.

Prabhupada's immediate response to the case in America was to fight it, honestly and vigorously, as he wrote to a disciple in the autumn of 1976: 'Regarding the point about whether our movement is bona fide, you can use the following arguments. Bhagavad Gita has got so many editions. Our books are older than the Bible. In India there are millions of Krishna temples. Let the judges and juries read our books and take the opinion of learned scholars and professors. Regarding the second point about the parents' jurisdiction over their children, here are some suggestions. Do the parents like that their children become hippies? Why don't they stop it? Do the parents like their children to become involved in prostitution and intoxication? Why don't they stop this? When the government takes the children for the draft neither the parents nor the children like it. This question should be raised. There are so many men over thirty. Are they brain-washed? It may be a minority in your country, but in other places it is the majority. The diamond seller caters to a minority. Why are they allowed to sell? Always when there is something valuable, only a minority will be able to purchase. Our books are not commercial, they are religion and philosophy. They are now feeling the weight of this movement. They thought these people would come and go, but now they see we are staying. Now we have set fire. It will go on, it cannot be stopped. You can bring big fire brigades, but the fire will act. The books are already there. Even if they stop externally, internally it will go on. Our first class campaign is book distribution. Go house to house. The real fighting is now. Krishna will give you all protection. So, chant Hare Krishna and fight. One movie expert has opined there are so many ideas in our movement. Try to get our ideas into movies. Get some Indian professors' opinions. Get a list of standing orders from Indian universities. Take this opportunity for being well advertised. They are afraid. So many young men are being affected. They have rightly said it is an epidemic. Let all the Indians say that this is bona fide. Have profuse testimony. Collect testimony in London and Toronto. Collect opinions that this is a bona fide Indian culture. This same attack came in Germany. By

propaganda you cannot suppress the truth. You cannot suppress
fire by propaganda. Now we have to become more strong to
defend. The fighting has become acute, but if you stick to the
regulative principles, Krishna will give you all strength. Whatever
is done is by Krishna's mercy. They are afraid that a different
culture is conquering over their culture. *Param drshtva nivartate.*
That is natural. If someone finds something better he'll give up the
old, how can he stop? It is a fight, do not be afraid.'[1]

So ISKCON fought it out in court to show that there had
been no coercion and its disciples had willingly taken to its path.
Srila Prabhupada had taken a strong stance against this court case,
telling one of his disciples in the course of a heated conversation,
the following:

Ramesvara:* They have a list of five or six conditions, and they
     say if all those conditions are there, then it is a suitable
     atmosphere for brainwashing. And they say we are
     imposing those conditions on our members.
Prabhupada: Yes. We are brainwashing from bad to good.
     That is our business. We are washing the brain from all
     rascaldom. That is our business. You are . . . Your brain
     is filled up with all rubbish things: meat-eating and illicit
     sex, gambling. So we are washing them. *Ceto-darpana-
     marjanam* [Cc. Antya 20.12]. *Srnvatam sva-kathah
     krishnah punya-sravana-kirtanah, hrdy antah-stho hy
     abhadrani* [SB 1.2.17]. *Abhadrani* washing. Abhadrani
     means bad things. The bad things should be washed off.
     Don't you cleanse your home? Don't you cleanse your
     room? Is not that brainwashing? So if you wash your room
     very cleansed, who blames you? But you are so rascal that
     'Why you are washing this garbage?' you are protesting.

* Disciple.

You are such an intelligent man. We are washing the
garbage; you are protesting, 'Why you are washing the
garbage? This is your intelligence. But intelligent men
wash the garbage. That is the law of nature, cleanse. That
we are doing'.[2]

Presumably, this is not quite the argument that ISKCON presented
in court. Instead, ISKCON offered the explanations offered
by some its own devotees, one of which to a noted psychiatrist
was this:

Dear Dr Lubin: In our recent telephone conversation you
asked me to articulate in a letter those questions concerning the
current brainwashing, deprogramming controversy which I feel
may be pertinent to psychiatrists interested in religious issues
and therefore a potential topic for discussion and or research
within the Committee on Psychiatry and Religion of the Group
for Advancement of Psychiatry. Speaking on my own behalf
and informally on behalf of the Hare Krishna religious society,
I might suggest that this issue raises some very serious questions
concerning possible abuses of diagnostic power in psychiatry
against religious practitioners and movements for what may
be social, political, and legal ends. Within the last ten years a
large number of new religious groups, sects, communities and
organizations have appeared on the American scene. Some are
totally new organizationally as well as theologically. And others
are, or allege to be, based upon some already existing spiritual
tradition. I myself am a member for six years of the International
Society for Krishna Consciousness, the Hare Krishna
Movement. The term Krishna consciousness is synonymous
with the term bhakti-yoga, a theistic form of yoga which finds its
scriptural authority in the Bhagavad Gita [sic] and other major

Indian devotional texts. The religious tradition represented in the West of the Hare Krishna movement, Vaishnavism, has centered the lives of hundreds of millions of Hindus for many centuries in India. This particular tradition has produced one of the world's largest and richest bodies of religious, philosophical, and mystical literature. The founder and spiritual leader of the movement, A.C. Bhaktivedanta Swami Prabhupada, has within the last ten years, offered more than fifty volumes of translation and commentary on major texts of the tradition: Bhagavad Gita, Srimad Bhagavatam, Sri Chaitanya Charitamrita, etc. These works are considered significant contributions to scholarship by specialists in the field and are studied in the universities throughout the world. See book reviews in the pamphlet, 'The Krishna Consciousness Movement is Authorized'. The members of the Hare Krishna movement, both men and women, single and married, live in strict adherence to Vedic and Vaishnava principles in regard to religious practice, chastity vows, diet, etc. The movement's nearly one hundred centers are mostly urban monasteries from which members in accordance with Vaishnava tradition perform evangelistic and proselytizing activities. The authenticity of the Hare Krishna movement has formerly been confirmed by numerous Hindu religious academic and cultural bodies both in India and U.S. Of the new religious movements which are prominent, most are allegedly based on either a Western religious tradition: the Children of God and Unification Church are Christian oriented; or an Eastern religious or philosophical tradition: Zen groups, yoga groups, Hare Krishna, etc. Of the groups based either on Western or non-Western spiritual traditions, some are seen as not accurately representing that tradition upon which they are ostensibly based. For instance, several Christian church organizations assert that the Unification Church, the Moonies, is not a bona fide Christian organization. Others, such as the Krishna consciousness movement, are accepted as legitimate, both by scholars and adherents of that tradition. As the public tends, however, to indiscriminately lump together whatever appears to be strange or out of the ordinary, the mass media refers to all such groups with the derogatory term, 'cult'. All questions of legitimacy aside, the parents of many members of such groups feel, for one reason or another, that their son or daughter has been brainwashed and they are under the "mind control" of the cult. Originally denoting the specific technique employed by Chinese Communists to effect ideological persuasion to extreme psychological and often physical coercion, the term brainwashing is defined as a colloquial term applied to any technique designed to manipulate human thought or action against the desired will or knowledge of the individual. That's from the *Encyclopaedia Britannica*.

In popular usage it becomes an imprecise, all-encompassing and pejorative term used to describe any kind of persuasion or behavior [sic] with which one may disagree. In psychology it is not generally accepted, I am told, as a legitimate clinical term. How does one wash another's brain? The dynamics of 'conversion' in the case of Krishna consciousness are quite informal. Talking with devotees, reading scripture, meditation, etc. and certainly do not include the application of any type of psychological coercion against the desire, will, or knowledge of the potential or novice devotee. Although life in a Hare Krishna community is communal and monastic with well-defined guidelines affecting the behavior and religious practice, it is in fact, a good deal more open then many or most types of monastic communities. The Hare Krishna member is totally free to increase or decrease his involvement with the Society at any time he or she wishes. Because full commitment, as in any religious tradition, is not easy. A high percentage of those who join eventually leave. If brainwashing is what we're doing, we're not very good at it. Distressed however by an apparent rejection of their own values and lifestyle, and unable to account for what may be radical or abrupt change in the lives of their offspring, some parents of cult members, believing that their sons and daughters have been brainwashed, hire someone like Ted Patrick to forcefully abduct and debrainwash [sic] or deprogram them. What is being called deprogramming involves extreme coercive tactics, including rather intense psychological and often physical intimidation aimed at inducing the cult member to renounce his or her religious beliefs and practices. (See affidavit enclosed.) During deprogramming the victim is isolated from his particular religious community and is physically restrained. His religious apparel and paraphernalia, scriptures, prayer beads, sacred pictures etc., may be confiscated and destroyed and his beliefs and religious convictions vilified. In one case a pregnant mother was physically beaten. In another, a Hare Krishna devotee who refused to violate his religious vow of reciting names of God, had his mouth filled with ice and gagged. Such deprogramming lasts often for several weeks with deprogrammers working in shifts while the deprogrammee [sic] is deprived of sufficient sleep. All this so that the brainwashed youth can be returned to a normal state and once again be able to make free choices. Deprogramming often ends with the victim signing a statement admitting that he had been brainwashed. Perhaps just as the confessions of those accused of being witches during the

Holy Inquisitions were proof of the existence of witchcraft, such confessions by members of religious groups are taken as sufficient proof of brainwashing by those committed to the idea of cultic brainwashing. But such tactics are a gross violation of fundamental human and constitutional rights . . .[3]

These were important points which shed light into the kind of questioning ISKCON had started to face by the mid-1970s in the West.

Such arguments and others in the same vein presented by ISKCON's lawyers convinced the judge that the movement, which at that time had around two thousand followers in the United States, was a 'bona fide religion with roots in India that go back thousands of years'.[4]

Judge Leahy pointed out in his judgment that, 'The freedom of religion is not to be abridged because it is unconventional in its beliefs and practices or because it is approved or disapproved of by the mainstream of society or more conventional religions.'[5]

He said that the brainwashing allegation was incorrect. 'It appears to the court that the people rest their case on an erroneous minor premise to arrive at a fallacious conclusion. The record is devoid of one specific allegation of a misrepresentation or an act of deception on the of the part of any defendant.'[6]

Therefore, to attack ISKCON and prevent its work, said the judge, 'be it circuitous, direct or well-intentioned or not, presents a clear and present danger to this most fundamental, basic and eternally needed right of our citizens—freedom of religion'.[7]

These allegations and this case were a landmark both for ISKCON, and for the broader question of freedom of Hindu groups in the West. It established that whatever work that ISKCON was doing was firmly within the contours of law and the framework for freedom of religion. But it was also an example of the kind of turmoil Srila Prabhupada was firefighting even as it seemed that his global movement was finally settling down with established centres around the world, and importantly, in India.

The news came at a time when Srila Prabhupada's body was increasingly breaking down. He suspected again and again that it might be time for him to go, that he could die any day. And yet, again and again he seemed to return from the brink. He could not, for the most part, walk any more without assistance and he felt, again and again, that time was running out.

And therefore his personal single-minded focus was on producing and publishing books. The story of Srila Prabhupada had two aspects—one, when he was out in the world promoting, building, preaching, teaching and then, another, his own private space, dead in the night, when he was relentlessly translating, without a hesitation offering his deep spiritual discoveries on the most profound Vaishnava texts.

During his lifetime, often working in the most adverse circumstances, Srila Prabhupada himself produced seventy-one books. This number would be astonishing for any writer but with Prabhupada it needs to be taken in the context that most of this was done in the last decade of his life when he was a septuagenarian, frequently unwell and building, simultaneously, a global movement.

Through his last decade, when ISKCON created more than a hundred centres around the world, Srila Prabhupada never slept for more than two hours in a night—between 10 p.m. to midnight, for at midnight he would rise to write, translate, compose till the break of dawn every single day in a feat which ought to be considered one of the greatest, and most taxing, in the history of the written word.

Prabhupada, through the course of the journey of ISKCON from its humble roots in Manhattan to its multimillion-dollar temples around the world, never forgot the fundamental purpose—to spread the word, in this case quite literally, of Krishna.

Therefore, when he urged his disciples to publish and sell more copies of the books, Srila Prabhupada saw it as a fundamental aspect of the practice of ISKCON. Taking books and going out into the streets to sell them, thus, became a rite of passage for monks within ISKCON.

By 1973, ISKCON was selling more than four hundred thousand copies of its books in one year. The following year, sales of their seminal magazine, *Back to Godhead*, hit four million copies. The Bhaktivedanta Book Trust was created as an independent entity with a strict rule that proceeds from the sales of the books would be divided half-and-half between funding more publication and sale, and building temples and other physical centres. When more and more people became life members of ISKCON, 50 per cent of the money was ploughed into the work of the Book Trust and the rest for other work. As sales exploded, new kinds of expensive papers were used for publishing books, especially for the Western market, where they could be distributed at high rates to raise funds for the growing organization.

In German, Spanish, Japanese and every other language outside India and at home, wherever Srila Prabhupada could find any interest, he would promote his books. The word of God had to be placed before every eye.

And like Ganesha with his broken tooth for Ved Vyasa,* writing incessantly the Mahabharata, so was Srila Prabhupada, the scribe of Krishna.

Ideally, Prabhupada would have liked to focus only on this writing but even after the creation of the Governing Body Commission, internecine quarrels continued to trouble ISKCON and its founder, who wanted nothing more than to go relatively quiet, kept having to keep the flock in check. Everything from the construction to book distribution kept throwing up problems.

---

* The story of Ganesha and Ved Vyasa.

In 1971, he wrote, 'GBC [Governing Body Commission] does not mean to control a center. GBC means to see that the activities of a center go on nicely. I do not know why Tamala* is exercising his absolute authority. That is not the business of GBC. The president, treasurer and secretary are responsible for managing the center. GBC is to see that things are going nicely but not to exert absolute authority. That is not in the power of GBC. Tamala should not do like that. The GBC men cannot impose anything on the men of a center without consulting all of the GBC members first. A GBC member cannot go beyond the jurisdiction of his power. We are in the experimental stage but in the next meeting of the GBC members they should form a constitution how the GBC members manage the whole affair. But it is a fact that the local president is not under the control of the GBC. Yes, for improvement of situations such as this I must be informed of everything.'[8]

In January 1975, for instance, in a letter from Bombay to Brooklyn, Srila Prabhupada wrote, 'Regarding the controversy about book distribution techniques, you are right. Our occupation must be honest. Everyone should adore our members as honest. If we do something which is deteriorating to the popular sentiments of the public in favor of our movement, that is not good. Somehow or other we should not become unpopular in the public eye. These dishonest methods must be stopped. It is hampering our reputation all over the world. Money collected for feeding people in India should be collected under the name ISKCON Food Relief. Not any other name. And every farthing of that money must be sent to India, or better yet, buy food grains there and ship them here and we will distribute. But every farthing collected for that purpose must be used for that purpose.'[9]

To accommodate people who could not immediately give up familial desires, Srila Prabhupada had allowed marriages but now

---

* One of the disciples.

children of devotees were crowding ISKCON temples. New rules had to be created. ISKCON could not become an extension of the family life of the devotees—it had been designed for Krishna bhakti and could not be entangled in the quagmire from which Abhay Charan De had once escaped.

But the answer was not to drive away anyone who could lead an austere ascetic life either—this was the dichotomy of ISKCON. Krishna consciousness was for everybody and even within the ashram, the various types of devotees—celibates and married couples—created confusion among what was the ISKCON way.

This was a pivotal point for the organization of ISKCON. A drastic change could have been made but Srila Prabhupada chose the path of openness. As he said, if he had been conservative or strict he could never have achieved what he did. The example he gave of how his life had made him open-minded was from his early days in New York, sharing a room and refrigerator with a hippie. The man kept pieces of meat for his cat in the fridge and, without a choice, Prabhupada, a man as determinedly against meat as is perhaps possible, kept his vegetarian food in the same fridge.[10] Yet he did it. The reasoning was simple—in his path to spreading Krishna consciousness that was where life had brought him in that moment—and so he embraced it.

As he embraced questions about race and gender, constantly trying to explain that divisions as they existed, including racism and patriarchy, were in the realm of the material world—before the beatific gaze of Krishna, everyone was the same. This was not an easy lesson to preach in America in the 1970s, abuzz with questions of racial equality and gender divide, but Srila Prabhupada's honesty was that of a preacher. If asked, he would have to offer his unqualified and unabashed opinion—and if someone did not want to hear his opinion, then too he had a fallback option, sing Hare Krishna, Hare Krishna, Krishna Krishna, Hare Hare/ Hare Rama, Hare Rama, Rama Rama, Hare Hare.[11] This was a simple solution to avoid any culture collisions—while chanting, one couldn't really argue!

What distressed him the most were sannyasis breaking the vow of celibacy. But he allowed them too to remain in the temples and within ISKCON as grihastha or householder monks, allowing them to get married. 'My Godbrothers and sannyasis in India criticise me for giving brahmana and sannyasa initiation and installing deities in the West and allowing women to stay in temples. But for all that, I am expanding Krishna consciousness. And for all their strictness, they are doing nothing. If I discriminate, then I will be alone again, as I was in Vrindavana, and "again become a mouse".'[12]

And becoming a mouse would not do. Instead, as had been recommended traditionally for Vaishnava ascetics, they had to be as soft as a rose and as hard as a thunderbolt.[13] Srila Prabhupada had to steer the ISKCON ship through words of wisdom, and where needed, chastisement. Whether meeting the scion of the Ford automobile fortune or Indian Prime Minister Indira Gandhi, fearful of attacks on her life,* or her successor Morarji Desai, Prabhupada in his last years had to play a very delicate and critical role to ensure the longevity of his movement.

His efforts—no matter where he was in the world—were to ensure that his designated GBC would be able to run the movement sensibly and without strife. But till the end, he had to be the guiding force, never quite able to completely detach from the day-to-day workings of ISKCON—whether it was commenting on the correct kind of wheels for rath yatra chariots in San Francisco or worrying about money being siphoned off by building contractors in Bombay.

Those were turbulent times, both for ISKCON and Prabhupada's home country India. From 25 June 1975 to 21 March

* From radicals and terrorists.

1977, India was under the rule of Prime Minister Indira Gandhi, who had declared Emergency, taking upon her office all political power. Srila Prabhupada, never acutely political, seems to have, interestingly, discussed the Emergency, albeit briefly. When the Emergency ended and Gandhi called an election, she was soundly defeated, which included losing her own seat in Parliament. Told by a senior disciple that Gandhi had lost the election held after the dreaded Emergency, Prabhupada heard about the developments in India intently.

Prabhupada, while rarely offering political commentary, seemed to have been prescient about the fundamental flaw in democracy, which is described as populism today, that popular support leading to power could be very damaging if the voters and the politicians are not intellectually evolved and morally sound. The idea that the person who gains power must rise above the trappings of the position is something Prabhupada seemed to have held high as an ideal for public life. He was acutely aware that without a spiritual core, leadership, especially in politics, could, indeed would, be damaging.

Srila Prabhupada was also acutely aware of the mortality of his body—a body he was not very attached to—and he often spoke about the time when he might die. But his emphasis on what would live on was unambiguous, as he said, 'I will never die. I shall live from my books, and you will utilize.'[14] His body, said Prabhupada, 'was an old machine. The more you cure it, the more it gets worse. But my work never stops. That keeps on going. My main work is to write these books, and that is going on.'[15] By this time, around 1977, ISKCON was about to hit cumulative book sales figures of sixty-five million; every year it was reaching sales of fifteen to twenty million copies. It had become one of the greatest single-institution publishing ventures that the world had known.[16]

Srila Prabhupada died in the autumn of 1977. Towards the end he moved to Rishikesh, the pilgrimage town in the Himalayas, where after a few blissful days in the clean mountains beside the gurgling river Ganga, he started to feel unwell.

An unperturbed and prescient Prabhupada—after all, it was only his body—asked to be moved immediately to Vrindavan. When he arrived there, he announced that most of his 'material' activities including the need to eat were fading out, he was being given, in his words, freedom from the material world by Krishna. And he insisted once again to his GBC members that they should now operate as if he were not there.[17]

But there were many loose ends to be tied up. What structure would save ISKCON in India from being taken over by vested interests when Srila Prabhupada was gone? A trust structure. What were the chances that ISKCON would come under attack from envious parties at home (especially) and abroad in a post-Prabhupada era? Significant. How would its global properties and money be distributed and organized? Equitably, making them independent but co-owners of ISKCON under one umbrella.

A will was created—after extensive consultation with the GBC group—to ensure that there were no future clashes.

Some of the concerns would come true, dangerously, in the weeks that followed when mobs of local miscreants attacked the ISKCON temple in Mayapur and viciously hurt some resident monks. The local chapter of ISKCON fought back—not least with one monk firing a gun at rampaging mobs who were attempting to injure male devotees and disrobe female devotees, and by gathering its many supporters for a mass protest. But concerns about life after Srila Prabhupada remained.

From spring through to summer of 1977, the devotees of ISKCON prayed and chanted non-stop for their guru who seemed frailer than ever, his food intake negligible and sleep nonexistent. Emotionally, Srila Prabhupada seemed in a deeper and more delicate place than before, frequently moved to tears or in a meditative trance before the deity. It was as if he was—almost literally—feeling a closer presence of the Godhead as he walked towards Him.

If there was only one true Vaishnava in the world, that person could save the world, Srila Prabhupada taught his disciples during his last months—and to his followers, he was that one Vaishnava. But he reminded them to 'follow' but not 'imitate'. That difference was, no doubt, acutely clear to him through his own life. He had followed the path of his guru but to have imitated it would have perhaps been to never set out for America without any real strategy for success.

That summer when Srila Prabhupada felt a little better, he made one last trip to England, even though he travelled lying on a mattress at the back of a car to the airport and on a wheelchair to the flight.

In England, reunited with many of his international devotees, Prabhupada learnt that book sales in European languages had surpassed sales in English in America. This, by all counts, was an astonishing feat, and Srila Prabhupada exclaimed, 'No author throughout the world has written so many books—Shakespeare, Milton, Dickens. Neither their books have been so widely read or with such appreciation.'[18]

But the strain was beginning to tell. For a man who had always been certain that he wanted to meet his creator while living on the pious land of Vrindavan, now, in England, he confessed to the feeling of not wanting to return to India. 'In India, whatever project I made the government has simply given me obstacles. I had to tax my brain so much . . . From the members of Parliament to the members of the street, everywhere there is suspicion that I have brought the CIA.* Such a mistake they have made!'[19]

---

* Central Intelligence Agency, the secret service of the United States of America.

This is a rare but startling revelation into some of the reasons why Srila Prabhupada found it problematic to expand ISKCON at the pace at which he wanted, even after he returned to acclaim and adulation from America. His dream Bombay temple was to be inaugurated.

Srila Prabhupada celebrated his eighty-first birthday in London with some talk of him going to America—but his health had been fluctuating and it was not clear that he would be able to take the exertion.

Instead, the Acharya of ISKCON, who was now barely able to move without help and a wheelchair, and was afflicted with problems in his kidneys and other related ailments, travelled to Bombay from London. He would try and see the opening of his dream Bombay temple.

But Srila Prabhupada landed in a Bombay where the finishing touches were still being given to the temple, and the construction, the heat and dust, imperilled his health even further. The best doctors were called, as were the finest Ayurvedic *kavirajas*. But not much improved. And the guru decided that without waiting any further for the opening of the Bombay temple, he would return to Vrindavan. Devotees even tried to reason with him by saying that if he remained in Bombay, his will to live (and see the temple opening) would be higher than if he left for Vrindavan but their spiritual master knew that it was time. And so it was that as summer turned to autumn, Srila Prabhupada returned to his beloved Vrindavan.

Conversations between key devotees on Srila Prabhupada's treatment is a good example of the kind of crisis his health was going through* veered from the various ailments that the Acharya might have—kidney failure was the common consensus—to what

---

* All the interlocutors in this exchange were prominent disciples of Srila Prabhupada.

kind of doctor would be right to treat him (while allopathy was considered but there was a strong sense that traditional Ayurvedic medicine and physicians or *kavirajas* would be able to help).

Bhagatji: So should we look for some good Ayurved physician?
Tamala Krishna: Well, Prabhupada had a dream this morning, and in this dream, he saw one ramanuja-vaidya preparing this makara-dhvaja medicine. So Prabhupada's dreams are transcendental. So that means Krishna has given some idea how to get Prabhupada treated. So we called one ramanuja here tonight. I don't know what the discussion was. I couldn't follow the meaning. But in any case, Prabhupada gave us an opportunity to try this allopathic medicine. He was never in favor of allopathic medicine, but all of his disciples were in favor to let us try it. So Prabhupada subjected himself to our treatment. And factually you saw he was vomiting, dizzy, and losing sleep. Then yesterday we didn't give any medicine, and he was much better off. You heard how he was speaking strongly. So we already got indication. Finally we spoke with Srila Prabhupada that "We want you to direct us." So Prabhupada said, "So you are ready to follow whatever I direct?" So we said, "Yes." He said, "Then no more allopathic. It is finished." We're trying allopathic from our side, but it didn't work. Factually it didn't work. This Dr Gopal* promised in four day he will sit up. And Dr Ghosh, afterwards he told me, "That is rubbish." He said, "How could he . . . He wants to gain the confidence of the patient." But this kind of promising, it's childish to say like that. Anybody could know Prabhupada was not going to sit up in four days. Dr Ghosh is a very competent, confident doctor, there's

_____
* The allopathic doctor.

no doubt. But that whole science of Western medicine is very speculative. It's guessing work. Anyway, so many devotees were telling their stories. I told that my father, a half a year ago, he had arthritis of the hip, so they put a new hip. Then it came on this side, they gave a new hip here. Then eight weeks he was in the hospital. They said, "Now you're better. Let's get you up and you can walk." After eight weeks, so many operations. They stood him up and immediately he had heart attack and died. They're so expert that that's how they killed him. Then we know one devotee, he is in New York temple, he was a nurse, head nurse assisting one of the biggest surgeons who was operating on the presidents. She said that during the operation they would joke with each other. One day one man came in and complained, "I have a pain in my side." They took x-ray and found that during the operation they had left a scissors inside. These are the mentalities of these people. The whole science is very . . .

Hamsaduta: Dubious.

Tamala Krishna: Doubtful. Dubious. So Prabhupada has more faith . . . Another thing, kaviraji medicine is not dangerous. Whereas these men, you can see how many side effects they have, these Western medicines. Prabhupada becomes dizzy, he cannot sleep, he vomits. And as soon as we agree to x-ray, x-ray is only the first step, then there'll be more and more and more. When you call in a doctor it means you are ready to take his treatment. When you ask for an x-ray it means that after the x-ray you're ready to accept whatever they advise. Otherwise why do you call for x-ray? That's the whole point. So the real issue we have to decide is whether Prabhupada wants to take the allopathic medicine or not. If he says, "I don't want allopathic medicine," what is the use of taking x-ray? Because the kavirajas don't care for X-rays. They say that simply by pulse they can see everything. Just like this man, he took the pulse and immediately he reached for the kidneys. We did not tell him anything, but he took the pulse and immediately he reached for the kidneys and the stomach. And he said, "Kidneys are completely malfunctioning, and the fire of digestion is nearly extinguished." I think that's a very practical statement if you think about it. Prabhupada, he's passing urine, he can pass stool, but what is the real problem, the biggest problem? There's no taste, no appetite. And that you have to admit, he has no idea how to get appetite, Dr Gopal. He has no idea. He's thinking this and this. He doesn't even understand there's a fire of digestion. Where does it mention that Krishna is sitting as the fire of digestion in the stomach? Where does it say that in the allopathic books? (laughs) It doesn't. But Prabhupada has said it from the very beginning: "I have no digestion." So the question is how to wake up that fire. And they can't do this, these allopathic doctors. Maybe the kavirajas can do it.

Bhagatji: So there is one Vedic kaviraja in Mathura. Should I bring him?

Tamala Krishna: Well I don't know. First of all there's now already two kavirajas involved. Maybe we should first let this ramanuji do his work.

Bhagatji: Today, he came today.[20]

When Srila Prabhupada left Bombay, the question that hung for a long time in the chanting-filled air was—shouldn't he be moved to a good hospital? But Prabhupada was adamant—he would not go to a hospital. He did not wish to submit the remaining part of his life to hospitals and modern treatments; he wanted to submit to Krishna.

At Vrindavan, his spirits were lifted by a devotee showing
his beautiful newly published books—one hundred and twenty
thousand copies of the Krishna trilogy, sixty thousand of the
Srimad Bhagavatam (Second Canto) and ten thousand Isha
Upanishads. All for distribution in . . . Yugoslavia.

News of the beautiful New Vrindavan in America came, as
did stories of successes from elsewhere, and at Vrindavan his
devotees constantly urged Srila Prabhupada to stay. Till the end,
questions of money and property and various tasks of ISKCON
kept floating up to its guru. For instance, this exchange only
days before Srila Prabhupada's death between a senior devotee,
Prabhupada's son Vrindavan De and Prabhupada himself. The
topic was payments taken from ISKCON and the money due to
it for the distribution of books (in which Vrindavan De played an
important role):

> Vrindavan De: . . . I want that loan for the time being. I shall
> pay it back.
> Tamala Krishna: But that loan . . . You have to understand
> something. The Society cannot loan . . .
> Prabhupada: All the money he can take, loan.
> Tamala Krishna: On the basis of that money.
> Vrindavan De: It is for a month or three or four months.
> Tamala Krishna: No, no, that's not what Prabhupada's saying.
> On the basis of those postal receipts. Is that what you're
> saying, Srila Prabhupada? You can put up those postal
> receipts, that money, to the bank, and they can issue you
> loan against that money.
> Vrindavan De: I don't think so. I don't know, actually, because
> I don't have any idea about it.
> Tamala Krishna: Because, Srila Prabhupada, our Society
> cannot loan money for a business like this. This is not
> our Society's business at all . . . We can't start loaning

money for these kind of businesses. It's against the Society's memorandum and rules that money can be given to individuals for their personal businesses. This is a charitable society. It's bounded by the Society's charity laws . . . I mean we would lose our charitable status, because the accounts are audited every year. So it will look very . . . In fact, if we do that, then they may raise objection to the stipend also . . . Furthermore, then we'll have to charge interest, and if we charge interest, that gets us into a lot of trouble also. As a Society, we're not supposed to be doing business, profit-making business.[21]

Srila Prabhupada had tried hard to leave such nitty-gritties to be dealt with by his senior disciples but they plagued him till the very end. It was clear that Srila Prabhupada was on the transcendental plane, in touch with his dear Lord. He was willing to offer till the very end of his life his instructions for the well-being of Krishna's organization.

His own preference was to give up eating and drinking altogether and survive for as long as, or to be more accurate, as little as, possible. He had made up his mind to go.

Perhaps the best way to understand Srila Prabhupada's behaviour in his final days and weeks is to consider the attitude of a parent who knows their time with their children is coming to an end and yet their love and desire to protect their children keeps them attached to their families.

Once or twice, on the coaxing of his devotees, he agreed to drink a little and eat a very small amount just to keep his vitals working, but his heart was not in it. He made his final apologies for his 'temperamental' behaviour (the use of the word 'rascal', for instance, to his devotees).

When he went back to the Godhead on 14 November 1977, it was in quietude and amidst the chanting that he had placed upon every lip he could, Hare Krishna, Hare Krishna, Krishna Krishna, Hare Hare/ Hare Rama, Hare Rama, Rama Rama, Hare Hare.

18

Conclusion: Going Back Home

'Our mission is to go back to home, back to Godhead,' said Srila Prabhupada frequently. [1]

This could be said to have been the theme of his life. Prabhupada had always urged his followers to be on a journey that, step by step, brought them closer to the final goal—a return home to his Krishna.

That was the spiritual direction of Prabhupada's inner life, even as he struggled to build a worldwide movement to pronounce and propagate Krishna bhakti. Even though chanting and kirtans, and the distribution of books and prasadam formed such a vital part of Prabhupada's external life, his inner life kept returning to the quietness of the night, to the ink scratch of his writing and his dictaphone. To present the purport of the Vedic scriptures to the world—go back home, back to Krishna.

Srila Prabhupada not only traversed the path home but he put words to the journey, creating a cartography of prayer, charting through tens of thousands of words a route, a roadmap, his eternal offering to Krishna—and a guide for all those who followed him.

His success was in his failures. He had tried to explain to his family the urgent pull he felt towards the worship of Krishna, and urged them to become part of it. Had tried to make his family part of something he believed fervently was the only means to salvation. He had tried to explain that from his very childhood this hunger to serve Krishna had been the one recurring factor in his life, even though he had tried many a path from nationalism to capitalism. He had tried to include them.

That failed, but the process liberated Abhay Charan De to become Swami Bhaktivedanta and then Srila Prabhupada.

He did not arrive in America looking to be a guru. He came, primarily, to share Vedic knowledge through distribution of his books. He had hoped that someone would listen; he was, in fact, wary of becoming a guru. As he said, 'One should go to a guru for spiritual advancement of life, not as a fashion. People go to a guru as a fashion. My Guru Maharaja used to say that "Don't make a guru just like you keep a dog, as a fashion." Nowadays it has become a fashion to keep a dog. In the European, American countries it is a compulsory fashion to have a dog. Everyone keeps a dog. And they love dog very much, more than anything!'[2]

But he did become a guru—to some of the most unlikely people. From his efforts at building a movement in India—which failed—Srila Prabhupada had drawn the lesson of not depending too much on the Indian community in the West but to reaching out instead to Westerners, Americans, the British, French and Germans, to teach them.

In this he succeeded more effectively than his wildest dreams.

As someone who grew up in a British colony struggling for independence, Prabhupada was conscious of the limitations of that legacy. He told the story of how a Calcutta High Court judge was asked in 1914 by a member of the British ruling class what he would do if the Germans came to India. Mukherjee replied that he would welcome them. When asked why, the judge replied, 'You [the British] have taught us to make like this, so we shall do that. Because you have simply taught us this, how to obey your orders. So anyone who will come, we shall do this. The idea is the slave mentality. The Englishmen, in an organized way, they taught the Indians how to become servant of the Englishmen. We have seen. It is Gandhi's movement that he dismantled this idea of white prestige; otherwise, we were taught like that. Formerly, in our childhood, it was the advancement of civilization if one could imitate the English fashion. So we should not make that a fashion. Guru is not a fashion.'[3]

Srila Prabhupada, therefore, worked to create a band of disciples and an organization where his followers could think for themselves, and be free to take their own decisions within broad boundaries. In this, he succeeded only partly as till the very end, he had to keep reminding his disciples that it was up to them to maintain the sanctity of ISKCON, and ensure that it stood for the right values and was able to operate without rifts.

Till the end, ISKCON needed his guidance in many ways. But through this process, he was able to achieve things that once seemed so impossible that they were magical—being able to procure land in Mayapur, Bombay and Vrindavan, being able to build his own temples, of the kind that he wanted, in the heartland of Vaishnavas. Even though he urged his disciples again and again to learn how to work, it was his own interventions and handholding at every step—whether it was to win legal battles or ensure that work was completed on time—that finally created the series of pivotal temples for ISKCON.

'Now you have everything, respect, philosophy, money, temples, books, all these things I have given, but I am an old man and my notice is already there. Now it is up to you all how to manage it. If you cannot increase it, you should at least maintain what I have given you. You cannot accuse me that I have not given you anything. So it is a great responsibility you now have,'[4] Prabhupada wrote to one of his key disciples in Los Angeles in the summer of 1975.

In 1976, only a year before his death, Prabhupada noted in a lecture, 'So it is said by parampara system . . . do not make any friendship, or . . . compromise with [the] mind. Do not do this. As I was saying yesterday, my Guru Maharaj used to say that, "When you get up, you beat your mind with shoes hundred times, and when you go to the bed, you beat your mind with broomsticks a hundred times." Then there will be no compromise, if you simply beat your mind. That is required. This is [the] Vedic system . . . Therefore, it is advised, "Either your son or disciple, you should always chastise them. Never give them lenience." So, little lenience, immediately so many faults will grow. Now for our practical life we are known all over the world as shaven headed. Is it not? Now we are becoming hair headed. We are forgetting shaving, because there is a little leniency . . . This is discrepancy . . . It is not desirable that in grown-up ages also you should be chastised. That is not desirable. That is also difficult, because when the disciple or the son is grown up, if he is chastised, then he breaks. So before being chastised, you should be conscious that this is our rules and regulation.'[5]

Prabhupada was prescient enough to understand that while his movement had succeeded in a manner which he could have scarcely imagined only a decade ago, the swiftness of his success meant that many of even the oldest disciples of ISKCON were but very new to Vaishnava life; they were, in his oft-used word, 'neophytes'. This remained one of his worries till the end.

But Srila Prabhupada was able to detach his own spiritual journey and message from even the boundaries of the physical movement that he gave birth to. Therein lies evidence of his spiritual strength. He led ISKCON till his death in the autumn of 1977 but especially in the later years, he kept on the process of detaching himself from the splendour and clamour of his movement.

The Prabhupada story is full of dramatic arcs and exclamatory moments. But perhaps its real radiance lies in Prabhupada's consistent efforts to keep alive, and intensify, his very private faith and devotion.

Again and again, he was pulled back into the issues and problems in running worldwide ISKCON every day when all he wanted was to be left alone to write his books in peace—but in a curious sort of way it only made his writing more determined, more urgent. He knew what he had to finish.

It was almost as if Srila Prabhupada knew that whatever the institutional issues of ISKCON—including quarrels between his designated core disciples—his work would live on, not least through his voluminous writings.

In more than one way, the life of Srila Prabhupada should be considered above and beyond the legacy and history of ISKCON, the institution he founded. Prabhupada was the most influential Vaishnava spiritual leader to emerge in the twentieth century; the scale of his influence in the Western world can be considered more expansive than that of Swami Vivekananda in promoting Hinduism around the world, even though the ISKCON movement does not yet have a history as long as Vivekananda's Ramakrishna Mission.

Prabhupada was a contemporary of other Hindu spiritual leaders from India like Maharishi Mahesh Yogi[*] and Paramahansa Yogananda.[†] But his footprint, in terms of the spread of ISKCON and its vast publishing efforts, outstripped the work of either Mahesh Yogi or Yogananda. Even though The Beatles first turned to the Maharishi for spiritual succour, it was with Srila Prabhupada that George Harrison continued a deep association till the end of his life. In both size and depth, Srila Prabhupada achieved much more than these contemporary gurus.

While choosing to keep his movement and himself away from engaging with the very politically explosive times in which ISKCON

---

[*] 1918–2008.
[†] 1893–1952.

grew, it might be worthy to consider that Srila Prabhupada did, in fact, respond to the politics around him. Only, he did so in an unusual manner. By continuing to focus on poorer communities to preach and embrace, even as ISKCON grew wealthier, Srila Prabhupada kept alive a deep commitment to public service. He decreed, for instance, that no one should go hungry within a 10-km radius of an ISKCON temple. Today, ISKCON Bangalore has created the world's biggest midday meal programme called Akshaya Patra, where vegetarian food following the recipes that Prabhupada himself so loved is served free of cost to underprivileged students. Srila Prabhupada understood that spiritual succour must be provided to those, like the hippies who he first worked with, who are perhaps most in need of it. This is a lesson he never allowed himself or his organization to ever forget. He instinctively and through experience understood that spiritual opinions or concepts might not be readily accepted depending on the politics of the time and therefore distilled the practice of his message to simple ideas: chanting or singing and feeding the hungry.

The life of Srila Prabhupada is also instructive in its detailing of the spiritual journey, from the temporal to the transcendental. Unlike Vivekananda, Mahesh Yogi and Yogananda, who all entered monastic life in their boyhood, so to speak, Prabhupada had a far more complex and, therefore real, journey. Certainly neither Vivekananda nor Mahesh Yogi or Yogananda married or had children, none of them engaged with familial responsibilities or worked to sustain a family in any serious way during their lives. Only Vivekananda worried about his mother's finances and that she should not be reduced to penury, but that concern, while potent, does not compare in intensity to the kind of familial responsibilities and hardships that Srila Prabhupada dealt with. At least one of his children, Vrindavan De, remained connected to him through his entire lifetime.

While he felt spiritual stirrings early in life, Prabhupada actually followed the template of Hindu life, leaving his family at an advanced age, which would be close to contemporary 'retirement age', to plunge into monasticism. By the time he took his monastic vows, Abhay Charan De had completed almost an entire cycle of what would constitute 'normal family life'.

By continuing an inner life simultaneously with his family activities and responsibilities, by being in God consciousness while being mired in the world, Srila Prabhupada's journey echoes our own hurdles as we confront the pressures of the world while perhaps ignoring the inner call.

Life in the world and life of the spirit have often been constructed as opposing forces, and indeed they often are. But Srila Prabhupada's life shows the possibilities for spiritual redemption even after, or along with, the fulfilment of familial life, a path for sannyasa for the ordinary man.

Srila Prabhupada's journey is not that of the precocious or the child prodigy, but it is the dogged, earnest path of the earnest believer whose faith lifts him to extraordinary heights. Thus, Prabhupada speaks to us not from the pedestal—though that is where he really belonged and his life finally took him—but from amidst the jostle and noise of the crowd.

Through the jostle of building and running a global movement, Srila Prabhupada recognized that as important as the logistics was to advance the cause of Krishna consciousness, the bigger it became, the more time and energy it could take up, which might, ironically, distract from the path of seeking the divine.

This recognition that is the underlying theme of his life is perhaps his greatest message—to serve the Supreme Godhead Krishna without a tinge of selfishness and to build with attachment to Lord Krishna an organization to exclusively serve His mission.

Therein lies his greatness.

Bibliography

Satsvarupa Dasa Goswami, *Srila Prabhupada Lilamrta*, The Bhaktivedanta
Book Trust, 1980, Vol. 1–6.

John Marriott, *The Other Empire: Metropolis, India and Progress in the
Colonial Imagination*, Manchester University Press, 2003.

Thomas R. Trautmann, *Aryans and British India* (Second Indian ed.),
New Delhi: YODA Press, 2006 (1997), p 117.

Rebecca J. Manring, *Reconstructing Tradition: Advaita Acharya and
Gaudiya Vaishnavism at the Cusp of the Twentieth Century*, Columbia
University Press.

Michael Edwardes, *Red Year*, London: Sphere Books, 1975.

Paul Oliver, *Hinduism and the 1960s: The Rise of a Counter-Culture*,
London: Bloomsbury, 2014.

David Lockwood, *Calcutta Under Fire: The Second World War Years*, Rupa
Publications.

Jeffery D. Long, *Hinduism in America: A Convergence of Worlds*, London:
Bloomsbury Academic.

Martin A. Lee and Bruce Shlain, *Acid Dreams: The Complete Social History
of LSD: The CIA, the Sixties, and Beyond*, Grove Press, 1992, p 97.

Lucy Sante, 'The Nutty Professor', *The New York Times Book Review*,
Timothy Leary: A Biography by Robert Greenfield, Harcourt,
Incorporated, 2006.

Eric Foner, *Reconstruction: America's Unfinished Revolution, 1863–1877*, The New American Nation, New York: Harper & Row, 1988.

Joshua M. Greene, *Here Comes The Sun*, New Jersey: John Wiley & Sons, 2010.

Ashley Kahn (ed.), *George Harrison on George Harrison: Interviews and Encounters*, Chicago, IL: Chicago Review Press, 2020.

E. Burke Rochford Jr., *Hare Krishna in America*, Rutgers University Press.

Forty Years of Chanting: A Study of the Hare Krishna Movement from its Foundation to the Present Day in *The Hare Krishna Movement: Forty Years of Chant and Change*, edited by Graham Dwyer and Richard J. Cole, London: I.B. Tauris, 2007.

Edwin F. Bryant and Maria L. Ekstrand, *The Hare Krishna Movement: The Postcharismatic Fate of a Religious Transplant*, New York: Columbia University Press.

Ravi M. Gupta (2014), Ravi M. Gupta (ed.), *Caitanya Vaiṣṇava Philosophy: Tradition, Reason and Devotion*, Burlington, VT: Ashgate.

Ferdinando Sardella (2013), *Modern Hindu Personalism: The History, Life, and Thought of Bhaktisiddhanta Sarasvati* (reprint ed.), New York, NY: Oxford University Press.

Phillip Murphy, Raoul Goff (eds.), *Prabhupada Sarasvati Thakur: The Life and Precepts of Srila Bhaktisidhanta Sarasvati* (first limited ed.), 1997, Eugene.

Notes

Introduction

1. Joshua M. Greene, *Here Comes The Sun*, New Jersey: John Wiley & Sons, 2010, p 91.
2. Ibid., pp. 87–88.
3. See https://youtu.be/GXfkdLZLqXg.
4. Ibid.
5. With incense and chanting filling the air he said 'hare krishna' and slipped away; two holy men flew from London 'to ease George's path into the next life'. The Free Library. (n.d.). Retrieved January 24, 2022, from https://www.thefreelibrary.com/With+incense+and+chanting+filling+the+air+he+said+%27Hare+Krishna%27+and...-a080505217.
6. Srila Prabhupada, *Easy Journey to Other Planets*, Chapter 2, 'Varieties of Planetary Systems'.
7. See Back to Godhead, 20 April 1967, Relevant Enquiries.
8. Satsvarupa Dasa Goswami, *Srila Prabhupada Lilamrta*, The Bhaktivedanta Book Trust, 1980, Vol. 1, pp. 3–4.
9. There are ten avatars of Vishnu or Dashavataars—Matsya, Kurma, Varaha, Narasimha, Vamana, Parasurama, Rama, Balarama, Krishna, and Kalki.

10. Gosvāmī Satsvarūpa Dāsa. (2017). Srīla prabhupāda-līlāmrta: A biography of his divine grace A.C. bhaktivedanta swami prabhupāda. Bhaktivedanta Book Trust.

11. See https://www.deccanchronicle.com/lifestyle/viral-and-trending/191217/significance-of-feet.html.

12. And then Puri in Odisha, and then in Vrindavan.

13. Satsvarupa Dasa Goswami, *Srila Prabhupada Lilamrta*, The Bhaktivedanta Book Trust, 1980, Vol. 2, pp. 6–7.

14. Food that is first offered to the gods and then distributed among devotees.

Chapter 1: Calcutta Boy

1. Satsvarupa Dasa Goswami, *Srila Prabhupada Lilamrta*, The Bhaktivedanta Book Trust, 1980, Vol. 1, p 8.

2. See https://www.iskconbangalore.org/srila-prabhupada/childhood-in-calcutta.

3. See http://www.backtogodhead.in/the-mango-season-by-syamananda-dasa/.

Chapter 2: A Different Kind of Revolutionary

1. Satsvarupa Dasa Goswami, *Srila Prabhupada Lilamrta*, The Bhaktivedanta Book Trust, 1980, Vol. 1, p 25.

2. 'Urban Segregation Levels in the British Overseas Empire and Its Successors, in the Twentieth Century', Transactions of the Institute of British Geographers, 1992, Vol. 17, No. 1 (1992), p 101.

3. John Marriott, *The Other Empire: Metropolis, India and Progress in the Colonial Imagination* (Manchester University Press, 2003, p 133.

4. Thomas R. Trautmann, *Aryans and British India* (Second Indian ed.), New Delhi: YODA Press, 2006 (1997), p 117.

5. Satsvarupa Dasa Goswami, *Srila Prabhupada Lilamrta*, The Bhaktivedanta Book Trust, 1980, Vol. 1, p 30.

6. Ibid.

7.   Syamal Chakrabarti, 'Shaping the Chemical Industry and Saving the Cotton Industry: Role of Sir P C Ray, a Visionary Entrepreneur of British India', *Indian Journal of History of Science*, Vol. 53, 4 (2018), p 103.

Chapter 5: 'Forbearance Like a Tree, Humbleness Like a Straw'

1.   Satsvarupa Dasa Goswami, *Srila Prabhupada Lilamrta*, The Bhaktivedanta Book Trust, 1980, Vol. 1, p 70.
2.   Ibid.
3.   Ibid., p 71.
4.   Ibid., p 85.
5.   Ibid., pp. 85-86.
6.   Ibid., p 105.
7.   Rebecca J. Manring, *Reconstructing Tradition: Advaita Acharya and Gaudiya Vaishnavism at the Cusp of the Twentieth Century*, Columbia University Press, 2005, p 6.
8.   Satsvarupa Dasa Goswami, *Srila Prabhupada Lilamrta*, The Bhaktivedanta Book Trust, 1980, Vol. 1, p 105.
9.   Ibid., p 106.
10. Ibid., p 107.

Chapter 6: 'Sugar Candy'

1.   Bhagavata Janananda Prabhu, Taped interview, 20–22 May 1977.
2.   In *Calcutta Under Fire: The Second World War Years*, Rupa Publications, p 1.
3.   Ibid., pp. 9–10.
4.   Lecture on Guruvastakam at Upsala University, Stockholm, 9 September 1973.
5.   Satsvarupa Dasa Goswami, *Srila Prabhupada Lilamrta*, The Bhaktivedanta Book Trust, 1980, Vol. 1, pp. 125–27.
6.   Ibid.
7.   Ibid., pp. 128–29.
8.   Ibid., p 133.

9. Ibid., p 130.
10. Ibid., pp. 130–31.

Chapter 7: 'Rotten Politics'

1. Satsvarupa Dasa Goswami, Srila Prabhupada Lilamrta, The Bhaktivedanta Book Trust, 1980, Vol. 1, pp. 125–27.
2. Ibid., p 128.
3. Ibid., p 87.
4. Ibid. p 130.
5. Ibid., p 149.
6. Ibid., pp. 150–51.
7. Ibid., pp. 151–52.

Chapter 8: The Reluctant Pharmacist

1. Michael Edwardes, *Red Year*. London: Sphere Books, 1975, p 119, citing Vishnubhat Godse *Majha Pravas*, Poona, 1948, in Marathi, p 67.
2. See https://niti.gov.in/planningcommission.gov.in/docs/reports/sereport/ser/stdy_mythpvty.pdf.
3. Satsvarupa Dasa Goswami, *Srila Prabhupada Lilamrta*, The Bhaktivedanta Book Trust, 1980, Vol. 1, p 314.
4. Ibid., pp. 316–17.

Chapter 9: Downtown Monk

1. See https://www.migrationpolicy.org/article/emigration-immigration-and-diaspora-relations-india.
2. Srila Prabhupada's *Jaladuta* diary, Sunday, 22 September 1965.
3. Paul Oliver, *Hinduism and the 1960s*, London: Bloomsbury, 2014, p 4.
4. See https://rodpush.wordpress.com/2015/08/16/srila-prabhupadas-butler-eagle-article-srila-prabhupadas-first-article-written-about-his-mission-in-the-west-sept-22-1965-butler-eagle-pennsylvania/.
5. Ibid.

6. Ibid.
7. Satsvarupa Dasa Goswami, *Srila Prabhupada Lilamrta*, The Bhaktivedanta Book Trust, 1980, Vol. 2, p 18.
8. Ibid.
9. Srila Prabhupada's diaries and excerpt from room conversation in Vrindavan on 9 September 1976.
10. Satsvarupa Dasa Goswami, *Srila Prabhupada Lilamrta*, The Bhaktivedanta Book Trust, 1980, Vol. 2, p 31.
11. From the diaries of Srila Prabhupada.
12. Satsvarupa Dasa Goswami, *Srila Prabhupada Lilamrta*, The Bhaktivedanta Book Trust, 1980, Vol. 2, p 45.
13. ISKCON archives, Other Books by Srila Prabhupada, Life Comes From Life, The Twelfth Morning Walk: 17 May 1973.
14. See https://www.bygonely.com/polluted-new-york-city-1970s/.
15. See https://www.collectorsweekly.com/articles/when-new-yorkers-lived-knee-deep-in-trash/.
16. Jim Dwyer, 'Remembering a City Where the Smog Could Kill', The *New York Times*, 28 February 2017.

Chapter 10: A Swami among Hippies

1. See https://web.archive.org/web/20110514031701/http://www.upress.umn.edu/sles/Chapter5/ch5-1.html.
2. See http://vanishingnewyork.blogspot.com/2010/03/64-e-7th.html.
3. Ibid.
4. See https://ny.curbed.com/2017/10/4/16413696/bowery-nyc-history-lower-east-side.
5. Ibid.
6. Srila Prabhupada's diaries, excerpt from his time at the Bowery in April 1966.
7. Ibid., June 1966.
8. Indian-style bread.
9. Satsvarupa Dasa Goswami, *Srila Prabhupada Lilamrta*, The Bhaktivedanta Book Trust, 1980, Vol. 2, p 75.

10. See https://www.nber.org/digest/sep04/how-1960s-riots-hurt-african-americans.
11. See https://www.encyclopedia.com/history/encyclopedias-almanacs-transcripts-and-maps/race-riots-1960s.
12. See http://scholar.library.miami.edu/sixties/urbanRiots.php.
13. See Srila Prabhupada's diaries, excerpt from his time at the Bowery in May 1966.
14. Srila Prabhupada's diaries, excerpt from his time at the Bowery in April–June 1966.
15. Ibid.

Chapter 11: Sami Krishna

1. Satsvarupa Dasa Goswami, *Srila Prabhupada Lilamrta*, The Bhaktivedanta Book Trust, 1980, Vol. 2, p 157.
2. Paul Oliver, *Hinduism and the 1960s: The Rise of a Counter-Culture*, London: Bloomsbury, 2014, p 5.
3. Jeffery D. Long, *Hinduism in America: A Convergence of Worlds*, London: Bloomsbury Academic, p 124.
4. Ibid., p 134.
5. Satsvarupa Dasa Goswami, *Srila Prabhupada Lilamrta*, The Bhaktivedanta Book Trust, 1980, Vol. 2, p 152.
6. Ibid., p 166.
7. ISKCON Cookbooks, Great Vegetarian Dishes.
8. Ibid.
9. Ibid.
10. Satsvarupa Dasa Goswami, *Srila Prabhupada Lilamrta*, The Bhaktivedanta Book Trust, 1980, Vol. 2, p 152 and Ibid., p 203.
11. Ibid p 204.
12. Ibid.
13. ibid pp. 214–15.
14. https://www.poetryfoundation.org/poems/49303/howl.
15. https://harekrishnarevolution.wordpress.com/2017/05/04/industrialism-and-capitalism-is-no-material-advancement-it-is-material-exploitation/, an excerpt from a letter dated 14 March 1969 to Rupanuga Das.

Chapter 12: The 'High' of Krishna

1. Satsvarupa Dasa Goswami, *Srila Prabhupada Lilamrta*, The Bhaktivedanta Book Trust, 1980, Vol. 2, pp. 217–18.

2. See http://www.prabhupadaconnect.com/Allen-Ginsberg-on-Srila-Prabhupada.html.

3. See https://news.gallup.com/poll/6331/decades-drug-use-data-from-60s-70s.aspx.

4. Donald R. Wesson, 'Psychedelic drugs, hippie counterculture, speed and phenobarbital treatment of sedative-hypnotic dependence: a journey to the Haight Ashbury in the Sixties', *Psychoactive Drugs*, April–June 2011; 43(2): 153–64.

5. See https://www.bbc.com/culture/article/20181016-how-lsd-influenced-western-culture.

6. See https://psychology.fas.harvard.edu/people/timothy-leary.

7. Ibid.

8. See Netflix, 'Ram Dass, Going Home', https://bit.ly/34cRVTs.

9. Ram Dass, *Be Here Now*, RHUS; latest edition, 12 October 1971.

10. Martin A. Lee and Bruce Shlain, *Acid Dreams: The Complete Social History of LSD: The CIA, the Sixties, and Beyond*, Grove Press, 1992, p 97.

11. Lucy Sante, 'The Nutty Professor', *The New York Times Book Review, Timothy Leary: A Biography* by Robert Greenfield, 26 June 2006.

12. Satsvarupa Dasa Goswami, *Srila Prabhupada Lilamrta*, The Bhaktivedanta Book Trust, 1980, Vol. 2, p 237.

13. Correspondence of Srila Prabhupada, Letter to Damodara from Delhi, 3 December 1971.

14. Eric Foner, *Reconstruction: America's Unfinished Revolution, 1863–1877*, The New American Nation, New York: Harper & Row, 1988, p 32.

15. Satsvarupa Dasa Goswami, *Srila Prabhupada Lilamrta*, The Bhaktivedanta Book Trust, 1980, Vol. 2, p 257.

16. Ibid.

17. Ibid p 261.

18. Ibid., p 264.

19. Ibid., p 293.
20. Ibid., p 308.

Chapter 13: 'I Am Nobody's Guru. I Am Everybody's Servant'

1.   Anthony Ashbolt, '"Go Ask Alice": Remembering the Summer
     of Love Forty Years On', *Australasian Journal of American Studies*,
     December 2007, Vol. 26, No. 2 (December 2007), p 35.
2.   Satsvarupa Dasa Goswami, *Srila Prabhupada Lilamrta*, The
     Bhaktivedanta Book Trust, 1980, Vol. 3, p 5.
3.   Ibid., p 10.
4.   Ibid., p 11.
5.   Prabhupada Stories, Govinda Dasi, 2003, ISKCON archives, Story
     6, Wild Kirtans.
6.   E. Burke Rochford Jr., *Hare Krishna in America*, Rutgers University
     Press, 1985, p 66.
7.   Satsvarupa Dasa Goswami, *Srila Prabhupada Lilamrta*, The
     Bhaktivedanta Book Trust, 1980, Vol. 3, p 49.
8.   Sheila Weller, 'Suddenly That Summer', *Vanity Fair*, 14 June 2012,
     https://www.vanityfair.com/culture/2012/07/lsd-drugs-summer-
     of-love-sixties.
9.   See https://www.theguardian.com/travel/2007/may/27/escape.
10. Memories Anecdotes of a Modern Day Saint - Volume 3 by
     Siddhanta Dasa.
11. Prabhupada Stories, Govinda Dasi, 2003, ISKCON archives, Story
     13, Draft board.

Chapter 14: Ginsberg and George

1.   Satsvarupa Dasa Goswami, *Srila Prabhupada Lilamrta*, The
     Bhaktivedanta Book Trust, 1980, Vol. 3, pp. 203–204.
2.   Ibid., p 240.
3.   Satsvarupa Dasa Goswami, *Srila Prabhupada Lilamrta*, The
     Bhaktivedanta Book Trust, 1980, Vol. 7, p 91.
4.   See https://www.enochpowell.net/fr-79.html.

5. See https://www.youtube.com/watch?v=vBpoZBhvBa4.

6. Ibid.

7. Ibid.

8. See https://back2godhead.com/c-bhaktivedanta-swami-prabhupada-poet-allen-ginsberg-conversations/.

9. Ibid.

10. See https://krishna.org/george-harrison-interview-hare-krishna-mantra-theres-nothing-higher-1982/.

11. Remembrances recorded by Richard J. Cole (Radha Mohan Das) at Bhaktivedanta Manor, United Kingdom in June 2003, published in the chapter 'Forty Years of Chanting: A Study of the Hare Krishna Movement from its Foundation to the Present Day' in *The Hare Krishna Movement: Forty Years of Chant and Change*, edited by Graham Dwyer and Richard J. Cole, London: I. B. Tauris, 2007, p 30.

12. Satsvarupa Dasa Goswami, *Srila Prabhupada Lilamrta*, The Bhaktivedanta Book Trust, 1980, Vol. 4, p 36.

13. Ibid p 37.

14. See https://www.lyrics.com/lyric/4372752/Within+You+Without+You.

15. See https://www.lyrics.com/lyric/33953569/The+Beatles/I+Me+Mine.

16. See https://genius.com/George-harrison-all-things-must-pass-lyrics.

17. See https://www.lyrics.com/track/743153/George+Harrison/My+Sweet+Lord.

18. Edwin F. Bryant and Maria L. Ekstrand, *The Hare Krishna Movement: The Postcharismatic Fate of a Religious Transplant*, New York: Columbia University Press, pp. 431–41.

19. Satsvarupa Dasa Goswami, *Srila Prabhupada Lilamrta*, The Bhaktivedanta Book Trust, 1980, Vol. 4, p 74.

20. Ibid., pp. 74–75.

21. Ibid., pp. 78–79.

22. BBT Archives - Letter to Satsvarupa, Los Angeles, 31 December 1968.

23. BBT Archives, Letter to Satsvarupa, Los Angeles, 24 December 1968.

24. Satsvarupa Dasa Goswami, *Srila Prabhupada Lilamrta*, The Bhaktivedanta Book Trust, 1980, Vol. 7, p 151.

25. BBT Archives, Letter to Archbishop of Canterbury, Los Angeles, 1969.

26. Greene, Joshua M., *Here Comes The Sun*, New Jersey: John Wiley & Sons, 2010, pp. 198–99.

27. Ashley Kahn (ed.), *George Harrison on George Harrison: Interviews and Encounters*, Chicago, IL: Chicago Review Press, 2020, p 543.

Chapter 15: 'Dry Grass Catching Fire'

1. Satsvarupa Dasa Goswami, *Srila Prabhupada Lilamrta*, The Bhaktivedanta Book Trust, 1980, Vol. 4, p 124.

2. Ibid pp 119-20.

3. BBT Archives, Letter to Cidananda, Los Angeles, 23 January 1969.

4. Satsvarupa Dasa Goswami, *Srila Prabhupada Lilamrta*, The Bhaktivedanta Book Trust, 1980, Vol. 4, p 127.

5. Ibid., p 128.

6. Ibid., p 248.

7. Ibid., p 259.

8. Ibid., pp. 191–192.

9. Ibid., p 205.

10. Ibid., p 223.

11. Ibid., p 238.

12. From 'Bringing the Lord's Song to a Strange Land: Srila Prabhupada's Strategy of 'Cultural Conquest' and its prospects, William H. Deadwyler (Ravindra Svarupa Dasa), Forty Years of Chanting: A Study of the Hare Krishna Movement from its Foundation to the Present Day in *The Hare Krishna Movement: Forty Years of Chant and Change*, edited by Graham Dwyer and Richard J. Cole, London: I. B. Tauris, 2007, p 104.

13. A.C. Bhaktivedanta Swami Prabhupada, Srimad Bhagavatam: First Part, Vrindavan and Delhi: The League of Devotees, 1962, p i.

14. Srimad Bhagavatam Canto 1, Vol. 2, 1964.

15. Satsvarupa Dasa Goswami, *Srila Prabhupada Lilamrta*, The Bhaktivedanta Book Trust, 1980, Vol. 4, p 252.

Chapter 16: Krishna in War and Peace

1. See https://www.youtube.com/watch?v=ezr3UNOryFw.
2. Satsvarupa Dasa Goswami, *Srila Prabhupada Lilamrta*, The Bhaktivedanta Book Trust, 1980, Vol. 4, p 26.
3. BBT Archives, Evening conversation, 8 August 1976, Tehran.
4. *Back to Godhead* magazine, #68, 1974, Secretary to a Pure Devotee, 21 June, Melbourne, Australia.
5. Satsvarupa Dasa Goswami, *Srila Prabhupada Lilamrta*, The Bhaktivedanta Book Trust, 1980, Vol. 5, pp. 12–13.
6. Ibid p 110..
7. See https://www.youtube.com/watch?v=8fk5J8xzsTA.
8. Ibid.
9. BBT Archives, Letter to Satyabhama—Hawaii, 30 March, 1969.
10. Satsvarupa Dasa Goswami, *Srila Prabhupada Lilamrta*, The Bhaktivedanta Book Trust, 1980, Vol. 5, p 121.
11. BBT Archives, Srimad Bhagavatam - 5.6.2, Vrindavana, 24 November 1976.
12. BBT Archives, Srimad Bhagavatam - 1.16.20, Los Angeles, 10 July 1974.
13. Satsvarupa Dasa Goswami, *Srila Prabhupada Lilamrta*, The Bhaktivedanta Book Trust, 1980, Vol. 5, p 152.
14. BBT Archives, Room conversation with Dr Arnold Toynbee, 22 July 1973, London.
15. Satsvarupa Dasa Goswami, *Srila Prabhupada Lilamrta*, The Bhaktivedanta Book Trust, 1980, Vol. 5, p 271.

Chapter 17: The Great Liberation

1. Tamala Krishna Goswami, *Servant of the Servant*, 'SOS 15: Dancing to the Brhad Mrdanga'.
2. Satsvarupa Dasa Goswami, *Srila Prabhupada Lilamrta*, The Bhaktivedanta Book Trust, 1980, Vol. 6, p 275.

3. BBT Archives, Room Conversation, 26 December 1976, Bombay.
4. See https://www.washingtonpost.com/archive/politics/1977/03/21/
    hare-krishna-cleared-of-mind-control/52548dea-08e0-4154-97cd-
    00122cd6895c/.
5. Ibid.
6. Ibid.
7. Ibid.
8. BBT Archives, Letter to Giriraja, London, 12 August 1971.
9. BBT Archives, Letter to Rupanaga, 9 January 1975.
10. Satsvarupa Dasa Goswami, *Srila Prabhupada Lilamrta*, The
    Bhaktivedanta Book Trust, 1980, Vol. 6, p 213.
11. Ibid., p 90.
12. Ibid., p 243.
13. Ibid., p 171.
14. Ibid., p122.
15. Ibid., p 377.
16. Ibid., p 394.
17. Ibid., p 383.
18. Ibid., pp. 461–462.
19. Ibid., pp. 463–464.
20. BBT Archives, Room conversation, Vrindavan, 20 October 1977.
21. BBT Archives, Room conversation, Vrindavan, 28 October 1977.

Chapter 18: Conclusion: Going Back Home

1. BBT Archives, Departure Address, Los Angeles, 15 July 1974.
2. BBT Archives, Letter to Jagannatha Suta das, Los Angeles, 26
    August 1975.
3. Ibid.
4. BBT Archives, Letter to Jagannatha Suta das, Los Angeles, 26
    August 1975.
5. See https://www.youtube.com/watch?v=K4PQ5WiiNfY.

Index

(Sengupta, Hindol. Sing, Dance and Pray: The inspirational story of Srila Prabhupada-Founder-Acharya of ISKCON. Gurugram: Penguin Random House/Penguin Anand. 2022/18032023)